FAIZ AHMED FAIZ

Love and Revolution

Love and Revolution

FAIZ AHMED FAIZ

THE AUTHORIZED BIOGRAPHY

Ali Madeeh Hashmi

RUPA

Published by
Rupa Publications India Pvt. Ltd 2016
7/16, Ansari Road, Daryaganj
New Delhi 110002

Sales centres:
Allahabad Bengaluru Chennai
Hyderabad Jaipur Kathmandu
Kolkata Mumbai

Text photos courtesy the Faiz Foundation Trust, Pakistan.
Cover portrait by Saeed Akhtar. Courtesy Moneeza Hashmi

ISBN: 978-81-291-4517-8

First impression 2016

10 9 8 7 6 5 4 3 2 1

Typeset by SÜRYA, New Delhi
Printed at Replika Press Pvt. Ltd, India

To the future—Hamzah, Mahir, Faiz, Zainab, Alina, Anya, Ahmer and Amr

'Bala se hum ne na dekha tau aur dekhen ge'

Contents

Preface

The idea of writing a biography of my Nana (grandfather) actually materialized gradually over a number of years. He had been a towering (in some ways an overwhelming) presence in our lives. The Zia dictatorship of the 1970s and 1980s was a difficult time for people like my family (liberal, Left-leaning). I remember being teased and taunted in my schoolyard about being the grandson of a 'communist' and an 'atheist' (and feeling mystified about what that meant!). At that time, my main concern was to distance myself from him as much as possible. Years later, living in the US, I could look at his life more objectively. I knew that in spite of all that had been written about him, there had never been a full-length biography. I had access to close family members and friends as well as his personal papers and books. It also gave me a chance to get into his mind and understand him from the inside out (which, as a psychiatrist, I'm interested in). I made a deliberate effort while writing the book to avoid making a family connection and keep myself 'out of the action', so to speak, for several reasons. I wanted the book judged on its own merit and not as a product of someone related to Faiz. I also wanted to avoid adding to the 'Faiz industry' where people have turned a brief meeting with him into articles or whole books about him, mainly employing Faiz as a prop to project themselves—which to me appeared distasteful (although Faiz probably wouldn't have minded!). I wanted to keep the focus where it belonged, on Faiz and his life. Being a psychiatrist is an advantage since we are used to peering beneath the surface of things and I was also very keen to write about the human side of Faiz. I paid close attention to the events in his life which were emotionally significant, like his father's death at a young age, his brother's death while he was in prison, his family life and his pain at the thought of his family suffering because of his political stance. Yet, I don't think the book 'psychologizes' Faiz and it is most definitely not a 'psychological analysis' of his life or work but if the reader does find some 'psychological' nuances in the book, it is because that is what I do every day so some of it may have seeped in. People often ask me about my personal memories of Faiz, but, regretfully, there are not too many. He was always travelling, and even when home, was always surrounded by friends and admirers. I do remember him giving me an Urdu lesson. It was probably in his last years. I remember he was a little breathless and wheezy because of his lung problem. He was explaining a poem by Allama Iqbal (I don't remember which one) and made a sarcastic comment about 'pan-Islamism'. Once we went to receive him at the airport didn't recognize me when I went up to greet him because he had been away so long and I had grown much taller in his absence. He kept laughing about it. Ironically, my sharpest memories are of his last night and his funeral. I remember him getting sick and my father and uncle and I taking him to the hospital. I was in the backseat and he was in the front, semi-conscious. I kept feeling his neck for a pulse and was relieved that it was there. Then, of course, the funeral a couple of days later—the crowds, the cameras; it was quite surreal. That's why I have started the book with his death and his funeral, which I remember most vividly.

The best part about writing the book was definitely to be able to really get to know him from the inside out. It really felt like he was there at times, speaking to me through his poems and other writings. It helped that his life has been documented so well (although in a scattered way). The prison letters were a revelation too. To be able to hold on to hope and happiness under those conditions was hugely inspiring.

It's been quite a journey through a tumultuous life, a life 'fully lived'. It's up to the reader to decide if I have been able to do justice to the life of this amazing man.

Needless to say, all those who helped in this book including those who are quoted in it are in no way responsible for any errors which may appear in it. Any errors are entirely my own responsibility.

Dr Ali Madeeh Hashmi
Lahore, November 2015

1
The Envy of the Kings of Ages

Ajal kay haath koi aa raha hai parwana.
Death is bringing a missive.
—Faiz Ahmed Faiz

19 November 1984, Lahore.

It was a mild November day in Lahore. The next day Faiz would be dead but no one knew that yet. Faiz's younger daughter Moneeza was celebrating her seventeenth wedding anniversary and, luckily for her, Faiz was in Lahore. Moneeza, and her elder sister Salima, were used to not having their famous father around for important occasions. Faiz had always made an effort to be involved in their lives but he was a man of the people. When they were younger, he would often be the 'guest' of military dictators in various prisons around Pakistan, starting with his arrest and imprisonment in the infamous 'Rawalpindi Conspiracy Case', in which he served four years in several different prisons under the threat of a death sentence for treason. He had since spent briefer periods in jail under other governments as well and had remained closely watched whenever he was in Pakistan. More often than not, he was not in Pakistan, travelling all over the world for conferences on literature, peace, workers' issues and the like. This year, though, he was in Lahore.

In fact, he had just returned from visiting his two ancestral villages. The better known was Kala Qader near the small town of Narowal, a little over 100 km to the north-east of Lahore. Kala Qader was where he was born and had grown up; it was the home of his ancestors and he retained a strong link to the village. Not too far from Kala Qader is the village of Jessar, the birthplace of his mother Sultan Fatima, known affectionately to all and sundry as 'Bebe-ji' (respected mother). Bebe-ji had been the youngest wife of Faiz's dashing adventurer father; the young girl he married upon his return from England. Faiz had been visiting both villages in the last couple of days and had been given a royal welcome, one befitting a prodigal son. Hundreds of people from surrounding villages had turned up for a glimpse of Pakistan's most famous poet. Faiz had charmed and humbled everyone who came to see him by declaring that he was not a guest; he was one of the hosts since he too belonged to the villages. And in fact, he was related to dozens of the villagers through birth or marriage. They were all his extended family—cousins, uncles, nieces, nephews—descendants of his father, Sultan Mohammad Khan.

Faiz, the man who had travelled to every corner of the world and lived in three continents wistfully asked the villagers to build him a room or two overlooking the lush sugarcane and mustard fields so he could live out the rest of his life there, where the spirits of his ancestors rested in peace. At the villagers' insistence, Faiz led the prayers at the local mosque. It had been built by Faiz's father and at the entrance to the mosque on a simple white marble slab was engraved Faiz's only Persian 'Na'at' or 'Ode to the Prophet':

Every grieved heart is indeed your abode;
I bring you yet another to lodge in now.

The king on his throne worries only [about] his riches;
On this dust sits your beggar and is his envy.

His older daughter Salima recalls that he was very cheerful upon his return, although in retrospect, the fact that he had gone and met everyone there and spent time with them seemed as though 'maybe he knew, somehow that the end was near'. When he came back though,

> he was very happy. He came straight here [to Salima's house]. He told me he had been to Jessar and this was his first visit after forty years. He was laughing and joking. He said there had been a woman who used to be the village beauty and now she was this old crone! And then he laughed and said, 'I wonder what I looked like to her?!' But he was very happy; there was not a hint of being unwell; he was full of joie de vivre. He kept saying, 'You should go back to the village, keep visiting.' He kept insisting that city people have no idea of the lives people lead in villages, of what it means to have to live in a rural area of Pakistan.[1]

Faiz had made more of an effort in recent months to stay in Lahore, close to his family and grandchildren. He had remarked to some of his family that he was tired of travelling. He had not been keeping very good health. A history of chain-smoking since his youth, non-stop travelling and a generally unhealthy lifestyle had taken their toll. In addition, the last five years had been tough for Pakistan and Pakistanis. General Zia-ul-Haq's harsh military dictatorship had strengthened its grip on the country after arresting and eventually executing the country's first elected prime minister, the charismatic and mercurial Zulfiqar Ali Bhutto. After the few years of relative political freedom under the Bhutto government, the Zia dictatorship seemed even more oppressive. Even though Faiz had returned to Pakistan at the personal insistence of the general who had promised that he would not be harassed, he could not help but be affected by the gloom and misery besetting the nation and its people. This was especially so since he had long been their most eloquent dissident, someone whose voice had carried to far corners of the globe; because of this, in spite of the general's assurances, Faiz was still trailed everywhere he went by the police and intelligence agencies.

Faiz's younger son-in-law, Humair Hashmi, spent a lot of time with Faiz in the last months since they lived next to each other and would see each other in passing almost every day. They shared a love of beautiful women and good drinks:

> We used to talk of everything under the sun—how to make homemade wine, poetry, the Zia government, politics, everything. The one thing he never talked about was his female friends and he never liked to talk about the 'Conspiracy case'. He would say '*Choro yaar*' [Leave it]. First of all none of them [the accused] was supposed to talk about it because of the statutes about the case and, of course, he did not like to think about it. As everyone now knows, there was no 'conspiracy'; it was an excuse to ban the [Communist] Party and prosecute all who were in disagreement with the government. Back then we had just two newspapers, *Pakistan Times* and *Nawai Waqt*, and the latter perpetually referred to Faiz as 'the convicted Faiz Ahmed Faiz'. Even when he was given the Lenin Peace Prize, it would always refer to him as the 'formerly imprisoned Faiz Ahmed Faiz' or something like that. That's not easy for anyone

> to tolerate especially for someone as sensitive as Faiz. It would happen whenever he was in Pakistan or when he was in the news—it would say, 'the Rawalpindi Conspiracy Case convict Faiz'.
>
> That last year, he knew he did not have long. Look at the pictures of him; you can tell it in his eyes, that faraway look as if the curtains are being drawn. When one would talk to him, he seemed to be detached, as if he wasn't really there listening to you. And he spent all of that last year going around seeing old friends. That's why he went to the village. Before that he had been there maybe ten years ago at my insistence.[2]

Faiz's physical health had also declined in that last year. 'He would say to me, "Take me to a doctor." I would say, "Okay," so I took him to a doctor but there was not much he could do. He had smoked all his life and he had such a dislike of physical activity, he would say exercise, no, that is for the labourers, we won't do that,' says Hashmi with a laugh. 'He wouldn't walk from here to the post office (about 400 yards away).' Of course, besides his health and the political conditions in Pakistan, Faiz could not have been unaffected by the path his beloved Soviet Union was taking. Even though the official dissolution of that original socialist dream was still many years away, as a sensitive artist Faiz could not have remained unaware of the internal decay in Soviet society. Undoubtedly, Faiz's sadness in his last days was also related to the fact of 'that Moscow, which on close inspection, proved to be so far away from the ideal social system that so many socialists had envisioned'.[3] Says Hashmi, 'He would say, "The Soviets never discuss politics with us." He thought that it was justified to some extent but he also thought they were taking it too far; that there should be open discussions about it; new ideas. But since they did not want to do it, he would not press the issue with them and he was very sensitive about approaching this topic with others. He would discuss it with close friends but otherwise he wouldn't say anything.'

Upon his return from his last visit to his village, Faiz had remarked rather dejectedly that he had not met Sher Muhammad Hameed, an old friend who had befriended the teenaged Faiz when he had first arrived to study in Government College, Lahore, as an eighteen-year-old and who, with a circle of friends, had consoled a grief-stricken Faiz upon the death of his father just a couple of years later. In a brief recollection titled 'Faiz say meri rafaqat' (My companionship with Faiz), published as a preface to Faiz's poetry collection *Shaam-e Shehray Yaaran* (Evening of the Beloved's City), Sher Muhammad Hameed movingly described his first meeting with Faiz in 1929:

> We all used to live in New Hostel. Every evening when we would go out for a stroll, we would see a young man standing by the railing, alone, unaware of his surroundings, gazing towards the college tower and far off into the horizon....after three or four days, Nabi Ahmad's curiosity persuaded us to talk to him. He went up and asked him 'Excuse me, who are you and why do you stand here looking lost and alone?' The young man, startled, answered, 'My name is Faiz, I have done my FA from Murray College Sialkot and have taken admission in the third year here. I do not know anyone here.'Nabi Ahmad immediately said 'Come, brother, from today we are your friends, this is Sher Muhammad Hameed and this is Agha Hameed, they are your class fellows too.' It has been forty nine years since that day, life has undergone a thousand ups and downs but our bond of friendship with Faiz has endured and it has been a source of great pride and joy for us.[4]

Just a few days earlier, Faiz had visited one of his oldest friends in hospital. Khwaja Khurshid Anwar (1912–1984) was a film-maker, writer, director and music composer who had achieved acclaim in both India and Pakistan for his inventive and original music. Anwar and Faiz had been friends since their days as fellow students in Government College where he had studied philosophy and actually taken the top position in the Master of Philosophy examination in 1935. However, earlier, he had been enamoured of socialist and anarchist ideas and had become affiliated with the Ghadar Party and its most famous supporter, the young Sikh revolutionary Bhagat Singh. At one time, Anwar used to stash his revolutionary literature under the young Faiz's hostel bed. He had also been arrested and prosecuted for the 'Acetic Acid' case where he was alleged to have supplied some of the chemicals that Bhagat Singh and his associates used to make the bomb for which they were eventually arrested and executed. Faiz's close friend and associate, I.A. Rehman, remembers accompanying Faiz on the hospital visit to Khurshid Anwar. Upon seeing Faiz, Anwar sat up in his hospital bed and said in Punjabi, 'Faiz, I'm leaving, I'll wait for you over there (in heaven).'[5] This upset Faiz a great deal. As it happened, Faiz died ten days before Khurshid Anwar.

Another old friend of Faiz's was in his thoughts in his last few days. Ustad Daman (real name Chiragh Deen 1911–1984) was a celebrated Punjabi poet and mystic who had started his career reciting his defiant poetry at gatherings of the Indian National Congress before Independence. Daman had, like most anti-establishment figures, spent his life in humble circumstances, and Faiz had informed his close friends and associates that he wanted to create a trust for Ustad Daman so some money could be raised to buy him a house. Faiz told I.A. Rehman that the deed for the trust had already been drawn up and that he wanted to have a meeting immediately after he got back from his village, so they could start working on the plan.[6] Ustad Daman survived Faiz by less than two weeks and passed away on 3 December 1984.

The next day was Moneeza's wedding anniversary and there was a dinner party at her house. On the evening of the party, Faiz felt unwell but since he lived right next door to Moneeza, he got dressed and walked over. He had never been much of a talker but he was unusually quiet that day. He had brought over a memento from a recent visit to Nigeria as a present. Moneeza's husband, Humair, offered to make him a drink but Faiz refused. He even refused a 7 Up, which was very unusual for him. He sat for a while on the sofa but was clearly not well. At one point, he closed his eyes and seemed almost to faint, scaring Moneeza. After a while, he got up and excused himself, telling the others to carry on. Moneeza, worried, saw him back to his house. A short time later, his panic-stricken wife, Alys, called Moneeza and Humair over. Faiz was very sick. He had gone into the bathroom and fainted. When she went to check on him, she found him lying on the floor, unconscious. By this time, his older daughter Salima and her husband Shoaib (Humair's older brother) had arrived. Faiz was put in a car and driven to Mayo Hospital, Lahore's oldest and most respected hospital. Faiz had been there before, most recently in 1982, after a heart attack. It was then he had written his haunting poem, 'Is waqt to yun lagta hai' (It seems, at this moment). It was, he said, 'Ek be-khwaab raat ki waardaat' (The experience of a sleepless night):

> It seems at this moment there is nothing.
> Not the moon, the sun, darkness or light,
> a film of beauty on the shades of the eyes
> or the repose of pain in the havens of the heart.

At Mayo Hospital, he was admitted and word quickly spread that Faiz was in hospital. Several senior medical professors showed up to offer their help. He was in bad shape. A lifetime of chain-smoking had ravaged his lungs and he could barely breathe. Salima stayed till late at night, then went home to sleep for a few hours. She returned early in the morning. Things had gone from bad to worse. The doctors had fought hard all night to save Faiz's life but he had no strength left. His last poem, written just days before he died, seemed to indicate that he was ready:

> Whatever we have received from life, why fret.
> As long as the treasure of pain is ours, why bother about more or less.

Salima and Moneeza took turns being with him. His wife, Alys, was at home. She could not bear to be in hospital. Salima remembers the last moments: 'Mizu [Moneeza] had stepped out of the room, he was lying in bed gasping for air as he had been all night and all of a sudden, he sat bolt upright, eyes wide open and staring at the ceiling. I rushed to him and threw my arms around him and felt him go limp. I screamed for the doctors and they all rushed in and pushed me away. They shooed us all out of the room and started working on him.'

I.A. Rehman had gone to the hospital with Mazhar Ali Khan, the editor of *Viewpoint,* and another close friend, to see how Faiz was doing. When Rehman arrived at the hospital around mid-morning, Faiz was nearly gone. The doctors were trying to revive him after what may have been a cardiac arrest. 'They had all these things in his mouth, tubes and instruments, trying to revive him and I remember Moneeza was screaming, "Don't hurt him, please, don't hurt my father."'[7] Soon after, Faiz was dead. Moneeza remembers that it happened just as the afternoon calls for prayers had started ringing out from the mosques.

News of his sickness had already spread. News of his death spread just as fast. By the time the family brought him home to be buried, people were already gathering, first in ones and twos, then in groups, then in dozens and hundreds until the streets to his home in Model Town, Lahore, were choked with people. The news had already reached Europe and beyond by the time he was brought home. A Labour Party activist, exiled at the time in Amsterdam, remembers that he received a phone call the same afternoon that Faiz died.

In Lahore, 1984 was not a good time for people to gather. General Zia-ul-Haq's brutal military dictatorship was at its zenith; there had recently been widespread arrests and repression in the wake of protests against the dictatorship, especially in the province of Sindh. Large gatherings of people were strictly proscribed and could lead to arrest, imprisonment or worse, but no one cared. Faiz was dead and everyone wanted to pay their last respects. It had always been thus with Faiz. His poetry, his life's work and his personality had combined to make him the most popular poet in the Indian subcontinent since Muhammad Iqbal, Pakistan's national poet. In addition, Faiz had always had a knack for making everyone, even his most stringent critics, feel welcome in his presence. His life had always been an example of turning the other cheek, never responding in person or in print to his numerous, vociferous critics. On the contrary, even those who had spent their lifetimes opposing his work had always testified to his courteousness, his unfailing good humour and his genuine affection for all and sundry. To everyone, friend and foe alike, he had never been just 'Faiz', he had always been 'hamara Faiz' (our Faiz).

Once he was brought home to be buried, the news media arrived as well. Pakistan's most famous poet since Allama Mohammad Iqbal, the man who had been a thorn in every Pakistani government's side since the country's formation in 1947, had died, and it was big news. There were many in the media who were secretly or openly sympathetic to Faiz's views but had held their tongues (and their pens) for fear of retribution from the authorities.

Pakistan Television (PTV), Pakistan's only television channel at the time, state run and monitored, did not announce the news until late at night. Doordarshan, India's state-run television, announced it much earlier as did the BBC in London. By the evening, the house was full of people, milling around in groups, talking in low voices, consoling each other. Faiz was to be buried the next day in the nearby Model Town graveyard. PTV finally announced the news at the end of a late-night news broadcast and kept coverage to a minimum, no doubt under strict orders from the military authorities. The man who had encouraged resistance and rebellion against oppression was just as dangerous dead as he had been when alive.

The Soviet ambassador in Islamabad wanted to attend the funeral since Faiz was a national hero in the USSR. He had travelled extensively there, his poetry had been translated into every language of the country and his books, printed in the thousands, had always sold like hot cakes. In 1962, he had been awarded the Lenin Peace Prize, the Soviet bloc's equivalent of the Nobel, in Moscow. In 1984 though, the Cold War was still in full swing and Pakistan was very much in the American camp. The Pakistani government refused the Soviet ambassador permission to travel from the capital to Lahore. He left anyway and permission was later granted.

The next day, the crowd swelled into the thousands; the small house was packed, as were the streets outside. Humair Hashmi remembers the day of his death:

> We were all devastated of course, my mother, Moneeza, Salima, Shoaib, all of us. And then the people started showing up and it was unimaginable. He died around one or two in the afternoon and people started arriving soon after that and just kept coming. There would be a knock on the door at 3 or 4 a.m. in the morning, and people would want to come in and offer their condolences. We knew he was famous, of course, but we never thought there would be so many people. It was just not possible to arrange anything. It was surreal; there was such a crowd. And then when the politicians heard that there was a crowd, they wanted to join in too! We got a call from the chief minister of the Punjab to delay the funeral prayer a little because he wanted to come and join. A couple of the generals in Lahore

called and they wanted to come too. I consulted Shoaib and we waited a few minutes and then we said, 'Let's go ahead with it, they can come whenever they want.'[8]

By this time, the local media had been alerted and it too showed up, taking pictures and interviewing people. The funeral prayer could not be held in the house; there were too many people, so it was shifted to the school playground next door. There were too many people to count, in the thousands. Salima remembers, smiling through her tears, that her husband Shoaib's pocket was picked. Apparently, not all the mourners had noble intentions!

Everyone wanted to accompany Faiz's funeral possession. Muslim tradition dictates that the deceased is carried aloft on the shoulders of mourners, lying on a 'charpai', a wooden string bed, after the burial absolutions have been completed. If the burial ground is far away, the funeral possession can be motorized but the body has to be carried over the last few yards in the old way. In addition, the body is always lowered to its final resting place by hand. In Faiz's case, the cemetery was about a mile away, and the procession started out on foot. By this time, the number of mourners was in the tens of thousands. Everyone wanted to 'lend their shoulder' (i.e. help carry the body) as a mark of respect and devotion. In the cemetery it was the same.

Even in death, Faiz was controversial. Some of his fellow Marxist friends later objected strenuously to Faiz being given a traditional Muslim burial since he had never observed traditional religious rituals. Faiz's attitude towards religion had been, to the chagrin of both his fans and his critics, maddeningly ambiguous. He had written poems replete with references to the Day of Judgment, divine reward and punishment and God. He had even named one of his poems 'The face of your Lord', a direct reference to a Quranic verse ('Ar-Rahman': The most gracious). However, as befits a Marxist, and upholding the proud tradition of Iqbal, he had also written verses challenging and exhorting God in his inspiring 'Rabba sacchiya' (True master):[9]

I do not desire kingship, Lord,
just an honourable livelihood.
I am not greedy for palaces,

just a solitary corner to live my life.
If you acquiesce to me, I will do the same
by you, I swear to never turn down any of your demands.
But, Lord, if this request is too much [for you],
then I shall return and send another Master [in your place].[10]

Thus, some of his old friends who were not believers were incensed in the midst of their grief at his traditional 'Muslim' funeral. Salima recounts their objections:

> They were very angry. They said, as an atheist, he would not have agreed to that [a traditional funeral]. But I said Abba [father] organized that for anyone in the family who died. His sister passed away, his mother passed away, all of that was done. He believed in observance because it was comforting to those who were left behind. When someone like that [Faiz] dies, what do you hang on to? It was peoples' way of showing their allegiance to him. Don't forget, it was Zia-ul-Haq's time and there were still 5 or 10,000 people at the funeral. If it had not been General Zia's time, there would have been 100,000 people. And all those who came would have had to think hard whether they wanted to be seen at Faiz's funeral but still they came.[11]

She laughs, 'But those diehard communists, they weren't convinced.'

In retrospect, she was probably correct. If Faiz had himself had a say in it, he would probably have done the same. Even though he was a rebel and a maverick with a stubborn independent streak which would sometimes aggravate his fellow travellers, he would probably not have chosen to end his life with a rebellious gesture like his fellow poet, Nazar Mohammad Rashed, who expressly chose to be cremated rather than buried, scandalizing many of his oldest friends and contemporaries. It probably helped that Rashed lived a large part of his life outside Pakistan and spent a lot of time in Iran, the original land of the fire-worshippers. In addition, he died in Europe and was cremated in England, thus avoiding the religious furore that such a decision would have caused in a place like Pakistan.

Another brilliant literary rebel who died young, the fiery short-story writer Saadat Hasan 'Manto', had actually written his own epitaph six months before he died: 'Buried here is Saadat Hasan Manto in whose bosom are enshrined all the secrets of the art of short-story writing. Buried under mounds of earth, he continues to contemplate who is the greater short-story writer: God or he.'[12] His family, fearful of a religious backlash, changed the text and had this engraved on his tombstone instead: 'This epitaph belongs to the grave of Saadat Hassan Manto, who still believes that his name shouldn't have been erased off the tablet of the universe like a word written twice by error.'

Faiz's religiosity (or lack thereof) had been a topic of discussion amongst his friends and foes alike throughout his life. One of his friends recounted an anecdote related to him by Faiz himself. Once, while incarcerated in Hyderabad jail for the infamous Rawalpindi Conspiracy Case, Faiz, who had memorized a part of the Quran in childhood, started giving lessons in it to the other inmates. One of his jailers, a young colonel, who had been told that the prisoners were godless communists, was mystified. He took Faiz aside and said, 'Faiz sahib, what is your religion?' To which Faiz replied, 'The same as that of Maulana Rum [the famous thirteenth-century Persian poet and mystic, Rumi].' The colonel was satisfied and said happily, 'We are Muslim brothers, you teach the Quran well.' Years later, Faiz met that same colonel at a dinner somewhere and he, again curious, asked: 'But Faiz sahib, what is the religion of Maulana Rum? To which Faiz replied, the same as mine!'[13] Faiz himself said of this, 'I have had a deep affinity for "tasawwuf" [Sufi thought] firstly because it is an invaluable part of our literary heritage and also because the point of view of the Sufi is of "wahdat-ul-wajood"[unity of oneness], therefore, in their own way, it is very consistent and scientific. Also, the worldliness and the compromises that are found in the Mullah's religion are absent from theirs.'[14] In this, Faiz of course was following in the footsteps of his great poetic predecessors, Muhammad Iqbal (1877–1938), Mirza Asadullah Khan 'Ghalib' (1797–1869) and Mohammad Mir Taqi 'Mir' (1723–1810), all of whom forcefully rejected religious orthodoxy in favour of an all-embracing spirituality typified by the Sufi saints of the subcontinent.

Salima recounts an exchange between Faiz and his beloved

wife, Alys, a much more pragmatic person, less inclined to flights of mystical fantasy.

> She [Alys] tried to pin him down about the Holy Prophet.
>
> What did he [Faiz] truly think of him? Did he truly think he was a messenger of God? Abba [Father] very sweetly and patiently said, 'It doesn't matter but as a Marxist, how I interpret the Prophet is that he was a tremendously effective political leader.' He said, 'If you look at his life, how he rose from what he was, a destitute orphan, to become a leader and a great force for reform, for egalitarianism and justice, for social reform, you will understand.' So he explained it in Marxist terms to mummy, in terms she would understand and accept. My mother being what she was, an avowed atheist at that time, she wanted to probe him, to get him to commit and he just said, 'Look at it in your terms, think of him as a great political leader, a reformer, a revolutionary for his times.'[15]

A written message of condolence was delivered from the general himself the day after Faiz's death, conveying '[my] personal sense of loss and grief...and my profound admiration of his poetic genius'. To be fair to General Zia, he had sent several messages in the last couple of years to Faiz to end his self-imposed exile and assured him that he would come to no harm should he return to Pakistan. Faiz, though, was wary of the promises of dictators and mindful of the fact that the general had more to gain from him than the other way around. Having come to power by deposing Pakistan's first popularly elected Prime Minister, Zulfiqar Ali Bhutto, Zia would, no doubt, have grabbed the opportunity to legitimize his rule by allowing Faiz back into Pakistan and perhaps even bestowing some official recognition on him. It had always been tricky for despotic Pakistani governments to deal with Faiz. They wanted to harness his immense popularity across classes and languages but would have liked his central message of struggle and resistance to remain opaque to people.

One commentator noted, 'The news [of Faiz's death] spread like wild fire through Pakistan and all over the world. At the time of his death, Faiz was the greatest poet in the Urdu language and now, after he is gone, there is no one of his stature, poet or author, on the horizon. This is why his death is such a tragedy. The memory of this tragedy will pain our generation the same way it will his family.'[16]

Faiz was at last buried, in a simple grave in Model Town, Lahore, the place where he had lived the last years of his life.

Notes

1. Salima Hashmi, personal recollection.
2. Humair Hashmi, personal recollection.
3. Ludmila Vasilieva, *Parvarish-e Lauh-o-Qalam: Faiz Hayat aur Takhleeqat* (Karachi: Oxford University Press, 2006), p. 285.
4. Sher Muhammad Hameed, 'Faiz se meri rifaqat'. *Nuskha hai Wafa* (Lahore: Maktaba Karvaan, 1985), p. 497.
5. I.A. Rehman, unpublished interview with the author, Lahore, 2014.
6. Ibid.
7. Ibid.
8. Humair Hashmi, personal recollection.
9. Faiz Ahmed Faiz, *Nuskha hai Wafa*, p. 578.
10. Translated by this author.
11. Salima Hashmi, personal recollection.
12. Ayesha Jalal, Nusrat Jalal (eds), *Manto* (Lahore: Sang-e-Meel Publications, 2012), p. 188.
13. Ayub Mirza, *Hum ke Thehre Ajnabi* (Islamabad: Dost Publcations, 1996), pp. 15–16.
14. Faiz Ahmed Faiz, 'Guftagoo—Faiz Ahmed Faiz', *Dunyazad*, no. 35 (Karachi: Scheherzade Publications, 2012), p. 64.
15. Salima Hashmi, personal recollection.
16. Jamil Jalibi, *Ma'asir Adab* (Lahore: Sang-e-Meel Publications, 1991), pp. 216, 219.

2
Fantasy and Reality

Mard-e Khuda ka amal, Ishq say sahib farogh

The action of the Man of God is radiant with Love

—Muhammad Iqbal

Faiz Ahmed Faiz's father, Sultan Muhammad Khan, travelled far from his land of birth and made his name and fortune in exotic foreign lands. From the remote village of Kala Qader (Now Faiz Nagar), Sultan Mohammad Khan travelled all over the world, becoming by turns 'mir munshi' (chief secretary) to the emir (ruler) of Kabul, his ambassador to England, a lawyer from Cambridge and then a gentleman of leisure back in Sialkot. Sultan Muhammad Khan's story was exciting enough to be immortalized as a novel by one of his close friends and confidantes, the Englishwoman Lillias Hamilton, the official court physician of Emir Abdul Rahman, the ruler of Kabul.[1] Faiz himself called his father 'a nineteenth-century adventurer, who had a far more colourful life than I have had'.[2]

Abdul Rahman Khan (1844–1901), emir of Afghanistan, had fought several fierce battles of succession for the throne since the death of his grandfather, Dost Muhammad Khan, in 1863. He had lived in exile for several years in Tashkent, then part of Russian Turkestan, until he reclaimed the throne in 1880 with the help of the British. It was in 1885 when he was in conference with the Viceroy of India, Lord Dufferin, in Rawalpindi, that he complained of aching joints to which the viceroy responded by requesting the imperial court to send an English physician for him. Dr Lillias Hamilton, a physician, writer and adventurer was that person and she remained at his court for many years, in the process becoming a close friend of Sultan Muhammad Khan's.

These were turbulent times in India and in the entire region. The British Empire, then at its zenith, and its counterpart in Asia, the Russian Empire, were vying for influence in the area. The rich, fertile plains of India with their natural and human wealth had attracted foreign invaders since ancient times. The armies of the ancient Persian empire, Alexander and the Mongols, had all found India irresistible. Now the Russians and the British were fighting over the same prize. Afghanistan was the natural buffer between the vast Russian Empire to the north and British India. It was thus a useful pawn in the 'Great Game' between the two imperial powers. As a result, any ruler of this area needed to carefully balance the interests of his own people (and himself) with those of the two empires. Abdul Rahman Khan was such a ruler, one who succeeded in suppressing (or buying off) all opposition to his rule and who created the first 'central' Government of Afghanistan, albeit at great cost.

In this stormy age, Faiz's father, Sultan Muhammad Khan, was born into a landless peasant family in the village of Kala Qader. His ancestors had been Kshatriya Rajputs descended, by family accounts, from Raja Sain Pal of Saharanpur. It is not known when the family converted to Islam but Sultan Muhammad Khan's grandfather's name was Sarbuland Khan, which points to his having been a Muslim.[3]

Some biographers of Faiz have highlighted that Sultan Muhammad Khan was born into a poor family, so poor that in order to conserve money, a kerosene lamp, the only light in the household, was lit for just a short time each night.[4] As others have pointed out though, such a state of affairs was by no means an exception in colonial India.[5] A few pockets of affluence existed in some of the larger cities, usually amongst the descendants of the old nobility or those who had managed to gain the favour of the colonial masters, but the vast majority of the population and almost all of the peasantry in the countryside remained desperately poor. However, the social and economic system the British had brought with them from England rewarded intelligence, ability and hard work as opposed to the pre-colonial feudal system prevalent in India.

The Rajput caste, from which Sultan Muhammad Khan was descended, was recognized by the British as a 'martial race'.[6] A fighting spirit and a fierce desire to rise above his conditions were thus no doubt a part of Sultan Muhammad Khan's genetic heritage.

Most of what we know about Sultan Muhammad Khan's early

life is from the later writings and speeches of Faiz himself. Faiz quotes his father on one occasion, 'Because my father was a landless peasant, he was employed by the people who had some land to tend their cattle. So he said "I used to take the cattle out of the village and I found there was a school, a little distance from the village. I would leave the cattle to graze and attend the school."'[7] His teacher at the village school must have recognized his innate intelligence and encouraged him to continue his studies. This then became his daily routine. He would take the cattle out to graze, leave them a while, go to school to have his work from the previous day checked, get the work for the day and go back to his cattle. His rapid progress persuaded the teacher to allow him to sit for the final examination, which he passed with flying colours ahead of all the other children. This earned him a scholarship of two rupees a month, a not insignificant sum in those days for a poor family. He was thus able to get admission into the local high school situated some distance from his village. For several years, he would walk back and forth to school, undeterred by the distance or inclement weather, until he passed the high school examination with flying colours as well. This was as far as he could go in his village; there was no college or any other institution of higher learning in the village.

There are differing versions of the events following his departure from his village for the bustling metropolis of Lahore. There is no authentic record available of the period between Sultan Muhammad Khan's bidding farewell to his ancestral village and family and his arrival in the court of Abdur Rahman Khan. Faiz's account, corroborated at least in part by one of his biographers,[8] has Sultan Muhammad Khan coming to Lahore and finding shelter in a local mosque. In those days, in many places in the subcontinent, boys from poor families in the countryside who came to the city to seek an education or livelihood often found a place to stay in rooms attached to the local mosque which then, as now, was often the central gathering place for the community. The community would undertake to provide food and thus the children (some barely more than ten years old) would receive basic shelter and food which would keep them from begging and sleeping on the streets. By all the accounts available of this part of his life, Sultan

Muhammad Khan found just such a place to stay upon his arrival in Lahore, Punjab's largest city. He was, by the descriptions available, a good-looking young man. His later photographs from London testify to this. In addition, he was intelligent, well-spoken and polite, just the sort who could easily make friends and find himself at home in any company. He also had a pleasing, melodious voice and soon began to receive requests for public recitations of the Quran. After his studies, he would return to the mosque to do whatever chores were assigned to him and, in the evening, would go to the railway station to earn extra money as a 'coolie' (labourer) that he would send home to the village. In spite of this exhausting routine, his passion for studying remained undimmed. He had a special aptitude for languages and was soon fluent in English and Persian, the two dominant languages of the region besides the local Urdu.

What happened next is again a matter of some conjecture. However, Faiz himself described it this way, 'When he [Sultan Muhammad Khan] was living in this mosque, it so happened that an Afghan grandee was counsel to the Government of the Punjab. He used to come and pray in this mosque. He saw this young boy and rather liked him and he said "Look, we want an English interpreter for Afghanistan."'[9] It seems reasonable to assume that if, in fact, an official from the Afghan amir's court did visit the mosque for Friday prayers as alleged'[10] he could have met Sultan Muhammad Khan. If such a meeting took place, it is reasonable to assume that the rest of the story is also true: that the official was impressed with the young man's bearing, his intelligence and his easy proficiency in both Persian and English. This was the time that the Afghan emir was trying to forge closer links with the British rulers in India to consolidate his own rule in Afghanistan and anyone who could help further that aim was a useful friend. According to the prevailing accounts, the Afghan official offered Sultan Muhammad Khan an immediate appointment as English tutor in his own household.

This was not necessarily actuated by philanthropy alone. During this same period, an event of momentous significance was taking place elsewhere. The Durand Line refers to the porous international border between present-day Pakistan and Afghanistan. This poorly marked line is approximately 1,640 miles (2,640 km) long. It was established after the 1893 Durand Line Agreement between a representative of British India and Afghan Amir Abdur Rahman Khan to delineate their respective spheres of influence. It is named after Henry Mortimer Durand, the foreign secretary of British India at the time. The single-page agreement contains seven short articles signed by H.M. Durand and Emir Abdur Rahman Khan, agreeing not to exercise interference beyond the frontier line between Afghanistan and what was then British India (now Pakistan). The line had already been a cause of two earlier Anglo-Afghan wars and the demarcation was an (unsuccessful) attempt at seeking a permanent cessation of hostilities.

A joint British–Afghan demarcation survey took place starting from 1894, covering some 800 miles of the border. The resulting Durand Line established the 'Great Game' buffer zone between British and Russian interests in the region. This poorly marked border cuts through the Pashtun tribal areas, dividing ethnic Pashtuns (Afghans) on both sides of the border and lies in what has been described as one of the most dangerous places in the world. It has never been accepted by the Pashtun tribes living on either side, and remains disputed to this day.

It would be safe to assume then that anyone who was fluent in English and could, therefore, intercede in the negotiations with the British would be considered a valuable ally by the Afghans. In fact, this was the position that Sultan Muhammad Khan eventually assumed when he became mir munshi (chief secretary) to Emir Abdur Rahman himself. He was brought to Kabul by the same official who had met him at the Lahore mosque. The emir was just as impressed with him as the official had been, and he was immediately appointed royal interpreter and put in charge of all correspondence with the British. His duties included translating all letters and correspondence from the British into Persian and all letters from the emir to the British into English. He was soon made chief secretary and then a minister to the emir.

It was at the court of the emir that he met and befriended Dr Lillias Hamilton (1858–1925). From the fact of her close friendship with Sultan Muhammad she has, by default, become an important source for an account of his days in the emir's court. She has been described as an influential woman, perhaps related to Queen Victoria. Others, however, have disputed this.[11] What is known for certain is that she was an Englishwoman who trained as a nurse in Liverpool before going on to study medicine in Scotland and qualifying as a doctor in 1890. She became court physician to Emir Abdur Rahman upon the request of Lord Dufferin, the Viceroy of India at the time. She wrote a fictionalized account of her experiences at the Afghan court in her book, *A Vizier's Daughter: A Tale of the Hazara War*, published in London in 1900.

While she herself was quite clear that the book was a novel, she was not coy about describing how some aspects of the central character, Ali Mahomed Khan, resembled her close friend and the emir's confidante, Sultan Muhammad Khan. She writes in the introduction to her book:

> I have tried to draw him (the emir's Chief Secretary i.e. Sultan Muhammad Khan) as he was then, not as he is now after a period of repose, surrounded with the luxury of the most refined and cultured intellects in the world. [She is writing of the period when Sultan Muhammad had left the Afghan court and was living in England as the Ambassador of the emir.] I have tried to picture him first as the self-satisfied Court favorite, flattered and sought after by everyone; then as the overworked official, intrigued against, accused of every conceivable and inconceivable crime, by enemies too unscrupulous and too numerous not to be formidable. On showing him the manuscript of this volume, which I would not have published without his permission, his only comment was : "I think it is very like what I was." I do not exaggerate when I say he did, after a fashion, of course, the work of twenty men. He had not only the mere nominal superintendence of a dozen most diverse kinds of works, offices, etc., but was responsible for the working, and for the actual detail of each, and in Afghanistan there is no method. None has an understudy in case of illness, or to provide for a much needed holiday, so that if an official is laid up, the whole of his work accumulates, and he rises from a bed of sickness to meet a task beyond his strength even when he was well. There is no one whom he can rely for anything. But besides those works, which were merely extras, the man whom I have called Ali Mohamed Khan had his Court duties to attend to; he was head of what we should call the Intelligence Department, and was

> Chief Secretary to the Ameer. There is a popular saying in Kabul that instead of receiving increase of pay or an additional holiday for special services rendered, an official is praised and congratulated in open Durbar, and receives as a reward for his labors an extra burden of work. That is really what happened in his case.[12]

Dr Lillias Hamilton is not a novelist of note in the annals of English literature. However, she was a member of that tradition of the British Empire which encouraged and required all its agents and citizens to closely study the habits, lifestyles and ways of thinking of the 'natives' they came in contact with. Part of this was, no doubt, the habits inculcated into a scientific mind by societies that were undergoing the Industrial Revolution after the explosion of knowledge that had been the Renaissance. There was also a hard-nosed practical aspect to such studies. It helped in governance of the Empire. Thus, English officers and soldiers, doctors and writers, wherever they found themselves, in the plains, in mountains, in deserts, even in places where no natives had ever set foot were busy documenting and analysing their surroundings and experiences.

While there is general agreement that Sultan Muhammad found favour with the emir soon after his arrival in Kabul as evidenced by his eventual authorship of the emir's biography, *The Life of Emir Abdur Rahman*, there are conflicting opinions about his departure from the Afghan court. A widely circulated but probably inaccurate version was that with the increasing favours that the emir was bestowing upon his chief secretary, jealousy and envy against him grew, especially given that he was not an ethnic Afghan and had no family or other connections within the court. Lillias Hamilton warned him of these intrigues against him and advised him to flee before he was arrested or worse. She agreed to transfer his accumulated wealth to London in her name and Sultan Muhammad secretly fled Kabul for Lahore where he was promptly arrested as an Afghan spy and placed in custody in the same Lahore Fort where Faiz was to be imprisoned many years later.

This is the version that Faiz himself has subscribed to in one of his interviews.[13] It seems unlikely, though, that the emir, who had created a strong central government in Afghanistan for the first time in history, partly by spreading a vast and extremely efficient network of spies throughout the length and breadth of the land, would have remained unaware of a large caravan carrying all the gifts and awards bestowed upon his chief secretary heading out of his kingdom through the only route then available: a trek overland to Lahore, then to Bombay to board a ship for England. In addition, if Sultan Muhammad Khan really escaped in the dead of night without the permission of the emir, why were his wives and concubines later safely escorted to his ancestral village? And why would the emir then appoint Sultan Muhammad his ambassador to England and also commission him to translate his biography and publish it from London? Not just that, the emir also invited him back to Kabul to discuss the biography and, after the meetings, sent him back to England.

A more likely explanation for Sultan Muhammad's departure from the Afghan court seems to be that owing to his diligence, intelligence and sincerity, the emir appointed him his ambassador to England. Sultan Muhammad came back home but, since his stay was short, did not bring his wives along.

Whatever the circumstances, sometime before 1898, Sultan Muhammad left Kabul and after a brief stay in Kala Qader, headed to England where, in addition to acting as the emir's ambassador to the English court, he also enrolled at Cambridge University and acquired a degree in law. Sultan Muhammad had already worked on the Persian version of the emir's biography, which the emir had partly dictated to him. He writes in the preface to the first edition of the book's English translation: 'A portion of the book was written by the Emir himself...the rest was written in my handwriting from the Emir's dictation.' The English translation was entirely the work of Sultan Muhammad. The book was finished in some haste in 1900 since the emir was seriously ill by this time. By the time of his death in October 1901, he had most likely seen the first publication of the book.

Sultan Muhammad's stay in London was, by all accounts, a period of carefree prosperity. As Lillias Hamilton noted, it was 'a period of repose, surrounded with the luxury of the most refined and cultured intellects in the world'. One of Faiz's biographers (Ludmila Vasilieva) has even termed it a period of somewhat dissolute indulgence. She writes, 'He received a considerable sum of money from Afghanistan and he began to spend more of his time in the salons of the English aristocracy. Travel, games of cards and frivolous entertainment became a daily occurrence. Being the Afghan ambassador to England, he had access to the highest levels of society, he was presented to Queen Victoria, made a member of the Royal Geographical Society and played croquet with the Duke of Windsor...It appeared that fate had decided to bless him with contentment for the rest of his life.'[14]

Vasilieva then wraps up her description of his life by noting that his extravagance led to penury, his erstwhile English friends abandoned him and he decided to return to India.

It is certainly likely that Sultan Muhammad aroused much curiosity and admiration in London. This was the height of the 'Victorian' era, a time when 'the sun never set on the British Empire'. The Queen ruled her vast dominion with the proverbial 'iron fist inside a velvet glove'. Britain was the mightiest imperial power the world had ever seen, and India was the jewel in its crown. For an Indian to be the Afghan ambassador to the imperial court, and that too someone who spoke English like a native, meant that Sultan Muhammad was surrounded by a mysterious aura. In addition, he had no problem adapting to royal customs since he had experience as a courtier in Kabul. The twentieth century was dawning and the rajas and maharajas of the exotic East with their many wives and vast harems of concubines and slave girls were a subject of envious puzzlement in monogamous Victorian society. Even though Sultan Muhammad's wives and concubines had stayed behind in Kabul, he was still invested with an exciting otherness.

Sultan Muhammad's singular academic achievement in those days is the publication of the emir's biography. It was also a great honour bestowed upon Sultan Muhammad that the emir dictated the manuscript to him and trusted him completely with its translation into English. The emir, by all historical accounts, was an intelligent man and a shrewd judge of character. The most obvious example of this is his ability to ascend the throne of Kabul and beat back numerous challenges to his reign while attempting successfully to create a functioning central government in Kabul.

All the while he was balancing precariously between the two huge empires, the Russian and the British, on his flanks. One way of achieving this incredible balancing act was to place the right people in the right positions and his choice of Sultan Muhammad certainly bore this out. His biography was fashioned after the *Tuzk-e Babri*, the memoirs of Zahir-ud-Din Muhammad Babar (1483–1530) the founder of the Mughal dynasty. The two volumes of *The Life of Emir Abdur Rahman* offered the people and rulers of England their first glimpse into Afghan life. It helped dispel many of the prevalent myths about Afghanistan and Afghan society, especially about the barbarity and cruelty of its rulers and the savages who were supposedly their subjects. The first proof of this was, of course, the person of Sultan Muhammad himself. In his carriage, his speech and his actions, he was living proof of the sophistication of Indian and Afghan society. His friend, Lillias Hamilton, one of his strongest supporters, also helped dispel some of these myths.

In 1901, Emir Abdur Rahman died and was succeeded by his son, Habibullah Khan. This had no effect on Sultan Muhammad's position as ambassador. The former emir had, in his time, with the help of his staff, including Sultan Muhammad, worked hard to lay the foundations of a modern centralized state in the region. As a result, the new emir had little difficulty in ascending to the throne and establishing his writ over the land. Habibullah was a relatively secular, reform-minded ruler who attempted to modernize his country while continuing the precarious balancing act between the British and the Russians. During his reign he worked to bring Western medicine and other technology to Afghanistan. Acutely aware of the 98 per cent illiteracy rate, in 1904, Habibullah founded the Habibia school, which educated several generations of Afghan leaders, as well as a military academy. He instituted various legal reforms and repealed many of the harshest criminal penalties. Other reforms included the dismantling of the repressive internal intelligence organization that had been put in place by his father. He accepted British help and money in instituting many of these reforms but staunchly refused their offers to build railways or a telegraph system in the country, suspecting that they would lead to increased influx of both British and Russian travellers.

Sultan Muhammad continued serving as Emir Habibullah's ambassador from 1901 till 1905. It was also during this time that he met Muhammad Iqbal, a brilliant young student from Sialkot, near Sultan Muhammad's ancestral village. Iqbal, too, was pursuing a law degree at Cambridge and was, at that time, a relative unknown, although his poetry had already begun to capture the imagination of his countrymen. Iqbal arrived in Cambridge in 1905 and their companionship was likely brief, since it appears that Sultan Muhammad returned to India for good around the same time. While Vasilieva[15] has implied that Sultan Muhammad returned to his native land because of financial troubles resulting from his profligacy, this does not fit well with the picture of his life that we have seen so far. It is just as likely that after the death of Emir Abdur Rahman, the changes in government instituted by his successor meant that Sultan Muhammad had less and less to do and felt that perhaps it was time to return home. At any rate, sometime in 1905 or 1906, he returned by the same route from England, by ship to Bombay and thence to Lahore and Sialkot. He brought along a large amount of the wealth he had accumulated in his years abroad and, in keeping with Punjabi tradition, bought several tracts of land in the area. Initially, he set up a legal practice in Jhelum. Very soon though, he decided to move his practice to Sialkot, the largest city near his ancestral village, and this was where his Afghan wives and consorts joined him. He had already been awarded the title of 'Khan Bahadur' and must have been one of the most prominent and respected citizens of Sialkot.

Here, Sultan Muhammad's Afghan wives finally joined him. There is some dispute regarding how many wives he had. Different authors have put the number of his marriages at two,[16] three[17] or five.[18] What is certain though, is that his first wife was a niece of Emir Abdul Rahman's and his last and youngest, barely older than some of his daughters, was Sultan Fatima, the daughter of a landowner in the nearby village of Jessar, whom he married after his return to Sialkot. Sultan Muhammad Khan's household 'was full of women. Life went on mainly in the "zenan khana" [the women's quarters] where outside men were not allowed to set foot...Silence and calm was preferred in the house. Other than wives and children there were aunts, nieces, nephews and brothers and sisters and the head of the household fed and took care of all of them.'[19] Before his marriage to Sultan Fatima, Sultan Muhammad had just one son from one of his Afghan wives. He has been identified in some books as 'Agha Gul'.[20] He was afflicted with tuberculosis, as were many of his Afghan relatives, and died young. Years later, Faiz would remember him fondly as someone who was quite a bit older than he but who loved to tell the younger children stories. He was kept in isolation from the rest of the family because of his illness and no one was allowed to go into his room. 'In the afternoon, when everyone was asleep, Abbu [father/Faiz] would go to his room, sit on the doorstep and listen to his stories.'[21] This may have been one reason that Sultan Muhammad felt obliged to marry again after his return to the Punjab. The patriarchal culture of the Punjab with its strong emphasis on the greater worth of sons as compared to daughters, along with the insistence of family, may have persuaded him, as some have implied.[22]

At any rate, Sultan Fatima did not disappoint them. In 1908, her first son, Tufail Ahmed, was born, followed three years later by the birth of Faiz Ahmed and then two more sons, Inayat and Bashir. Sultan Muhammad was well aware that it was his education that had allowed him to rise from the villages and fields of the Punjab to the courts of Afghanistan and England. His children's education was, in his eyes, his primary responsibility. Endowed as they were with his genes and his thirst for knowledge, his sons rose to positions of prominence in the professions. Tufail Ahmed rose to become a judge, Faiz became a teacher, a journalist and a world-renowned poet, Inayat became a major in the army; the youngest, Bashir, was physically and mentally disabled since birth.

Sultan Muhammad Khan, in addition to possessing an indomitable spirit, perhaps a legacy of his Rajput ancestry, was also a true son of the soil. After his adventures in Afghanistan and then England, he chose the land of his birth as home and never entertained thoughts of leaving again. Faiz wrote about his early upbringing:

> In the morning, I would go the mosque for the Fajr prayers with Abba [father]. We would usually be up with the azan [the call to prayer before dawn], go to the mosque, say our prayers then

> read the Quran with Maulvi Ibrahim Sialkoti who was a great scholar of his era. I would then stroll for an hour or two with Abba then to school. In the evening, Abba would call me to write some of his letters since he was having some difficulty with it in those days so I was his secretary. I would also read the paper to him. These activities helped increase my knowledge greatly.[23]

Thus did Sultan Muhammad and his household live till the end of his days. The young shepherd boy with dreams of a better life for himself and his family had come a long way.

Notes

1. Lillias Hamilton, *A Vizier's Daughter: A Tale of the Hazara War* (London: John Murray, 1900), p. 112.
2. Sheema Majeed (comp. and ed.), *Culture and Identity: Selected English Writing of Faiz* (Karachi: Oxford University Press, 2005), p. 3.
3. Ludmila Vasilieva, *Parvarish-e Lauh-o-Qalam: Faiz Hayat aur Takhleeqat* (Karachi: Oxford University Press, 2006), p. 2.
4. Ibid.
5. Ashfaq Bokhari, *Faiz Ahmed Faiz: Chund Nai Daryaaftain* (Lahore: Saanjh Publications, 2012), p. 157.
6. Heather Streets, *Martial Races: The Military, Race and Masculinity in British Imperial Culture, 1857–1914* (Manchester: Manchester University Press, 2004), p. 241.
7. Majeed, *Culture and Identity: Selected English Writing of Faiz*, p. 4.
8. Vasilieva, *Parvarish-e Lauh-o-Qalam: Faiz Hayat aur Takhleeqat*.
9. Ibid.
10. Ibid., p. 3.
11. Bokhari, *Faiz Ahmed Faiz: Chund Nai Daryaaftain*, p. 160.
12. Hamilton, *A Vizier's Daughter: A Tale of the Hazara War*, p. 86.
13. Majeed, *Culture and Identity: Selected English Writing of Faiz*, p. 4.
14. Vasilieva, *Parvarish-e Lauh-o-Qalam: Faiz Hayat aur Takhleeqat*, pp. 5–6.
15. Ibid., p.5.
16. Ibid., p.6.
17. Mirza Zafarul Hasan, *Umr-e Guzishta ki Kitaab* (Karachi: Idara Yaadgar-e Ghalib, 1978), p. 36.
18. Sehba Lakhnavi, Kashish Siddiqui (comps), *Afkar*, Faiz number (Karachi: Maktaba Afkar, 1965), p. 26.
19. Khaleeq Anjum (comp.), *Faiz Ahmed Faiz: Tanqeedi Jaaeza* (New Delhi: Anjuman Taraqqi Urdu [Hind], 1985), p. 18.

20. Salahuddin Haider, *Jinhen Jurm-e Ishq pay Naaz Tha* (Lahore: Sang-e-Meel publications, 2011), p. 48.
21. Salima Hashmi, personal recollection.
22. Bokhari, *Faiz Ahmed Faiz: Chund Nai Daryaaftain*, p. 207.
23. Faiz Ahmed Faiz, 'Ehd-tifli se unfavan-e shabab tak—Preface: Shaam-e shehr-e yaaran', in *Nuskha hai Wafa* (Lahore: Maktaba Karvaan, 1985), p. 483.

3
Arrival

Naara-zad ishq ke khoonee jigar-e paida shud.

Love declared: a fiery lover is born.

—Muhammad Iqbal

Sialkot, one of Pakistan's ten largest cities, is an ancient city founded, according to one account, 5,000 years ago by a ruler named Shaal. It finds mention in the Mahabharta: 'Shaakal Nagri on the banks of Upkandi in the Madra region'.[1]

During the reign of Chandragupta Vikramaditya (375–413 CE), at the height of the Gupta empire, the ruler of the city, Shal Bahan, formerly of Ghazni, Afghanistan, built a castle here named 'Shaal-kot'. In the local dialect, 'kot' means fortress. Over time, the name changed to 'Sialkot', its modern-day name. Like all cities, Sialkot saw its fortunes rise and fall. Hindu rajas ruled it until the fourteenth century. They were deposed by Sultan Feroz Tughlaq. In the nineteenth century, Maharaja Ranjeet Singh and his armies occupied it, and still later, it came under the sovereignty of the British.

Sialkot was an active participant in the uprising of 1857. Lasting from 1857 till 1859, this was the first organized revolt of native Indians against their British rulers. After the fall of Delhi, uprisings all over the Punjab, including Sialkot, were brutally crushed. The inhabitants of the city were fined the then exorbitant sum of Rs 50,000. Two officers of Sialkot's militia were hanged and 139 soldiers were tied to cannon and blown to bits.[2]

This was the colourful past of this ancient city. Before Sultan Muhammad Khan ever arrived here, Sialkot had the distinction of being the birthplace of poet-philosopher, Allama Mohammad Iqbal, born in 1877, with whom Sultan Muhammad Khan had had a brief acquaintance in Cambridge.

As already mentioned, Sultan Mohammad had acquired several wives during his travels, although his biographers disagree on the number. His first wife was the niece of the emir of Afghanistan and Faiz's mother, Sultan Fatima, whom he married after returning to Sialkot, was his youngest and last. This is the reason that three languages—Urdu, Persian and Punjabi—were spoken in Sultan Muhammad Khan's household. This was to serve Faiz in good stead later, since he never required any formal instruction in either Urdu or Persian, being naturally fluent in both languages since childhood.

Until he married Sultan Fatima, Sultan Muhammad Khan had no sons who lived to a healthy adulthood, a significant setback to a prominent man in those times (and in some ways, still a social handicap). If he had lived on in England, he may never have felt the need to marry again. However, the lack of male progeny to carry on the family name was something which he was likely reminded of repeatedly once he came back to settle in the Punjab. This may have been the main reason he sought (or consented to) another marriage to the daughter of a prominent landowner in the adjoining village of Jessar.

Of this, Dr Aftab Ahmad, one of the grandsons of Sultan Muhammad Khan (the son of his daughter Bilquees from his Afghan wife Sanobar Jan), recalls:

> When our Nana-ji's [Sultan Muhammad Khan's] proposal was sent [to Sultan Fatima's house], her mother was all in favor of it but her father said he's too old for her. Bebe-ji [Sultan Fatima] was about 18 at the time and Nana-ji was fifty-plus, so her father was not in favor of it but her mother put her foot down. She said 'he's a famous man, a well known lawyer; I want to give my daughter to him'. So the marriage happened. And then, in retaliation, her father married a much younger woman who became her stepmother and from whom her step-brother, Iqbal was later born.[3]

Sultan Mohammad's first son from his youngest wife, Tufail, was born two years before Faiz. Regarding the birth of Faiz himself, there is some uncertainty. However, in 1965, at the request of Sehba Lakhnavi, editor of the journal *Afkar,* Faiz himself cleared up the confusion. The journal was in the process of preparing a special Faiz number. This was to be the third in a series of special numbers celebrating the lives and services of stalwarts of Urdu literature. The first two had honoured Shabbir Hasan Khan, also known as 'Josh Malihabadi', and Hafeez Jullundhri, the composer of Pakistan's national anthem. For a prestigious journal like *Afkar*, it was imperative that the information be accurate. The Faiz issue carried a copy of the note that Faiz sent to the editor, which stated:

'[My] date of birth in school papers is listed as January 7, 1911 and elsewhere as January 7, 1912. I had recently requested a friend to go the office of the Sialkot Municipal Corporation to try and obtain a copy of the records to find the correct date. According to his research, the date is listed as February 13, 1911 in the Corporation records.'[4]

Vasilieva states though, that the date 7 January lends itself automatically to some speculation.[5] We should recall that Sultan Fatima was a landlord's daughter who had spent most of her life prior to her marriage in her village. She would, perhaps naturally, have felt somewhat uneasy in the city. It is quite plausible that she left for her village some days before her son was due to be born to be closer to her family. It was in the village that Faiz may have been born as he has himself stated.[6] She may have stayed in the village with her newborn for a few weeks, perhaps up to a month, and then returned to Sialkot when the date of birth was registered at the city offices as 13 February, even though by then, the young Faiz was over a month old. The date of birth registered later in school was 7 January. The confusion over the birth year could perhaps be a clerical mistake or perhaps an erroneous statement by the relative who accompanied the boy to school for admission.

The boy was named Faiz Ahmed Khan, although with time, the surname 'Khan' disappeared. As with most Muslim names, Faiz Ahmed, too, has a religious significance. 'Ahmed' is one of the given names of the Prophet of Islam, Muhammad. The name, in Arabic, then, means, 'generosity of the Prophet'. When he began writing poetry, Faiz chose his first name as his 'takhallus' or pen name. In Urdu, the word 'Faiz' means 'bounty, beneficence or plenty' and thus, with time, the religious overtones of the name faded into more universal meaningfulness.[7]

Faiz recorded his memories of his Sialkot home in an audio cassette addressed to his two older grandsons. He recalls a huge house with lots of rooms and passageways on one of the larger highways of the city near Kanak Mandi (wheat market). Outside, there was a wide ledge where his father's legal clients as well as idlers would sit and gossip. Just in front of the large entrance was an exterior room where his father's elegant Victoria would be parked. In front of that was a large courtyard with stables on all four sides. On the right hand side was his father's large sitting room or 'divan' where all business matters would be conducted. The room was lined on all sides with books. This was where the children's tutors would sit as well. The next room on the right was the 'zenan-khana', the women's quarters. Two rooms below were used as storage areas. The upper floor was divided into two. In one portion lived Faiz's mother and in the other, the rest of the women of the house. His father's bedroom was upstairs as well. If he felt particularly affectionate someday, he would have Faiz sleep in the same bed with him. Next to his house was the house of Lala Hardev Sarai, the local moneylender from whom Sultan Muhammad Khan would borrow money from time to time. In the same house, there were several female cousins as well as all the daughters born of Sultan Muhammad's Afghan wives. Most of the Afghan wives were sickly. The climate of the Punjab did not suit them and, in spite of treatment by physicians, in the space of a few years, they all died one by one.

Faiz's older half-sister, Bibi Gul remembers the young Faiz:

> [He] was a plump baby, with a rosy complexion and very active. He was very attractive with large shiny eyes. He would turn towards anyone who addressed him and start gurgling and laughing. The house was full of women amongst whom he was a favorite plaything, first in a lap, then on someone's shoulder, someone else tickling him, another rocking him back and forth and another worrying about his massage or his grooming. Once he started crawling, we would watch him closely since he would crawl around all over the place. All children are curious and so was he; whenever he would see something shiny or new, he would leap at it.[8]

According to Bibi Gul, Faiz was the responsibility of one of the ladies in charge of the house by the name of Sardar Jan (affectionately referred to as Nana Jan). She had been part of the retinue of servants Sultan Muhammad Khan had received when he married his first wife, Saira Jan (the mother of Bibi Gul). Sardar

Jan was related to the family of the fifth emir of Afghanistan, Shah Shuja Durrani (1785–1842), and had helped raise one of his daughters. She had herself been raised in the royal harem, spoke fluent Farsi and Arabic, and had never married. Faiz used to listen to her tales with great interest.[9]

As was the tradition in Muslim households, Faiz's initial education began with a study of the Quran. In the early-morning hours, his father and other members of the household would recite the verses of the Quran out loud, which he would listen to while still in bed. Later, he started learning the customary duas (prayers) from his mother and then, at the age of five, his father took him to an Islamic school to begin regular instruction and later memorization of the Quran. About this phase of his education, Faiz later said, 'My first teacher was Maulvi Mir Ibraheem Sialkoti. His mosque was near our house, so I learned alphabets and the first *qaeda* [Quranic chapter] from him. Subsequently, I attended his Quran classes for years. He used to teach after the Fajr prayer. This was my initial education [and] he is my first teacher.'[10]

Unlike many other Islamic schools, in Maulvi Mir Ibrahim Sialkoti's school, children were not only taught the Quran but were also given regular instruction in the Farsi and Arabic languages. Faiz studied here for five years, learning the Quran, its proper pronunciation and meaning, and Farsi and Arabic as well. In later years, he had no difficulty speaking, understanding or writing either of these languages. The five daily prayers were in Arabic and many of his family members conversed in Farsi. When once asked why he had decided to get a master's degree in Arabic (rather than the usual Persian or Farsi), Faiz explained,

> One reason was that Persian was spoken in my household and I thought why study a language that I can learn at my house. This was because my father spent a significant portion of his life in Afghanistan. He was associated with the court of Emir Abdul Rehman, the grandfather of Emir Abdullah. When he returned, a few women from there came with him. The oldest of them we used to call Amma Jaan, she was the caretaker of the house, and the second whom we called Aapa Jaan was like our elder sister. Technically they were servants but in reality they were responsible for all the administration of the house. They didn't

> know Punjabi, so they spoke Persian, and we were forced to speak Persian with them. There were one or two Afghan families in Sialkot as well, and we used to converse in Persian. Although now I feel difficulty [speaking the language], in those days I didn't feel the need to learn it formally as I had learned it at home.[11]

Since his younger days, Faiz was known for his extreme reticence and shyness, bordering on faintheartedness. This was something friends and acquaintances would later remark on repeatedly. It arose from his desire to avoid conflicts at all costs and to settle any clash peacefully. About this aspect of his personality, he was to later say:

> When I think about childhood, one thing that stands out is the crowd of women in our home. Out of the three of us [brothers], my younger brother [Inayat] and the older one [Tufail] would rebel against the women and stay busy playing. I was the one the women got hold of. That was both good and bad. The good thing is that the women forced me to adopt an extremely civilized attitude to life because of which I could never, in those days, think of doing something rude or uncouth. I still cannot. The bad thing, something I still regret, is that in my childhood, I never indulged in all the mischief and shenanigans that children usually do.[12]

Bebe-ji

Much has not been written about Faiz's mother, Sultan Muhammad Khan's last and youngest wife Sultan Fatima, affectionately referred to all her life as Bebe-ji (Respected mother). Like most women of her time, she was uneducated but had an abundance of qualities that are just as precious as those one may hope to attain through a formal education: love and affection towards all and sundry, honesty and integrity; and she was forever trying to pass on these qualities to her children. She was especially fond of the shy and intelligent Faiz and he loved her with all his heart as well. Many decades later, reading his letters to Alys from jail, one can feel his love for his mother shining through.

One of Bebe-ji's nephews (the son of her elder brother Sardar Khan) remembers her thus:

As a young child I have many fond memories of childhood when she would come to Jessar (her ancestral home) every summer with Bashir (Faiz's younger brother) who was incapacitated by epilepsy. She would stay at our house for a month and then go to Kala Kadar(Sultan Muhammad Khan's ancestral village) to stay there for about the same length of time.

Jassar railway station is about half a mile from our home. My dad would especially arrange a 'doli' or a tonga to bring her home.

Every summer she would also go and stay for a week in Saed Mittha (inner city Lahore). This house belonged to her maternal grandparents. She had claimed part of her estate (one room) that she kept under lock and key. She would go and stay in that room with the family for a week; it was her way of keeping in touch with her family.

What I remember most about her was how incredibly kind she was. My sisters and I would look forward to her arrival. She would always bring small packets of presents for all the children. They were small bags, beautifully hand sewn by her, of velvet or some other pretty cloth. Inside would be all kind of sweets and goodies.

She would also bring small presents for everyone else in the family. Her suitcase was always full of tasty snacks and goodies. She was a really good cook. I used to love her cooking. She would make exquisitely delicious pickles from all sorts of fruits.

She kept herself busy doing chores around the house, like sewing small bags or making tasty snacks. If she was making something or getting ready to wash clothes, my sister would offer to do it for her. She would smile and wave to her to take over.

Another aspect of her personality which stood out to me was that she was extremely patient; and she was a woman of few words. On hot afternoons when the ladies of the house and friends would sit around in the big family room under a huge 'Punkha' (ceiling fan) being tugged by one of the servants, most of the women would be chattering away but Bebe-ji would sit quietly in the middle, and would only smile and respond in a short sentence if someone asked for her opinion. She never was one to engage in idle talk [the similarities with Faiz's later life are obvious].

At some point she had lost most of her hair. So I always saw

> her with a handkerchief tied over her head and a dupatta tightly wrapped round it. She was religiously observant and very punctual in her prayers and most of the day she would have a 'tasbeeh' [rosary beads] in her hands.
>
> She spent the last moments of her life with us. She had come to Jessar to attend her niece's marriage. She asked my sister and me to accompany her back to Lahore. It was a hot summer day. I, my sister and Bebe-ji set off from Jessar for Lahore by train.
>
> My sisters and I had rented a small house in NawanKot during our studies in Lahore. We arrived in Lahore in the mid-afternoon. I think it was the time of the afternoon prayer. Bebe-ji asked my sister to make a cup of tea while she went to say her prayers.
>
> I ran out to buy some milk. When I returned after few minutes, our world was upside down—Bebe-ji was gone!
>
> My sister told me that while making a cup of tea in the kitchen, she saw Bebe-ji's feet on the musallah [prayer mat]; she thought that Bebe-ji had finished her prayer and was stretching her legs after such a long hot journey.
>
> A few minutes later she went into the room and saw Bebe-ji laying flat on the musallah—lifeless!
>
> My sister was crying hysterically when I got back to the house with a carton of milk in my hand.
>
> We called our uncle Iqbal, who came and arranged an ambulance to take Bebe-ji to Bhai Tufail's house. My sisters spent the night beside Bebe-ji's bed reading the Quran. Faiz bhai came and sat for a long time beside his mother's body weeping quietly. The next day she was buried a few yards away from Tufail, her older son.[13]

These gentle qualities of Sultan Fatima (Bebe-ji) have been described elsewhere as well. Mazhar Jameel writes:

> Just as intrepidity, intelligence and courage were a prominent feature of the personality of Faiz' father, his mother was the personification of sacrifice, altruism, patience, generosity and love. In addition, she was an efficient manager of her household and her family who saw and lived through both the affluence of her husband's life as well as the penury that accompanied his death and during all this time, never allowed these circumstances to affect the education of her children nor ever to poison her relationship to his Afghan family. On the contrary, she looked

> after all the children from his Afghan wives as well as her own children, eventually marrying off the girls to well settled households. One of her own children [the youngest, Bashir] was developmentally disabled and she spent a large portion of her time looking after him until his early death.[14]

She wanted Faiz to be married into an affluent household, preferably part of her own biradari but she eventually accepted Alys, Faiz's British wife, gracefully, and in a short time, despite their obvious communication problems owing to language, she and Alys developed a strong bond. During Faiz's first (and longest) imprisonment, when Alys and her two young daughters struggled to get by, it was Bebe-ji's steadying hand behind Alys which kept her hopes up. During those times of economic hardship, it was the savings from her frugal habits which would come to the aid of the struggling family. In her book, *Over My Shoulder*, Alys spoke with the highest regard of everyone's beloved Bebe-ji, writing how, despite growing up in a traditional, somewhat stultifying, atmosphere, she had within her the capability of moulding an adverse situation to her advantage.[15]

Faiz wrote how, like most mothers, Bebe-ji too wanted her sons to have more male children but in the households of all three of her sons, only daughters were born. However, she never allowed this to worry her.

Her elder son Tufail's untimely death from a heart attack (when Faiz was incarcerated) hit her hard but she chose to stay on with his family. She was always ready to lend a hand to the poor or the unfortunate and she maintained a strong link to her village and her poorer relatives. Faiz was always pained by the fact that his mother had to bear more than her share of hardship in her life and that he could never serve her as much as he would have liked before her death at the age of eighty.

Faiz's younger daughter Moneeza remembers her grandmother thus:

> She lived until I was engaged although she didn't live to see me married. I was very fond of her and she was very fond of me in her own way. I got a lot of my religious leanings from her, just by looking at her: praying, fasting and all; and she was a sort of silent phantom in the house. She rarely spoke, she would just be

> around. I remember she was the very model of patience, she would just sit, chew on her 'niswar', say her prayers, sit quietly; she would even laugh without sound. I used to love making her laugh. Like my father, she would just giggle and start shaking when she laughed. I have a picture when I got a hold of her 'burka', put it on and she just loved it; she laughed her head off. And then we would go to Bawapark [Tufail's house] where she used to live and she would be there; I rarely heard her speak, never ever heard her raise her voice. She would always be wearing her black 'chador' and white 'lattha' (rough cotton) in the summer, shalwar kameez made of 'lattha' as well, she probably sewed it herself. Sometimes I would ask her about Abba [father] and she would say 'Faiz, well, he just used to sit there quietly. If you gave him some milk, he would drink it but he rarely asked for anything'. She was always more concerned with my younger 'chacha', Bashir; she used to feed him, bathe him, clean him, put him to bed. Until he died, she was utterly devoted to him, there was no one else to take care of him. And I used to be afraid to go near him because he frightened me; he wasn't aggressive or anything but just the sight of him, you know, drooling and all, it scared me. Even now I can remember his face clearly. But he scared me so until he died, I never really was very close to her. Sometimes I think she must have been a very lonely woman but at that time, nobody thought about these things. She would just sit and read the Quran quietly.[16]

Faiz's older daughter Salima remembers:

> She lived at our uncle Tufail's house so those girls [Tufail's daughters] got to spend a lot more time with her especially Cheema [Yasmin], she was very naughty so she used to get a lot of reprimands from Bebe-ji but she was also the one closest to her. After Uncle Tufail's death which was a terrible blow to everybody but especially to Bebe-ji, he was her eldest son after all, she felt honour-bound to stay with the girls. She was a very, very patient person. When Tufail died, it fell to my father and mother [Faiz and Alys] to help take care of all the family members in her household. There were fourteen people in the house and they used to live in a house in Ichchra [central Lahore]. So Bebe-ji had a lot on her plate and what I remember was that she was very, very kind; able to assimilate and absorb people's troubles, like a sponge, because she had this very saintly character so the

people in the village used to also care for her a lot; and of course, she had her cross to bear which was Uncle Bashir who was nightmare when I was a child because he was so frightening to behold, with a strange, wild look in his eyes and always drooling. And he was totally dependent on Bebe-ji to feed him and take him to the bathroom and stuff. And that was the only thing my mother [Alys] was not keen about, to have him in our house, around us. So then she put him in the mental hospital but that used to be a medieval place in those days and Bebe-ji was very unhappy, she didn't want to keep him there; so she used to go to the village and take him there because it really wasn't possible for her to live in someone else's house with him. The strange thing is that when she used to go to the village with him in the train, people used to think he is a 'Saeen baba' [Holy man] and they would come up and make offerings to him, which used to really make her mad [chuckles]. But you know she was this woman who was a lot younger than her husband but she was also the only one whose sons survived and so she had this special position in the clan. She was extremely religiously observant with her prayers and her 'rozas' and always telling everyone to do the same. And she tried her best for as long as she could to not have my father marry my mother, not because she disliked her or anything but because she felt it would be very hard. And, of course, my father because he was so close to her, he said I'm not going to do it until she gives permission, so they waited for two and a half years. First she said she was very ill, she said 'I'm dying', so he [Faiz] went off to Gurdaspur to see her and he realized she was making it up. There was nothing wrong, she was just trying to pressure him, you know; please marry so and so before I die, some cousin. But he just said, no, you'll be fine because he was as stubborn as she was.

And she saw with her own eyes the riches-to-rags story and all the poverty after her husband died. So she had a very hard life. And she wasn't educated in the formal sense but she could read and write letters. I would write to her when I was in England and she would be so delighted because it was such a novelty for her to receive letters from someone. I still remember, I used to address them to 'Sultan Fatima' and it would be a PO Box in the next village, because our village didn't have a post office. The other day I found a letter from her in which she had given me the recipe for 'Gosh-e Feel' [an Afghan dish which was

Faiz's favourite]. She would bring baskets full of that when she came from the village and we would send them to father in jail and we loved them too.

So in her own way, she was a soft version of the grand matriarch; understated, soft spoken, never heard her voice raised, even if she scolded someone, she would do it softly.'[17]

In a letter to Alys, Faiz recalled some memories of his childhood:

> As I was changing this morning, long forgotten memories crept out of their hiding places and I saw the Eid gathering and my father giving the Eid sermon under the cool shade of lush trees and Tufail and I sitting in the front row wearing our velvet coats.
>
> After the prayers, our elegant ride sets out from the 'Eid-gah' [the prayer gathering place], the bells on the horses' neck are tinkling, our servant is throwing money on both sides of the road and the street urchins are running after us yelling and trying to grab the money. Then another memory surfaces of entering the courtyard of the 'zenan-khana', crammed full of women. My sisters, their children, the maids and many of the poor women of the village visiting there as guests; as soon as my father enters, a hush falls over the room and everyone kisses his hand in turn. Then my grandmother enters, feeling her way around and my father stands in front of her respectfully and bows his head. She pats his head and gives him her blessing and my father leaves for his quarters and all of a sudden the silence shatters and everyone starts chattering and laughing and talking nineteen to a dozen again. I recalled all of those lives, those sorrows, those joys and I felt an intense desire to embrace all of them and grieve but before that could happen, I bid them farewell. Later there was a dinner and we talked and laughed and joked but time passed with difficulty and it was only when the sun went down that I felt some relief.[18]

Perhaps, as is natural, some of these memories acquired a rosy glow with the passage of time. It seems clear though, that Faiz's childhood was a time of carefree gaiety in a household which was prosperous and harmonious. This was later to make the hardships he faced more traumatic, especially after the sudden and unexpected death of his father. However, the affection he received in those early years was also to stand him in good stead in the adversity both he and his young family were to face in later years. The love that he received in his formative years would also indelibly mould his personality and his poetry, and would play a significant role in the admiration and adoration he was to be showered with all his life.

Notes

1. Javed Iqbal, *Zinda Rud* (Lahore: Sheikh Ghulam Ali and Sons (Pvt) Ltd., 1989), p. 46.
2. Ludmila Vasilieva, *Parvarish-e Lauh-o-Qalam: Faiz Hayat aur Takhleeqat* (Karachi: Oxford University Press, 2006), p. 11.
3. Dr Aftab Ahmad, personal recollection.
4. Sehba Lakhnavi, Kashish Siddiqui (comps), *Afkar*, Faiz number (Karachi: Maktaba Afkar,1965), p. 25.
5. Vasilieva, *Parvarish-e Lauh-o-Qalam: Faiz Hayat aur Takhleeqat*, p. 13.
6. Khaleeq Anjum (ed.), *Faiz Ahmed Faiz: Tanqeedi Jaeza*. (New Delhi: Anjuman Taraqqi-e Urdu, 1985), p. 21.
7. Vasilieva, *Parvarish-e Lauh-o-Qalam: Faiz Hayat and Takhleeqat*, p. 13.
8. Mirza Zafarul Hasan (comp.), *Khoon-e Dil ki Kasheed* (Karachi: Maktaba Asloob, 1983), p. 40.
9. Mirza Zafarul Hasan, *Umr-e-Guzishta ki Kitaab* (Karachi: Idara Yadgaar-e Ghalib, 1977), p. 8.
10. Faiz Ahmed Faiz, 'Guftagoo-Faiz Ahmed Faiz', *Dunyazad*, no. 35 (Karachi: Scheherzade Publications, 2012), p. 44.
11. Ibid., p. 47.
12. Mirza Zafarul Hasan, *Umr-e Guzishta ki Kitaab* (Karachi: Idara Yadgaar-e Ghalib, 1977), p. 8.
13. Mohammad Rafi, personal recollection.
14. Mazhar Jameel, *Zikr-e Faiz* (Karachi: Culture Department, Government of Sindh, 2013), p. 68.
15. Alys Faiz, *Over My Shoulder* (Lahore: The Frontier Post Publications, 1993), p. 303.
16. Moneeza Hashmi, personal recollection.
17. Salima Hashmi, personal recollection.
18. Faiz Ahmed Faiz, *Saleebain Mere Darichay Main* (Karachi: Maktaba Daniyal, 2011), pp. 157–8.

4
Bewildering Dream

Childhood shows the man, as morning shows the day.

—John Milton

Faiz's traditional religious education had been in progress for a while. In addition, he had become fluent in Persian and was being taught the basics of Urdu at home by a tutor by the name of Master Atta Muhammad. Faiz's father Sultan Muhammad Khan was the president of a welfare organization in Sialkot by the name of Anjuman-e-Islamia. He wished Faiz to begin his formal education in the religious school affiliated with this organization. When the time came, Faiz was appropriately dressed and sent to the school. Faiz remembered his memorable first day in school thus:

> For my first day at school, all kinds of preparations were made. I was dressed in fine clothes with my hair combed and 'kajol' was put in my eyes. After being dressed up, I was put in a two horse buggy and sent off to school. When I got there, it was quite a shock. In the madrassa, there was an old, worn out carpet on the floor on which a group of children wearing filthy clothes were huddled together. When I entered the class, the astonished children looked at me, wide eyed, as if to say 'what manner of creature is this?' I had never seen anything like it in my life nor ever met children like this.[1]

It was Faiz's first experience of economic and social inequality. Since he did not know what else to do, he sat down on the carpet with the other children. After the other children's surprise subsided, they made fun of him relentlessly, sometimes touching his fine clothes, at other times touching him to see if he was real. He recounted a similar experience another time:

> Once I went to our ancestral village, Kala Qadir with bhai Tufail. Our dress and our manner of talking and behaving was like those of other 'Raees-zadas' (children of the rich); we were the sons of Khan Bahadur, raised in opulence and luxury but our

> village relatives were all poor; after all, everyone in the village cannot be a Khan Bahadur. We were walking along royally and everyone was lavishing attention and affection on us, especially the women. It was a strange experience, they were all half-starved, had nothing except the clothes on their backs and lived in narrow dark abodes; their heads were bare except for filthy caps or threadbare 'dupattas', their bodies exuded strange, unpleasant smells; they used the ash from their cooking places to clean not only their utensils but often their hands as well. There were boys and girls our age, pale-faced, wrapped in soiled clothes, bare foot, staring at us from a distance and laughing, saying God only knows what. Their hesitation and fear all of sudden boiled up into an ocean and I realized for the first time in my life why kings are kings and why they turn these simple, poor, loving people into their subjects. I realized how easy it was to become a prince or princess. All you had to do was to be the offspring of a king. But to become like these sincere, selfless people, you had to work hard and struggle and sacrifice. Suddenly, my father's being a 'Khan Bahadur' became like a burden to me, it started bothering me. I felt myself being drawn to these simple village people. My various village aunts surrounded us and I liked it. One of them grabbed me and kissed my face so hard that the sounds resounded throughout the area.[2]

In this village Faiz saw a chakki (two millstones used to grind wheat or other grain) for the first time.

> It was a strange contraption, this 'chakki' in which they used to grind wheat and millet seeds and it was all done by the women! You cannot imagine how astonished the both of us were, fingers between our teeth, watching the chakki going around and round, two women together grinding the grain and the flour emerging from the other side. One night, the two of us decided we would use the chakki. We did not know where to put the grain. We picked up some grains and my brother picked up one of the stones while I dropped the grains in there but before I could remove my hand, the stone slipped from the brother's hand and crushed one of my fingers. Instead of flour, my blood ran out of the chakki. We both got scared and decided not to let anyone know of this mishap, especially not Khan Bahadur. We went straight to bed. The next morning, my finger was in agony

> because of the pain and it had spread throughout my body, the white bed sheet was soaked with blood. My finger bled the whole night while I lay there in pain. In the morning, when all the aunts came to wake me up, I was already awake. They saw the blood-soaked sheet and got scared. We were caught. They asked what had happened and I told them the whole story.[3]

After that first day, Faiz decided that if he was to come to this school, it would be in simple dress, like all the other children. At any rate, he did not stay in that school long. He did not like the style of teaching there, nor the atmosphere. He also felt that the teachers there were extra deferential to him to the point of being ingratiating because he was the son of the president of the organization. After a few days, he told his father that he had already learnt more at home than was being taught at the school and he wanted to be sent to a better school. By this time, Sultan Muhammad Khan had reached the same conclusion. After a few months, when school admissions started, Faiz was admitted directly into class four of the Scotch Mission School.

Faiz was to encounter social inequality in a far more personal and painful way after his father's death.

Scotch Mission School

The Scotch Mission High School initially started in 1868. It was situated in Kanak Mandi, Sialkot, and in 1889 it was upgraded to the status of an Intermediate College (and renamed Scotch Mission College) at the request of the Government of the Punjab. It was established by Scottish missionaries belonging to the Church of Scotland Mission.

The school was considered the best in the area, reputed for its educational excellence, discipline and orderly environment. Faiz entered the school in 1921 at the age of ten and studied here until 1927. Scotch Mission School had the distinction of being the alma mater of Allama Muhammad Iqbal as well, who had graduated from there in 1893. The school's faculty boasted many of the most renowned scholars of the era including Maulvi Mir Ibrahim 'Sialkoti', one of the great Islamic scholars of the late nineteenth and early twentieth centuries from whom Faiz received his initial lessons in the Quran and Arabic. In addition, one of Iqbal's most beloved teachers was still teaching at the school when Faiz became a pupil there. 'Shams-ul Ulama' (the Sun of Scholars), Maulvi Syed Mir Hasan (1844–1929), was a Quranic scholar as well as a teacher of Sufism, Persian and Arabic. The title Shams-ul Ulama was awarded to him in 1922 at the insistence of Allama Muhammad Iqbal who, when he was offered a knighthood by the British Crown, agreed to accept it only if Mir Hasan was also awarded a title. When the English governor of the Punjab remarked that Mir Hasan had not authored any books, Iqbal responded that he, Iqbal, was Mir Hasan's work. An estimate of Mir Hasan's ideas and the breadth of his vision can be made from the fact that he had joined Sir Syed Ahmad Khan's Aligarh Movement as early as 1873. His students would later tell many tales about his unique teaching style, one being that his instructions continued well after school hours. He would even go shopping for groceries with a crowd of students around him so that instruction could continue uninterrupted.[4]

Faiz described his association with Maulvi Mir Hasan in this way:

> When I entered school in sixth, seventh class [*sic*], my father took me to Shams-ul-Ulema Maulvi Mir Hassan and requested that he take me into his tutelage. He looked at me and asked me to recite a particular *gardaan* [conjugation of a verb]. I did so, and he accepted me as his student. When I finished school, I used to go to Maulvi sahib's mosque. His routine was that after the Asr (afternoon) prayer he would shift from his living quarters to the mosque and there the students would form a circle around him. There were students from diverse places such as Khorasan, Kabul and Turkey, studying a variety of subjects such as Hadith, Fiqah, and I would also sit there at the end, studying the Arabic alphabet. The picture still exists in my mind. Subsequently I spent the first two years of college in Murray College, Sialkot. Shams-ul-Ulema was the Arabic teacher there as well, so I had the honor of being his student again.[5]

Scotch Mission School was known for its strict discipline and emphasis on educational excellence. In addition, students were expected to participate in extracurricular activities as well. There would often be literary or other kinds of events happening in the school. Within a couple of years, Faiz became a favourite with his teachers for his quiet personality and educational achievements. In classes seven and eight, he was appointed class monitor, a job for which he was singularly ill-suited since he had no taste for disciplining others.

It was during his days at Scotch Mission School that he also acquired a lifelong love of reading. He said later:

> When I was in sixth, seventh class, there was a bookstore adjoining our house. There was an elderly person who ran it who was called Bhai sahib by everyone. He belonged to Brahmo Samaj[6]. He must have been a man of refined taste, as his store possessed all the works of novelists and poetry collections. [Abdul Haleem] Sharar and [Ratan Nath] Sarshar's novels, *Fasana-e-Azaad*, all the classics were available there for just two paisas. That is, he had made a reading library. I believe I had read all of these books by sixth, seventh class but I used to read them secretly. In those days it was not considered decent activity to read novels (laughing). By 6th, 7th class I had read the classical literature and by 7th, 8th class I had read all these novels. Then it so happened that my father had a *munshi* [secretary] who was also the treasurer. We used to take pocket money and money for books from him. One day we had a disagreement, and he complained to my father about my novel reading. I was summoned. My father inquired about my novel reading and I confessed. He said it's a good habit, but instead of Urdu novels I should read English novels. After that I started reading English fiction. I read Dickens for the first time in 8th or 9th class. In those days Rider Haggard was very popular. I read those and romantic novels, and Conan Doyle and detective stories. When I came to college, there was an exam of fiction. For that I read all the fiction of Europe from Tolstoy to Hardy. So I have been very interested in this and still am. For instance, I have read Tolstoy's War and Peace about 12 times, 10 times definitely.[7]

It was also during this time that he began to be interested in poetry, beginning (by his own account) with Ameer Minai and Nawab Mirza Khan 'Daagh Dehlavi'. His innate poetic talent can be judged by a story that he himself later narrated:

> Once, when I was in class 8, my older brother Tufail and a class fellow Nazir Ahmad said to me 'You read a lot of poetry and

> your Urdu is pretty good. Can you write poetry as well?' I said 'no, I have never written poetry'. So Nazir said to me 'Listen, we have a class fellow named Chajju Ram, he is very annoying. We want you to write a parody of him. Write some verses that his head is like a big pan, his belly is like a "matka", his legs are like reeds and that his hands are like this and his eyes are like that'. I had never done anything like it but I liked the idea and the next day, I made up 8 or 10 verses into a poem; Nazir Ahmad read it and was delighted. He said 'you're a poet!' He read it all over school. It got famous but I was distraught. I did not even know Chajju Ram. I went looking for him and when I found him, I apologized profusely. He laughed and said, 'I was looking for you too. What are you apologizing for? Because of your poem, I'm famous all over the school!'[8]

Faiz was thirteen at the time. Around the same time, he had developed a love of theatre and would often get home late. There would be theatre troops from Lahore and Delhi and sometimes from as far away as Bombay performing in the city somewhere. The plays of Agha Hashar Kashmiri were particularly popular. Faiz would often head to the theatre after school with his friends and stay there until late. This later developed into an enthusiasm for writing plays as well. Faiz remembers, 'Whatever I would watch on stage, it would stay in my mind for a long time. I would imagine myself the hero of the play and feel the dramatic tension again. The hero of Agha Hashar's plays would be a brave, steadfast fellow, willing to risk his lives for his principles.'[9]

His older sister remembers one of the consequences of his coming home late. The orders were that if the boys did not get back home by a certain time, they would have to go to bed hungry. His older brother Tufail would get home, make a ruckus and demand food. The younger, Inayat, would head to the kitchen and get something for himself. When Faiz got home, he would change and go lie down. His sisters would feel sorry for him and would ask him if he would like something to eat. Faiz would reply 'Yes, if something is available.' They would serve him his dinner and he would go to sleep happy.[10]

One of Faiz's fellow students in Scotch Mission School, Surendra Nath Rekhi, later penned some memories of his days with Faiz in a letter to Faiz's wife Alys. He writes how Faiz's father, Sultan

Muhammad Khan, was one of the first batches of graduates to pass out of Murray College. He goes on:

> It was our college convocations in 1928/29 and a big 'shamiana' was erected in the college compound. Dr. Garrett, the Principal of the college invited Sultan sahib [Faiz's father] to be the Chief Guest and to deliver the convocation address. Among other things, the most amusing thing he said in his address was that during the first year Sultan sahib was a student at the college, 2 students got admission, during the second year, 4 students joined, during the third year 9 students joined and during the 4th year, 16 students joined the college. That is to say, the yearly admissions in the college were square roots of the digits of the year, 2, 3, 4 etc. This fact provoked hearty laughter amongst the audience, especially the students of Mathematics, of which I was one.[11]

In class ten, a poetry competition was organized in school. One of his teachers, Bihari Lal Ji, selected a verse upon which the participants had to construct a poem. Those who came first, second and third were to receive medals as well as cash prizes. Maulvi Mir Hasan was appointed judge for the competition. Faiz won first prize and a special prize of one rupee from Maulvi Mir Hasan which he cherished all his life.

Love of poetry

Although Sultan Muhammad Khan had a deep affinity for literature and the arts and counted many poets, including Allama Muhammad Iqbal, amongst his friends and acquaintances, it would not be accurate to state that the atmosphere in his home encouraged a love of poetry in his children. In fact, recitation of the Quran was heard more often in the house than poetry. Still, poetry was very much a part of the culture of the city of Sialkot and Faiz heard it often enough when he was out of the house. As stated earlier, when Faiz developed his love of reading in Scotch Mission School, he also started reading poetry. His introduction to classical Urdu poetry was somewhat superficial since he could not understand all the nuances of the words but these initial forays did help awaken the poetic potential inside him that he was not even aware existed:

> I did not understand much of Ghalib at the time. The others also, I only half understood but they all had a strange effect on my heart. This was how I developed a love of poetry and an interest in literature. Another curious thing which really affected me happened around the same time when I repeatedly entered a state in which I saw a sudden change in the color of sunlight and experienced an illusion in which very near objects appeared very far and far objects appeared near. I remember that state even now, we were playing cricket and suddenly instead of keeping my eyes on the ball, I saw a light from afar and saw a tree. Now I do not experience such a state, however, up to a time I used to experience such things as sudden shifts in the colors of the world, dimming of the sunlight instead of it turning yellow, and a play of fog and lights. It was as if the world was a stage in a theatre or a screen.[12]

Of course, Sultan Muhammad Khan soon discovered his son's love of poetry and started taking him along on cold winter nights to the city's mushairas usually held in the large haveli of his neighbour, Pandit Raj Narayan Arman.[13]

As in most cities of the subcontinent, the 'mushaira' or poetry recital was a central feature of Sialkot's cultural life. It was considered a badge of honour to be fluent in Urdu poetry and to be able to recite a sher to underline one's point. Poetry would be recited everywhere: in the city square, inside homes, in schools, in the drawing rooms of the rich, in offices. It was considered even more of an honour to be able to recite one's own poetry in a formal mushaira. In a small mushaira, there could be anywhere from thirty to forty participants. The larger annual ones or those commemorating special occasions would attract thousands of devotees. One of the village squares would be taken over and a large canopy or shamiana would be erected over it. In the front rows, there would be carpets while in the back rows, straw mats would be placed for the attendees. On the raised stage, where the poets were to be seated, there would be carpets from end to end as well as comfortable cushions.

Most of the bigger mushairas would be held in Raj Narayan Arman's large haveli.[14] These were usually presided over by Allama Iqbal's close friend and the former mir munshi of the maharaja of Kashmir, Sirajuddin. Faiz heard the poetry of most of the poets in the city in these gathering and soon felt like writing his own. By the time he was sixteen, he had written some poems and read a few of them in the mushairas. However, Munshi Sirajjuddin was unimpressed and gently advised the young Faiz to dedicate his attention elsewhere. Faiz must have been hurt at hearing this, since he never forgot those words. Years later, he recalled, 'Munshi Sirajjuddin said to me, "Son, it's alright, you try very hard but give this [poetry] up. Concentrate on your studies and when your vision is deeper, perhaps then you can return to it. Right now, it's a waste of time". So I stopped writing poetry.'[15]

Fortunately, his period of giving up poetry was brief. It came to an end soon after he passed his matriculation (class ten) examination with flying colours and headed to Murray College.

Murray College, Sialkot

Murray College was then the most prestigious college in the area. Allama Iqbal had also spent two years here. It was in Murray College that Faiz rediscovered poetry writing when his teacher, Professor Yusuf Saleem Chishti, who had founded a literary organization called Ikhwan-ul Safa (Brothers of Purity), organized a mushaira. The ghazal read by Faiz at the mushaira received vociferous praise. He remembered the occasion years later, 'I remember him [Yusuf Saleem Chishti] because he started the tradition of *mushaira* in the college, based on a given hemistich, and it was there that I recited my first ghazal, and he appreciated it so much that I suspected that there might be a risk of my becoming a poet [laughs].'

Upon being asked if he remembered that first ghazal, Faiz replied: '[No] I did not remember any of it, but a friend of mine, Faqeer Mohyeddin (late), he wrote a book "Anjuman" in which it is mentioned that he met Molvi Yusuf Saleem Chishti somewhere and Molvi sahib remembered a particular verse. The other verses of the ghazal are forgotten, but this is the one:

Lab band hayn, saaqi mujhe aankhon se pilaa day
Woh jaam jo minnat kash-e-sehba nahi hota.'[16]

It was in Murray College that Faiz's love of poetry and literature was able to blossom, since literary and cultural activities were a regular feature on campus. Professor Yusuf Salim Chishti, who was a devotee of Iqbal's poetry, taught Urdu literature while Maulvi Mir Hasan taught Arabic and Persian literature. It was under his tutelage that Faiz developed an interest in classical Persian poetry and began a study of the ancient masters of Urdu and Persian literature.

It was around the same time that he also began to spend more time at home with his father. Faiz relates: 'It was beginning during my school years that father used to call me to his room at night to read his correspondence to him. He used to have some trouble writing at that time so I was, in effect, his secretary. I used to read the paper to him as well and all of these things really helped me. Reading both Urdu and English newspapers really helped me learn.'[17] By the time Faiz reached Murray College, his father relied on him more and more due to his advancing age (he was approaching 70) and Faiz, too, felt duty-bound to devote more time to his care. At last, in 1929, Faiz passed the bachelor's 'entrance' examination from Murray College in first division.

'Whoever loved that loved not at first sight?'

There was another important aspect of Faiz's time in Murray College. During his time there, he experienced 'what everyone that age experiences'; he fell in love for the first time. It was probably when he was around seventeen or eighteen years old and many years later, talking to renowned Punjabi poet and writer Amrita Pritam, Faiz confessed that it was love at first sight.[18] It happened in Lyallpur (now Faisalabad), where Faiz would often go to visit his sister and her family:

> I fell in love as happens to everyone at that age. I was 17 or 18 and I fell in love with an Afghani girl who was my playmate when I was a child. Her family had moved from Afghanistan about the same time as my father. They lived in a village near Lyallpur and my sister was married in that same village so I would go there often to see her. One morning I awoke and saw a beautiful girl feeding her parrot. One look and I was smitten. We would look at each other and eventually progressed to holding hands in secret but it never went beyond that. Her parents married her off to a rich 'zamindar'. It was a great blow and depressed me for quite a while.[19]

When Amrita Pritam asked him why he had not made any effort to further his love, Faiz replied, 'In those days, I could never dare to open my mouth and anyway, I was still studying, why would the girl's family wait that long. So before anything could be said, they married her off. A few years after that, I liked another girl. She was a small-statured, delicate type girl but after a while I began to feel that she is not just a girl but an intelligent and sensitive woman. She, too, married some high official.'[20] Faiz actually never considered this second attraction love. For him, that feeling was reserved for the Afghan girl.

Another close friend of Faiz's from his later years in college, Sher Muhammad Hameed, described Faiz's first experience with love thus:

> This was maybe 9 or 10 years ago. Faiz used to come to Lahore from Amritsar repeatedly, hoping against hope and would always return disappointed. Every fifth or sixth day he would write me a letter in which he would mention his unrequited love; at last, he wrote (his poem) 'Marg-e Soz-e Muhabbat' [Death of love's lament] to mark the end of this love. He traversed all the milestones of love during this time; all the joys and agonies inherent in this journey and yet never complained. The initial poems of 'Naqsh-e Faryadi' are products of this era.[21]

Thus, his early poems in *Naqsh-e Faryadi* (The Lamenting Image)—'Anjaam' (Ending), 'Aakhri khat' (Last letter), 'Haseena-e khayaal se' (To a beauty of imagination) tell the story of this first love. Faiz himself was not too impressed with these early creations in later years. Most of these were romantic poems first published in the *Ravi*, the prestigious literary journal of Government College, Lahore. Faiz included only a few of these poems in his published collections.

Faiz's father never discouraged his growing love for poetry but neither did he ever actively encourage it. For Sultan Muhammad Khan, it was probably natural that his son should be attracted to poetry; it was all around him. Sultan Muhammad Khan was much more concerned about his son's formal education. Faiz had finished school and then high school with flying colours. This was as far as he could go in the city of Sialkot. It was time to move on.

The next stop was Lahore, the ancient capital of the Punjab.

Sultan Muhammad Khan wanted his son to study in the most prestigious college in the city: Government College, Lahore, affiliated with the equally prestigious and ancient Punjab University. Despite the fact that Faiz had passed his high-school examination with distinction and was clearly academically gifted, there was no guarantee that he would be admitted into Government College. His father thus prevailed on his friend Allama Muhammad Iqbal to write a letter of introduction for the boy to the principal of Government College, Qazi Fazal ul Haq, who was, at the time, the head of the Persian department. In the letter, Iqbal particularly appreciated Faiz love of learning and his bright intellect. Armed with this letter, Faiz headed off to Lahore.

It must have been wrenching for him to have to leave his ancestral home where he had spent his childhood and boyhood amidst the loving women of his family. It might have been his grief at leaving his loved ones and his home behind that spawned these lines:

> Sadness spreads over the heart
> Grief pierces down into the soul
> Life's deceit shows nature's purpose
> Youth is departing, it's obvious.[22]

Notes

1. Ayub Mirza, *Faiz Nama* (Lahore: Classic Publishers, 2005), p. 25.
2. Mazhar Jameel, *Zikr-e Faiz* (Karachi: Culture Department, Government of Sindh, 2013), pp. 57, 58.
3. Mirza, *Faiz Nama*, pp. 443, 444.
4. Javed Iqbal, *Zinda Rud* (Lahore: Sang-e-Meel Publications, 2004), p. 39.
5. Faiz Ahmed Faiz, 'Guftagoo—Faiz Ahmed Faiz', *Dunyazad*, no. 35 (Karachi: Scheherzade Publications, 2012), p. 44.
6. A Hindu reformist movement.
7. Faiz, 'Guftagoo—Faiz Ahmed Faiz', p. 65.
8. Jameel, *Zikr-e Faiz*, p. 55.
9. Ludmila Vasilieva, *Parvarish-e Lauh-o-Qalam: Faiz Hayat aur Takhleeqat* (Karachi: Oxford University Press, 2006), p. 16.
10. Ibid., pp. 15, 16.
11. Surendra Nath Rekhi, unpublished letter to Alys Faiz from New Delhi, 24 January 1991, Faiz Ghar Archives, Lahore.

12. Vasilieva, *Parvarish-e Lauh-o-Qalam: Faiz Hayat aur Takhleeqat*, p. 19.
13. Jameel, *Zikr-e Faiz*, p. 66.
14. Ibid.
15. Khaleeq Anjum (ed.), *Faiz Ahmed Faiz: Tanqeedi Jaeza*, p. 36.
16. Faiz, 'Guftagoo—Faiz Ahmed Faiz', p. 45.
17. Anjum, *Faiz Ahmed Faiz: Tanqeedi Jaeza*, pp. 21, 22.
18. Sheema Majeed (comp.), *Baatein Faiz Say* (Lahore: Rohtas Books, 1990), p. 19.
19. Salima Hashmi, *Adbiyat*, vol. 82, no. 1, January–March 2009 (Pakistan Academy of Letters), p. 217.
20. Majeed, *Baatein Faiz Say*, p. 20.
21. Sehba Lakhnavi, Kashish Siddiqui (comps), *Afkar*, Faiz number (Karachi: Maktaba Afkar, 1965), pp. 6–12.
22. Faiz Ahmed Faiz, *Nuskha hai Wafa* (Lahore: Maktaba Karvaan, 1985), p. 37. Translation by this author.

5

Lahore, My Love!

Aye roshnion ke shehr...

O City of lights...

—Faiz Ahmed Faiz

Even though he had been a brilliant student in Sialkot, Government College, Lahore, Faiz's next stop was known for its high academic standards. Thus, armed with a letter of introduction from Allama Muhammad Iqbal to Government College's Principal, Qazi Fazal-ul Haq who also happened to be the head of the Persian department there, Faiz set off for Lahore. Iqbal and Qazi Fazal-ul Haq had been friends since their days as students in London. In the letter, Iqbal especially extolled the academic brilliance and enthusiasm of the young Faiz. Even at that time, Faiz knew the value of the document he carried. Years later he recalled: 'I am still grieved about the fact that Qazi sahib swiped that letter from me. When the interview was finished I said "Give the letter back to me". He said "No, it shall remain with me".'[1]

The letter was thus lost. However, Faiz's entry into Government College was assured. Faiz had had the chance before this time to get to know Allama Iqbal but he had always hesitated because of his natural diffidence. He felt the difference in their ages (Iqbal was fifty at the time) to be an insurmountable barrier. He wrote at one point: 'He was such a great poet and he was my father's friend as well, that I felt some misgivings approaching him.'[2]

And now, in 1929, he had become a student at Government College, Lahore, the same college where Iqbal had studied thirty years earlier.

'On the shoulders of giants'

Government College was renowned for its democratic atmosphere. It was usual for students and teachers to mingle freely outside the college. This may have been one reason that the students of

Government College excelled in their examinations and it was the top-ranked college in the Punjab. Government College, at that time, boasted a galaxy of literary luminaries, most of whom were diligent, affectionate teachers. Foremost among them were Professor Ahmad Shah Bokhari (known by his nom de plume, 'Patras') in the English department and 'Sufi' Ghulam Mustafa 'Tabassum'. Later, Faiz was also to develop an affectionate relationship with another brilliant teacher in Lahore, Dr Mohammad Deen Taseer. About his teachers, he was to say later:

> After that I went to Government College in Lahore, and Mr. Langhorn[3] was an English teacher there. I was under the impression that I have great command over the English language. When I started studying under him, all that I had learned previously he dismissed as rubbish. *laughter* He declared that I knew nothing, so I started learning the language anew and believe that I gained much insight from him. Then in Literature there [was] Patras Bukhari. I had the closest relationship as a student with him, Dr. [MD] Taseer and Sufi sahib. This was probably in 1928.[4]

Patras Bokhari

Ahmad Shah Bokhari Patras, affectionately known as 'ASB' came to Lahore's Government College in 1916, did his BA, then, after debating it a while, changed his focus from physics (his parents' choice) to English literature. After his MA in English, he proceeded to Cambridge, England, for his Tripos and soon distinguished himself there as well. He returned after finishing his education and was eventually appointed Professor of English. He was, in his time, a teacher, a writer, a translator, a broadcaster and finally a high-level UN diplomat. His arrival, in addition to strengthening educational standards, heralded an immediate renaissance in the literary and cultural activities of the college.

As proof of ASB's intellectual prowess, Muhammed Tufail, publisher of *Naqoosh*, recounted how on one occasion the young ASB, recently returned from Cambridge, engaged Allama Iqbal in a debate on the philosophy of Bergson, with both Iqbal and Patras putting forth their respective arguments and logic. Finally, Iqbal relented. Iqbal's poem, about ASB, 'Ek falsafa zada Syed-zaaday ke naam' (To a philosophical son of a Syed), was written after this incident.[5]

Faiz writes: 'Bokhari sahib had no special interest in journalism or politics but he spent many a night in the offices of "Pakistan Times" [where Faiz was Chief Editor immediately before and after partition]; the night Gandhi-ji was assassinated, the night of 13/14th August [Independence] and there is no harm in saying [now] that three or four editorials of the time plus several columns under different names were penned by Bokhari sahib.'[6]

He had no special affinity for children either ('Forget it, yaar, it's a woman's department') but on nearly every holiday, he would come and play with the Faiz and Taseer children, inventing all kinds of games with them, singing songs and telling stories.

He was even more allergic to the elderly but incidentally, when Alys's parents showed up from London, he charmed them in the first meeting. They were old-fashioned English people who had nothing in common with him. Faiz and Alys were concerned that the evening would be rather boring. After the introductions and a few niceties, he said suddenly, '"Mrs George! Do you remember any post World War I old song? E.g. that one...' and he started humming an old English song. My mother in law, who loved singing, immediately warmed up and they both sang until they were out of breath. When this act finished, Bokhari sahib turned to her husband and said "Mr. George, forget these women, let us, you and I, go". "Where are you taking my old man" called out Mrs. George?" "To paint the town red, Mrs. George!" and took him out gallivanting around all of Lahore's restaurants to watch the Anglo-Indian girls dancing.'[7]

ASB formed a new literary organization upon his return to Government College, called Majlis (gathering), in which, in addition to the intellectually gifted students of the college, experienced poets, authors and intellectuals were also invited, the purpose being the grooming of the literary abilities of students.

Later in life, Faiz paid ASB the ultimate compliment. When people would say disparagingly that ASB had not left behind enough books to match his intellectual talents, Faiz would repeat what Iqbal had said about Mir Hasan, that he, Faiz, was ASB's book.

'Sufi' Ghulam Mustafa 'Tabassum'

Another mentor to the young Faiz, Ghulam Mustafa, had initially adopted 'Sufi' as his nom de plume but later changed it to 'Tabassum' (smile) at the advice of his poetry teacher. He was a renowned teacher of Persian poetry, language and literature and an ardent lover of music. He was as lively, affectionate and friendly as ASB. He was also a reputed poet in his own right. His later nom de plume matched his personality perfectly, even though the first one (Sufi) also stuck and he is still remembered in the annals of Urdu literature and poetry simply as Sufi Tabassum. It has often been pointed out that the chosen pen names of many of the East's greatest poets bear a striking similarity to their poetic inclinations. This was certainly the case with Sufi Tabassum who had an abiding love of Sufi poetry. He always carried around the books of Amir Khusro[8] and Naziri[9] with whom he was extremely impressed. His enduring achievement is the Urdu translation of Amir Khusro's Persian ghazals as well as the Persian poetry of Mirza Asadullah Khan 'Ghalib'. He was on friendly terms with Allama Iqbal and would visit his house often. In fact, 'Allama Iqbal often called upon [Sufi Tabassum's] knowledge of both these languages [Persian and Urdu]...and he was the only member of the inner circle at Allama's house to be allowed to take an occasional puff from Iqbal's hukka.'[10] He singled out Faiz for special attention perhaps because he had heard of the brilliance of Faiz's father (and possibly Faiz himself) from Iqbal. Faiz considered 'Sufi sahib' his foremost teacher of poetry and the two later became close friends. To the end of his days, despite having achieved worldwide acclaim as a poet, Faiz would turn to Sufi Tabassum for an opinion or correction of his poems. This devotion was in no small measure due to the encouragement that Sufi Tabassum had shown the young poet at the beginning of his poetic journey.

Sufi Tabassum had appreciated Faiz's poetic genius early on. In 'My first meeting with Faiz', he wrote:

> It was October, 1929 and I had been at Government College for about 3 months. After the suffocating atmosphere of my previous employment, I felt a wave of joy sweep through me when I arrived. Bokhari sahib had organized a huge Mushaira. On the stage were the literary luminaries of the day and in the audience

> sat the leading members of all the notable literary organizations of Lahore...then a young man came on stage; fair of color, with a broad forehead, his movements fluid, his eyes and lips languorous. He read out his verses with great composure and poise. Looks were exchanged, Patras glanced meaningfully at the other people on stage and [afterwards] Faiz was invited back on stage to recite again. He recited a nazm as well as a ghazal. In both, his style of thought and expression was quite unique.[11]

Mohammad Deen Taseer

M.D. Taseer was born in 1902 in Amritsar, grew up in Lahore and was the first person in the Indo-Pak subcontinent to get a PhD in English literature from Cambridge University. He had been a favoured pupil of Allama Iqbal's and the latter had urged him to go to England for further studies. While in London, he had become friends with Syed Sajjad Zaheer and had been present when the draft manifesto of the All-India Progressive Writers' Association was discussed and approved. Although he was later to dissociate himself from the Association (for a number of reasons), he remained a dear friend and mentor to Faiz and later, of course, his brother-in-law, when Faiz married Alys, who was the younger sister of Taseer's wife, Christabel.

About all of these beloved teachers, Faiz later said:

> It happened that I met Taseer sahib around 1928. I met him in the first *mushaira* that happened at Government College after my admission. Bukhari sahib was the president. Taseer was there as well, along with [Abdul Majid] Salik (late), Chiragh Hassan Hasrat and Pandit Hari Chand Akhtar...Hafeez Jullundhari was there as well. The point is that all the teachers were present, so I got introduced to them in that first *mushaira*. Afterwards Taseer sahib invited me to their company and I got to meet Salik sahib and Sufi sahib. The situation was such that there wasn't much learning during college hours but more so outside college. Taseer sahib had a library in his house, which was open to all. Any person could take a book or inquire if he had a question to ask. Entry into Bukhari sahib's house was relatively difficult, but a few special students had the permission—not like the freedom of Taseer sahib's house, but after informing him and taking his permission we could visit. I

> used to visit him, and in those days he started a circle which is called Majlis-e-Iqbal but was previously named Majlis-e-Urdu. Every month there used to be a gathering in which students read out their essays and poetry, and the senior people there used to express their opinions on it. It was very educational. Then there was the house of Sufi sahib where people used to gather in the evening. Near the end of college days the boys who had passed BA were almost treated there as teachers. So whatever I learned, I learned from these people.[12]

Friends and rebels

Even though Government College offered many more opportunities for Faiz to flourish educationally, it was still the first time that he had been away from his family. In addition to his natural shyness, he was still suffering from the pangs of unrequited first love. His friend Sher Muhammad Hameed described how Faiz had been a loner in college until he and his friends Nabi Ahmad and Agha Hameed approached him and sealed a lifelong bond of friendship with him with the words, 'Come, brother, from today we are your friends.'[13] According to Sher Muhammad Hameed, it still took Faiz another five or six months to open up.

It was also in Government College that Faiz became friends with a young man by the name of Khwaja Khurshid Anwar, an ardent lover of music. It was in his company that Faiz learnt the finer points of music and in later life Faiz was to call him 'my dearest friend'.

These were turbulent times for the country. In the later part of the 1920s, especially in the Punjab and Bengal, revolutionary activities were at their peak. The ruling British termed all those involved in such activities as 'terrorists'. After the end of the First World War, Indian soldiers, radicalized and angry, were returning to their villages. Many of them bore the scars of battle and were physically disabled. In addition, the Great Depression that had originated in New York with the stock market crash of October 1929 had spread around the world including British India. The prices of agricultural goods had slumped, farmers had become destitute and the rural economy of India, which depended largely on agriculture, had been destroyed. The British had no interest in reviving it; they were instead focused on repaying their war debts as quickly as possible. Calls for Indian independence had again reached a crescendo. In addition, the October Revolution in the newly established Soviet Union had inspired toilers the world over. All over the country, trade unions and kissan sabhas (farmers' unions) were being organized but the English maintained a firm, brutal control over affairs, epitomized by the earlier massacre (in 1919) at Jallianwala Bagh. In response, many young men had turned to terrorism not just to answer force with force but with the ultimate goal of driving the British out of India. They would occasionally succeed in inflicting a blow upon the hated rulers but would usually be swept up by the vast imperial spying network that the British had set up all over the country. Thus, the young men arrested in cases like the Chittagong armoury raid and the Kakori train robbery were all awarded exemplary punishments to serve as deterrents to future offenders. However, this only served to fan the flames and young men like Bhagat Singh and his associates became heroes to the people of the Punjab for their activities against the British.

The movement had spread from the villages to the cities and had influenced many young people, among them Khwaja Khurshid Anwar. He was from an affluent family and he loved music. He counted among his close friends, in addition to the young Faiz who was a budding poet, Rafiq Ghaznavi, Agha Hameed, Nabi Ahmad and Sher Muhammad Hameed, all of them fond of music and poetry and none the least bit interested in politics. Once Khwaja Khurshid came under the influence of the radicals, banned literature began to be smuggled into college. Sometimes a poster would appear on the college noticeboard inciting action against the British; at other times, pamphlets would be distributed secretly inside newspapers. Gradually, Faiz's room began to be used for storing this contraband and later for secret meetings. Eventually, the hostel was raided but fortunately, nothing was found in Faiz's room, or in Khwaja Khurshid's. However, Khwaja Khurshid was arrested on the basis of secret reports that alleged that he had been smuggling acetic acid out of the college laboratory and supplying it to the radicals to make bombs. After the usual cursory trial, he was awarded three years rigorous imprisonment. He served a few months but was freed on appeal due to lack of evidence. He completed his education and later applied for entry into the Indian Civil Service but was denied it owing to his criminal record. He decided to try his hand at music and became one of the foremost musical composers and directors of his time, creating tunes that remain immortal to this day.

Poetry's origins

It was in Government College that Faiz began to pay attention to writing poetry. This was also the time when he was in the throes of his first, adolescent love. His initial poetic experiments (most of which he later discarded) reflected this preoccupation. His natural poetic inclinations flowered in the fertile artistic soil of Government College. Just a few months after his admission to the college, his first verses were published in its prestigious literary journal, *Ravi*. It was October 1929 and the verses were titled simply 'Ash'aar'.

Mai ho, tanhai dil afroz ho, main hun, tu ho
Chandni raat ho khamosh kinaar-e ju ho
Ek ho jaen khamoshi main hamari roohain
Jaise do phool hon aur ek hi si khushboo ho

[Let there be] wine, refreshing solitude, me and you
[A] silent moonlit night, a river bank
In silence, our souls mingle as one
Like two flowers with the same fragrance[14]

These are the earliest published verses of Faiz. The verses from the mushaira he participated in as a teenager, which Faiz himself referred to (see chapter 3), are the earliest (unpublished) verses on record. Some commentators have stated that the poem 'Mere masoom qaatil' (My innocent assassin) was Faiz's first nazm.[15] However, given that no such poem exists, this conjecture seems to be a mistake.

From this time, Faiz's poems appeared regularly in *Ravi*. A Bazm-e Sukhan (literary society) was already active under the patronage of Qazi Fazlul Haq. Later, monthly gatherings were also held at the home of 'Patras' Bokhari where Faiz would recite his poetry in the presence of notable litterateurs such as Imtiaz Ali Taj, M.D. Taseer, Hafeez Jullundhri, Chiragh Hasan Hasrat and Sufi Tabassum. In addition to Faiz, another poet Nazre Muhammad

(NM) Rashed was also a fixture at these gatherings. Rashed was a year older than Faiz and thus a year ahead in college and was studying economics. Faiz later referred to Rashed as Government College's malik-us shoara (king of poets) and admitted that he had learned a lot from him. The participation of older, more experienced scholars and teachers helped raise the level of these gatherings and played an important part in the development of the young students. In later life, Faiz repeatedly acknowledged his debt to his teachers, particularly Sufi Tabassum, Ahmad Shah Bokhari 'Patras' and M.D. Taseer.

Faiz and Iqbal

In January 1931, Allama Iqbal was the chief guest at the much-anticipated annual Government College mushaira. He was a fervent supporter of literary activities of this sort and often accepted such invitations. Faiz had just written a poem about Iqbal, in a rather long metre, which had already been published in *Ravi*. Sufi Tabassum was insistent that Faiz read it in front of Iqbal. When his turn came to recite, however, Faiz panicked and decided to flee the mushaira. Luckily, Sufi Tabassum was nearby and prevailed upon his young friend to recite the poem to the audience, which erupted in appreciation. Even Iqbal offered his quiet appreciation. In later years, this would form one of Faiz's fondest memories.

Iqbal, of course, was a well-established and much respected figure by the time Faiz was born. Faiz's devotion to him was, in part, due to the friendship between Iqbal and his father Sultan Muhammad Khan. In addition, Faiz had followed in Iqbal's footsteps and studied at the same schools and then the same college. Both also shared a devotion to the same teachers including Shams-ul Ulema Maulvi Mir Hasan and Maulvi Ibrahim Mir Sialkoti (and both were proud of this fact). Faiz remained a devotee of Iqbal's poetry throughout his life. As proof, one can point to the numerous scholarly essays of critical appreciation that he wrote on Iqbal's work. Faiz had a deep understanding of Iqbal's poetic thought and the far-reaching changes in Urdu poetry that he fashioned.

Thus, while Faiz never agreed with Iqbal's political philosophy of pan-Islamism, he remained a firm admirer of Iqbal's poetic prowess.

'Your Faiz has been orphaned'

Faiz remained in Government College for approximately five years (1929–33), completing his BA in Arabic and then MA in English. He later spent a year doing his MA in Arabic from Punjab University's Oriental College but spent most of that time in Government College as well. During this time, he was under the tutelage of some renowned teachers (some of whom we have already met). He was now regularly being published in *Ravi* and garnering accolades at various mushairas and gatherings inside and outside college. It must have been a happy time for him.

He had just moved into the fourth (final) year of his BA when he suffered the most devastating loss of his young life.

It was the occasion of the wedding of his younger sister, Bali. Sultan Muhammad Khan's house was full of visiting relatives and he was personally supervising the arrangements. The entire village was festive; after all, it was the wedding of Sultan Muhammad Khan's youngest daughter. Suddenly, Sultan Muhammad Khan fell, stricken by a pain in his chest. The doctor was fetched but it was already too late. Sultan Muhammad Khan was dead and the house of festivities suddenly turned into a house of mourning.

The death of a parent is, by all accounts, a terrible thing. The feeling of deprivation it generates can never be overcome, but Sultan Muhammad Khan's death brought the family face to face with a more urgent and much more calamitous problem. He was considered one of the area's most affluent men. It now dawned on the family that all of their luxury and opulence was being financed by debt. The creditors started lining up even before Sultan Muhammad Khan's grave had been dug. It turned out that he had left behind a huge (for those days) amount of debt totalling Rs 80,000. Most of the property had already been quietly sold or placed as collateral against the debt. The lands around the village were occupied by poorer relatives and could not immediately be vacated. Only the land which Sultan Fatima had brought in her dower was unencumbered, but it was wholly insufficient to feed the large family.

Sultan Fatima, her elder son Tufail and Faiz did not give up under these trying circumstances and decided they would repay every penny of the debt. Faiz humbly requested his mother and elder brother that he be allowed to leave his studies and start working. Both of them strictly forbade it. Sultan Fatima took some immediate emergency measures to bring the finances of the house under control. The large staff of servants was disbanded. Tufail and Faiz decided to take the financing of their education into their own hands. Tufail finished his law degree, took his civil-service exams and accepted a post as a judge. Faiz, too, began looking for part-time work. Sultan Fatima would do her best to get hold of grain, ghee, fuel, vegetables and other daily essentials from the village to feed the family. The household properties, including land, horses, buggies, cattle, all were quickly sold off to repay the debt.

The impact of this sudden loss on Faiz cannot be overestimated. In later years, he would point to this calamity as a watershed in his life when his personality underwent a sea change. At that time, though, he expressed his anguish far more simply in a letter to Sher Muhammad Hameed, 'Your Faiz has been orphaned.'[16]

This was also the time that smoking, which was to become Faiz's lifelong habit, became ingrained. Sufi Tabassum recorded an anecdote in this regard. It was exam season in college and Patras Bokhari was chief examiner. Sufi Tabassum was assigned one of the smaller rooms on the second floor where some of the MA English students including Faiz were taking the exam. Smoking was prohibited inside the examination room and Sufi Tabassum writes how he had brought along a paan to compensate for the lack of cigarettes. 'But Faiz would sometimes look at the paper and then glance contemplatively at me, then scratch his head with his pen or quietly inquire after his neighbors. Sometimes his left hand would move as if he was feeling for something.' Sufi Tabassum then writes that he was about to ask Faiz what was wrong when Faiz stood up and asked, 'Are we allowed to smoke here?' Sufi Tabassum responded, 'I will let you know presently.' Just then, Patras Bokhari came and stood outside the room and asked if everything was OK. Sufi Tabassum asked him 'Professor sahib, some students want to smoke, is it permitted?' Patras Bokhari responded, 'Until Professor Jodh Singh becomes the college Principal, yes, its allowed.' He then smiled and walked away. Sufi Tabassum walked back into the classroom and indicated to the students that they could smoke. 'A cigarette appeared in Faiz' hand as if by magic and both pen and cigarette started speeding along. The fragrant tobacco smoke spread all over the room. I was the teacher, chained by discipline. I forgot my "paan" and started enjoying the cigarette smoke. How was I to know that the clouds of this smoke would spread far outside the college walls along with the spirits of the smokers and would engulf the world of poetry and literature.'[17]

His father's death was a terrible blow for Faiz but in later life, he rarely ever referred to either the incident or his feelings, except perfunctorily, even though it imposed some very severe financial burdens on him, forcing him to take up part-time employment from time to time. He even took some help from a welfare agency based in Lyallpur (now Faisalabad), known colloquially as the 'Qila Fund'. This was all done to spare his family from any additional financial worries and to help them in any way he could. He had also become far more serious about life and his education. In 1933, he passed his BA (Honours) from Government College, with Arabic as an optional subject.

MA in English and Arabic

After his graduation, once again Faiz wished to seek employment to help his family out financially but his older brother Tufail again forbade it and asked him to concentrate on his education. Friends and well-wishers also reminded him that after a BA (Honours) degree, he could do an MA in one year and not pursuing that opportunity would be a waste. He would be able to find many more opportunities for employment, especially in the department of education after an MA. Faiz thus enrolled in an MA in English in Government College. He had studied a large cross-section of English poetry by this time and Milton, Keats, Shelley, Byron and Wordsworth were his favourite poets. In addition, under the tutelage of ASB, Professor Dickinson and Professor Harish Chand Katapalia, he had received a thorough grounding in English fiction and literature. He would make it a point to attend ASB's classes but for the rest, he would prefer to meet them outside class. In addition, he had developed an interest in reading books that were outside the syllabus. This reflected in his MA English result in which he attained a second division, his most inferior result so far.

After MA English, Faiz decided to pursue a master's in Arabic. About this decision, Faiz later said, 'One reason was that Persian was spoken in my household and I thought why study a language that I can learn at my house. Also, it was generally thought that those who studied Arabic had a better chance of going into the Indian Civil Service (ICS).'[18]

However, Arabic was not offered as a subject at MA level in Government College, so Faiz sought admission in the MA Arabic classes at the nearby Oriental College, affiliated with Punjab University. The principal of Oriental College as well as the head of the Arabic department was Maulvi Mohammad Shafi, a strict disciplinarian. Every candidate had to convince him that he was worthy of admission by demonstrating his love of the language. Faiz later wrote how he and his friend Hameed ud Din were summoned before Maulvi Mohammad Shafi. Hameed ud Din's father, Dr Sadruddin, was a teacher of Arabic in Government College so he was let off relatively lightly but, said Faiz, 'Maulvi sahib argued with me for quite a while mainly about the fact that young people considered Arabic an easy subject and avoided the hard work required to master it before pestering a teacher. I pleaded that I had been a student of Shamsul Ulema Maulvi Mir Hasan and Maulvi Ibrahim Mir Sialkoti and reminded him about my BA Honors in Arabic and he reluctantly agreed.'[19]

This was, however, just the beginning. In those days, MA students in Government College were considered 'junior teachers' and were given the latitude to attend classes as they chose. Punctuality, too, was not a priority. Maulvi Mohammad Shafi, though, was an old-fashioned teacher who enforced all the rules with relish. Faiz writes, 'He was very authoritarian and punctual to a fault. We were Government College's spoilt brats and, as usual, showed up 5 or 10 minutes late for his class. Maulvi sahib took out his gold watch from his pocket and glared at us for a few minutes and then, without saying anything, put it back. It was the same during class. He was a strict perfectionist but despite this unpleasant introduction, the beauty of his teaching style more than made up for any faults.'[20]

Unlike the teachers in Government College, he would rarely grant anyone an audience outside college, often standing on the balcony of his home behind the college to address anyone who showed up with a query. Faiz was to say affectionately later in life, 'Even after I had a head full of white hair, I would feel nervous if summoned by him.'[21]

By the time Faiz finished his education, his older brother Tufail had also graduated with a law degree and been appointed a senior civil judge in Lyallpur. Faiz's mother and other relatives had shifted to Lahore from Sialkot. Faiz, however, was not yet free of financial worries. In spite of his stellar academic qualifications, he still did not have a job and at the height of the worldwide Great Depression, there was no guarantee that he would find one. Unemployment was rampant, government departments were shrinking and Faiz joined the long line of educated, unemployed young men with an uncertain future. It was at this time that he was offered a position as a lecturer at Mohammadan Anglo-Oriental (MAO) College, Amritsar, which he accepted without hesitation. Soon, his carefree student days in Lahore would be distant memory.

Notes

1. Faiz Ahmed Faiz, *Mataa-e Lauh-o Qalam* (Karachi: Maktaba-e Daniyal, 2011), p. 106.
2. Ibid., p. 107.
3. Professor Langhorn Firth, head of the Department of English whose most famous contribution to Faiz's educational development was when, in Faiz's third year in Government College, he gave Faiz 165 marks out of a total of 150. When asked why he did it, his reply was 'because I could not give more'. In those days, the head of department could award an additional fifteen marks.
4. Faiz Ahmed Faiz, 'Guftagoo—Faiz Ahmed Faiz', *Dunyazad*, no. 35 (Karachi: Scheherzade publications, 2012), p. 45.
5. 'Patras and Iqbal', http://www.patrasbokhari.com/content/patras-bokhari-allama-iqbal. Retrieved 2013-12-25.
6. Faiz Ahmed Faiz, *Meezan* (Karachi: Urdu Academy, Sindh, 1987), p. 294.
7. Ibid., pp. 295–6.
8. Amir Khusro 'Dehlavi' (1253–1325), Hindustani poet; revered teacher of Persian literature and poetry, considered the founder of Urdu and Hindi poetry; beloved disciple of Sheikh Nizamuddin Aulia, the head of the Sufi Chishtia order.

9. Naziri of Nishapur (d. 1612), one of Hindustan's most popular Persian poets, patronized by the Mughal kings Akbar and Jahangir (his son) and also closely linked to Sufi circles of his time.
10. Salma Mahmud, *The Wings of Time* (New Delhi: Har Anand Publications, 2012), p. 28.
11. Faiz Ahmed Faiz, *Nuskha hai Wafa* (Lahore: Maktaba Karvaan, 1985), pp. 491–2.
12. Faiz,'Guftagoo-Faiz Ahmed Faiz', p. 46.
13. Sehba Lakhnavi, Kashish Siddiqui (comps), *Afkar*, Faiz number. (Karachi: Maktaba Afkar, 1965), p. 203.
14. Translation by this author.
15. Ibid., p. 27.
16. Faiz, *Nuskha hai Wafa*, p. 499.
17. Sufi Ghulam Mustafa Tabassum, 'Faiz say meri pehli mulaqat', in Mirza Zafarul Hasan (comp.), *Khoon-e dil ki kasheed* (Karachi: Maktaba Asloob, 1983), pp. 23–4.
18. Faiz, 'Guftagoo—Faiz Ahmed Faiz', p. 47.
19. Faiz Ahmed Faiz, 'Maulvi Mohammad Shafi', in *Mataa-e Lauh-o Qalam*, p. 94.
20. Ibid.
21. Ibid., p. 95.

6

An End and a Beginning

To make an end is to make a beginning.
The end is where we start from.
—T.S. Eliot

When Faiz joined Mohammadan Anglo-Oriental (MAO) Amritsar in 1935 as a lecturer after finishing his education, the entire world, including the Indian subcontinent, was in the throes of the Great Depression which had started with the Wall Street crash in America in 1929. Unemployment, poverty and fear stalked the land. Faiz later wrote that this was a time when 'ruined farmers flocked to the cities in search of employment, women from respectable households started selling themselves for food and refined young men wandered the streets unemployed'.[1] Under these conditions, he was happy to accept any job offer that came his way. He taught at the MAO College from 1935 to 1940 and in those years, according to his close friend and translator Ludmila Vasilieva, 'a new Faiz was born...who perceived the world entirely differently from before'.[2]

In the 1935–6 academic year, the total number of faculty members in MAO College was eighteen and in a group photo, Faiz is identified as a lecturer in English and in charge of the cricket team. This is the first documentary proof of Faiz's love of cricket and his regret, laughingly expressed in a later interview, that he could never become a cricketing star. The college at that time was headed by its vice-principal, Sahibzada Mahmooduzzafar, who had recently returned after completing his MA in English literature from Oxford University. The position of principal was vacant since it required a PhD degree. It remained vacant until 1937 when Dr M.D. Taseer returned from England after completing his PhD and assumed that post, by which time, Mahmooduzzafar had left for Delhi to assume secretarial duties for Pandit Jawaharlal Nehru. Thus, Faiz's time with Mahmooduzzafar and his wife, Dr Rashid Jahan, lasted barely two years in Amritsar. This, though, was a turning point in his life, a time that left a deep impression on how he perceived himself and the world around him.

In the third decade of the twentieth century, in the Punjab, Amritsar was second only to Lahore in terms of population and cultural and educational importance. They were twin cities and the intellectuals, poets and teachers of the area knew each other well. Faiz, therefore, found it relatively easy to fit in. Some people already knew him in Amritsar and had heard his poetry; others he knew by name or by their work.

Mahmood and Rashida

The two people Faiz remembered most fondly from his days in Amritsar had already been there for about two years by the time he got there. 'Sahibzada' Mahmooduzzafar was the scion of a distinguished family from Rampur and the son of Dr Saiduzzafar, a professor of anatomy at Lucknow Medical College. Mahmooduzzafar (1908–1954) was both a comrade and an Englishman to the core. He was sent off to school in Dorset at the age of twelve and eventually graduated from Oxford University. He finally returned to India in 1931 only to become an active nationalist, choosing to wear khadi (a rough, handwoven cotton fabric) and refusing to sit for the Indian Civil Service examination, as was expected by his family. He had been betrothed to his cousin Zohra (who later became the brilliant actress, Zohra Sehgal) in childhood, but was swept off his feet by the charismatic Dr Rashid Jahan, a gynaecologist posted at Lady Dufferin Hospital, Lucknow, with the provincial medical service, 'a forceful woman of formidable wit, intelligence, charm, and beauty'.[3] An intelligent and hard-working doctor, Rashid Jahan was also a dedicated member of the Communist Party and many other things besides, including a founder member of the All-India Progressive Writers' Association (AIPWA), an active member of the Indian People's Theatre Association (IPTA) and a lifelong campaigner for women's rights, who died an untimely death from cancer at the age of forty-seven.

Unlike Faiz's friends in Lahore, Mahmood and Rashida were not too keen on Urdu literature. One reason was that

Mahmooduzzaffar's familiarity with Urdu was basic, to say the least. Years later, in the heyday of the Progressive Writers' Association, Mahmood would argue passionately about English literature and poetry but whenever the conversation turned to Urdu poetry and those assembled would start reciting, 'a forlorn look would appear on Mahmood's face'.[4] It is no surprise then that he and Faiz never discussed literature or poetry and neither Rashida nor Mahmood was aware of the poetic talents of their new lecturer in English.

Together with Syed Sajjad Zaheer and Ahmad Ali, Mahmooduzzafar and Rashid Jahan had authored *Angarey*, an incendiary collection of short stories, which, when first published in Lucknow in 1932, created a storm. There was an immediate outcry and only a few hundred copies had been printed before the booklet of ten short stories was banned by the British authorities under pressure from India's leading Muslim clerics and conservative associations. Almost all printed copies were destroyed and the four authors of the collection, all Muslim, came under fierce attack for their criticism of religious orthodoxy, traditional social and sexual mores and the prevailing attitudes towards women and the poor. The booklet, with polemical stories that were of dubious literary merit, was to become the nucleus of the twentieth century's most significant politico-literary movement in the subcontinent.

This unusual couple, who became the young Faiz's mentors and friends, was responsible for first introducing him to communist ideas. He frequently visited their house and the topic of discussion there was often the successful workers' revolution in the Soviet Union and what lessons could be drawn from it to better the lives of India's teeming millions. Later, when they had become aware that Faiz wrote poetry as well, his old friend Khadija Begum remembered her first introduction to Faiz at the house of Mahmood and Rashida:

> When I got there, I saw a slightly built young man standing by the door wearing 'khaddar',[5] smiling quietly. Suddenly Rashida Apa said to me 'Khadija! Meet Faiz, our young poet'. I looked him up and down but couldn't convince myself that he was a poet. I had always imagined poets to look different from this:

> long hair, swaying from side to side, lost in thought, like Jigar sahib.[6] I thought, this cannot be a poet; I didn't look at him or talk to him. Faiz didn't drink, didn't recite any poetry, didn't make a ruckus, what kind of poet was this?[7]

Being energetic socialists and members of the Communist Party, it was Mahmood and Rashida who introduced Faiz to working for the poor. Sometimes Rashida would take him along when she went to a village to treat patients saying he could help write applications for some labourers who had lost their jobs. At other times, Faiz would sit quietly in a corner of Mahmood's office while he would be discussing the political situation in India with some young people or how they could help the kisan conference to be held shortly in Amritsar. Mahmooduzzafar had founded a small Marxist discussion group whose members included labourers. The main topics of discussion in this group were those revolutionary writings of Marx and Lenin that had been banned by the government and which they had succeeded in obtaining illegally. Many such study circles had come into existence all over the country and two of Faiz's close friends and comrades were being introduced to socialism through them. One of them was Makhdoom Moheyuddin, who, along with his peers Majaz, Ali Sardar Jafri, Jazbi and Faiz, would achieve renown as an eminent poet and writer. The other was Syed Sibt-e-Hasan who would go on to become one of the most distinguished and respected journalists and historians of his time and an untiring member of the Progressive Writer's Association.

Faiz began going to Mahmooduzzafar's study circle and, to his own surprise, became interested in politics. Many of his contemporaries, including Syed Sajjad Zaheer, Makhdoom, Ali Sardar Jafri and Krishen Chander had been passionate about politics since their adolescence and had been participating actively in the Independence movement. Faiz, well read as he was, had been unaware of national and international political conditions in his student days in Lahore. These were discussed frequently in college but for Faiz and his immediate circle of friends, poetry, music and cultural activities held more interest. In college, his room had even been used for hiding banned literature and he had become close friends with Khwaja Khurshid Anwar who had been associated with the Bhagat Singh movement but still, Faiz had remained untouched by the revolutionary zeal of his friends. At that time, his mind was occupied with poetry and literature and the turmoil of his first, failed, love.

Faiz later remembered how Mahmooduzzafar introduced him to communist ideas:

> One day, [Mahmood] handed me a small book and said read this and next week, we will discuss it but it has been banned by the government so be careful. The book was[Karl Marx and Friedrich Engels] 'The Communist Manifesto' and I read it in one sitting, in fact I read it two or three times. Man and nature, the individual and society, society and classes, classes and the means of production, the means of production and the relations of production, the evolution of society, the many layers of human relations, values, beliefs, thoughts and actions, it felt as if someone had handed me the key to a treasure of the unknown. Thus I became interested in socialism and Marxism. Later I read the works of Lenin and felt a great longing to see the land of Lenin and the October Revolution.[7]

This was the nudge that pushed Faiz towards socialist ideas and gave birth to those beliefs that later helped him become one of the driving forces behind the All-India Progressive Writers' Association. These were also the ideals that guided him throughout his life. Many people in Pakistan assume that Faiz was a communist since he had been in the company of communists since his youth; while he agreed with most of their ideas, Faiz was never a member of a communist party.

With Mahumooduzzafar and his circle, Faiz not only attempted to understand society, he also became active in trying to promote socialist ideas and to engage in activities that furthered those ideas.

Among the workers

Amritsar was also where Faiz got his first taste of dealing directly with labourers and factory workers. He was already enamoured of socialist ideas thanks to Mahmood and Rashid's influence. Once he became involved in the day-to-day lives of workers and saw how they lived, those ideas crystallized into dreams of a society based on economic and social equality, brotherhood and justice.

Most of the workers Faiz came in contact with were poor brick-kiln labourers who had been bonded into near slavery for generations. Some worked in government or semi-government offices and needed help with paperwork or other such matters. Sometimes Faiz would write an application for them or go with them to their offices to try and sort out their problems. This became a pattern; sometimes they would show up at the teacher's hostel where Faiz was living, at other times he would go to their localities. Once Faiz shifted to his new quarters near Company Bagh, they would come there. He had no prior experience, so once he decided that he wanted to do something practical for workers, he met renowned labour leader Fazal Elahi Qurban for guidance. Since the Communist Party was banned, most of its leaders including Qurban were living underground. He was delighted to meet Faiz though, and put him in touch with a well-known labour leader in Amritsar, Bashir Ahmad Bakhtiar, the secretary of the Amritsar textile workers' union. Most of the factories and workers' dwellings were located outside the city. In the industrial area were several large textile mills with thousands of workers, most of whom were Sikhs. Muslim workers mainly worked on looms and in other small industries. It was decided that Faiz would start teaching in the workers' villages. With the help of friends, he developed a system of teaching that would attract workers to learn, both those who were already semi-literate and others who were illiterate. Later, Faiz described his experiences thus:

> [We] began with starting study circles in various factories of the Industrial area, a few kilometers from Amritsar, and I started teaching the workers. There was a town there called Islamabad. In the middle of the city was the center of the trade union, whose administrator was [my friend] Basheer Bakhtiar. The routine was that after getting free from college and games, I used to teach in the evening from 7-8 pm to 11-12 o' clock. [Instead of] teaching them politics, we would provide them general knowledge, such as geography, history, social evolution, conditions of the contemporary world etc...This was 1937 and there was a strong threat of war. Hitler's popularity was at its

> peak and it was clear that this volcano would explode someday soon. Instead of telling them about Hitler and this or that, we tried to educate them about how a conflict takes place, and how the social conditions that exist were created in the first place. I did this for three, four years.[8]

In later years, describing his trade-union activities in Amritsar to renowned journalist Mohammad Shafi (Meem Sheen), Faiz recounted how, soon after he started working in the workers' colonies, he was made a member of the Amritsar Labour Federation, affiliated with the All-India Trade Union Congress (AITUC) which, after partition, became the Pakistan Trade Union Federation, in Pakistan. The AITUC, run by the Communist Party, was the largest workers' body in the country and represented workers from all over India. Because of this, it had remained under strict surveillance by the imperial authorities since the founding of the Communist Party in India in 1920.

Faiz lived in Amritsar for about six years (1935–40). He often described this as one of the happiest times of his life. This was where he was first introduced to Leftist ideas, where he became involved in the All-India Progressive Writers' Association and where he met and fell in love with his wife, Alys. This was also the time when Faiz and his 'subversive' activities first came to the notice of the authorities. Since trade unions and Communist Party members were under constant surveillance, it was only natural that Faiz's activities would be noticed as well. Intelligence agents even showed up at his college to investigate and see if anything incriminating could be found against him. Dr M.D. Taseer was principal at the time; he told them off in no uncertain terms and sent them packing. He also sent a vigorous note of support in Faiz's favour but the warning had been sent.

'Bhadka rahen hain aag lab-e naghmagar se hum'

This verse by famed Progressive poet Sahir Ludhianvi translates loosely as 'Here we go, stoking fire through song-laden lips'[9] is an apt anthem for the AIPWA.

It all started with the publication of a slim booklet of short stories titled, appropriately enough, *Angarey* (Embers). When first published in Lucknow in 1932, Angarey' created a storm. The authors, Syed Sajjad Zaheer, Ahmad Ali, Rashid Jahan and Mahmooduzzafar, all belonged to 'respectable' middle class families. That these four young friends would publish such an incendiary collection was remarkable enough. What made the ensuing furore even stranger was that the stories themselves were largely forgettable, possessing little literary or artistic merit. One commentator has noted that 'the book suffers from all the problems of early, polemical writing. Many of the stories are poorly conceived and the writing is a thin veneer for an angry, though important, political critique'.[10]

In addition, most of the stories are written in a 'stream of consciousness' style which is ironic, given that adherents of the AIPWA would later condemn just this style as 'modernist' and 'reactionary' and would exclude writers like Manto, Ismat Chughtai and Mira-ji from their fold for this 'sin'. Many of the stories are, quite clearly, meant to shock and provoke. It must have been obvious to the writers, all of whom grew up in Muslim households, that their work would enrage Muslim opinion, but it appears that they underestimated the impact. As Ahmed Ali later noted, 'We knew the book would create a stir but never dreamed it would bring the house down. We were condemned at public meetings and private...we were lampooned and satirized, condemned editorially and in pamphlets...our lives were threatened; people even lay in wait with daggers to kill us.'[11]

London

The question of a 'people's art' is not a new one. In fact, the debate around it began soon after the Industrial Revolution and matured in the nineteenth century to include questions such as what constitutes people's art? What is the role, if any, of art in bringing about social change? Is the artist obliged to pitch his art to a certain level of simplicity or complexity to suit his intended audience? What should such an art look like? As Sajjad Zaheer later wrote, questions similar to these were posed to those who were attempting to organize an All-India Progressive Writers' Association in some of their earliest meetings with artists in 1935. Describing a meeting in January 1936 in Lahore at Mian Iftikharuddin's house, attended by, among others, Abdul Majeed Salik, Chiragh Hasan Hasrat,

Sufi Ghulam Mustafa Tabassum and 'Dada' Firoz Din Mansoor, he writes: 'The questions raised at this small gathering assumed great importance in the Progressive Movement...whether it was necessary for a writer to participate in a political movement for independence. Another question was, how did we view ancient classical literature...and...what was the Progressive view of Ghalib or Shakespeare? Somebody objected that the language we used was not understood by the common man...what was our stance on religion? Was it necessary for a Progressive writer to be a socialist or a communist?'[12]

The central draft manifesto of an All-India Progressive Writers' Association had already been prepared before Sajjad Zaheer returned to India in 1935. On the evening of 24 November 1934 at Nanking Hotel in London, a group of young Indian intellectuals had engaged in intense debate over a draft document that had been circulated by the convener of the meeting, Sajjad Zaheer. He had left India in 1933 after the furore caused by the publication of *Angarey* and had proceeded first to Switzerland for a tuberculosis cure and then to England for law studies at Lincoln's Inn. In London, he came in contact with a number of writers and intellectuals, notably Ralph Fox (1900–36; noted British novelist, biographer of Lenin and one of the founders of the Communist Party of Great Britain), Mulk Raj Anand (1905–2004; pioneer of Indo-Anglian writing, known as India's 'Charles Dickens') and Rajni Palme Dutt (1896–1974; leading theoretician of the Communist Party of Great Britain). With the encouragement of Fox and the help of Anand, he formed the Indian Progressive Writers' Association in London with thirty to forty members, mainly students from Oxford and Cambridge and some expatriate Indians living in and around London. For his organizing efforts, he was awarded membership of the Communist Party as well.

The first meeting took place at Nanking Hotel and sought approval for the manifesto of the association, which aimed to do no less than articulate the future of Indian literature. In attendance at the meeting were names that would go on to achieve global prominence. Jyotirmaya Ghosh would become a key figure in Bengali literature. Mulk Raj Anand would gain global recognition with his first novel *Untouchable*, published the following year.

Mohammad Deen Taseer would become the first person from the Indian subcontinent to get a PhD in English literature from Cambridge and would become the co-editor of the famed literary magazine *Nairang-e Khayaal* in Lahore before his untimely death from a heart attack at the age of forty-seven. There were others in attendance as well, although their names have been lost in the fog of history.

As the nerve centre of the British Empire, until then the largest and richest in all of human history, London had attracted students, travellers, adventurers and fortune seekers from all over the world and India was no exception. In addition, compared to the rest of Europe, the relatively liberal atmosphere in London encouraged the free exchange of ideas and information. London was also where many of British India's best and brightest minds came to study, work and learn the ways of their overlords. It is thus no surprise that the foundations of the All-India Progressive Writers' Association were laid in this city. The following year, Zaheer and Anand travelled to Paris to attend the International Congress of Writers for the Defense of Culture, a massive conference of 200 writers, organized by, among other, André Gide, Henri Barbusse and André Malraux, to protest the rise of fascism in Europe. Encouraged by the speeches of writers such as E.M. Forster (a friend of Anand's), Boris Pasternak, Aldous Huxley and Ernest Toller, they returned to London to redouble their efforts. Later in 1935, Zaheer returned to Paris on his way home to India with the firm intention of organizing the Association there.

Upon his return to India, copies of the manifesto were circulated to Delhi, Allahabad, Lucknow, Calcutta (now Kolkata), Bombay (now Mumbai), Hyderabad, Kashmir and other places. It was decided to hold the first conference of the All-India Progressive Writers' Association (AIPWA) in Lucknow in April 1936, where Indian writers writing in all languages would be invited. Sajjad Zaheer came to Amritsar to meet writers from the Punjab and stayed with Rashid Jahan and Mahmooduzzafar. This was where Sajjad Zaheer met Faiz for the first time and was impressed by the depth and breadth of his knowledge. All four of them travelled to Lahore and, with Faiz's help, during their two-to-three-day stay, they met nearly all well-known authors, poets and intellectuals.

At Faiz's suggestion, Sufi Tabassum was made secretary of the Lahore branch while Faiz remained in charge of the Amritsar branch.

'We will have to change the standard of Beauty'

At the AIPWA's first national conference held in Lucknow, the Punjab was represented by Mahmooduzzafar, Rashid Jahan, Faiz and Mian Iftikharuddin. Besides the train fare to Lucknow, Faiz did not have any money, even to buy cigarettes. The great Indian short-story writer Munshi Premchand, who died later that same year, presided over the conference and read an erudite address from which one sentence became the motto of the AIPWA: 'We will have to change the standard of Beauty.' His inaugural address on the uses and purpose of literature was later termed by Sajjad Zaheer as the best exposition of the purpose of progressive literature written until that time. Since the address was in Urdu with many references from Iqbal's Persian poetry, Faiz connected with it immediately, unlike many delegates from other areas of India who had only a conversational familiarity with Urdu or Hindi and had to wait until it was translated into English to understand its true power. The address served as an inspiration for many of Faiz's later essays and editorials and he referred to its influence in many of his poetical works. The manifesto approved in Lucknow incorporated political as well as literary elements. The progressive movement defined itself as a struggle in favour of independence and against British rule and was also termed a guide in building a post-independence society free of oppression, exploitation and injustice—a society free of the brutal dictates of capitalism and imperialism.

Congratulatory messages were read out to the AIPWA from stalwarts of Indian literature such as Rabindranath Tagore, Allama Iqbal, Sarojini Naidu, and Maulvi Abdul Haq. The manifesto that was approved was basically the same as the one from 1935, with some important modifications by Faiz, who was nominated the secretary of the Punjab branch.

The provincial conference of the AIPWA was later held in Amritsar where Faiz again played an instrumental role. It was due to his efforts that Amritsar became, after Lahore, Punjab's second leading literary and cultural centre.

Adab-e Latif

With the founding of the AIPWA, it was as if a sea of Progressive literature emerged from out of nowhere. Branches of the AIPWA were established in all major and many smaller cities with regular conferences being held. Writers had discovered a new platform and new ideas for their writing. An acute need for new journals and magazines to publish these new creations began to be felt. Thus, Chaudhry Bashir Ahmed established a new journal by the name of *Adab-e Latif* and asked Faiz to be its first editor. Faiz accepted at the insistence of friends, partly because it was necessary to select those writings which represented the best of Progressive literature. With this in mind, he also persuaded older, well-established authors to write for the journal and, within a short time, *Adab-e Latif* became one of the leading literary journals in the country. Faiz's editorial tenure was short but tumultuous. For instance, in the 1941 annual edition some memorable pieces including Saadat Hasan Manto's 'Kaali Shalwar', Ismat Chughtai's 'Lihaaf' and Mumtaz Mufti's celebrated short story, 'Badmaash' were published. As a result, not only were Manto and Ismat Chughtai taken to court for indecent writings, *Adab-e Latif* itself was proscribed and shut down. Faiz refused to back down and in his deposition to the court noted that the writings banned by the court were masterpieces of Progressive literature and would be recognized as such by history. He assembled an impressive list of witnesses, including writers and law experts to serve as witnesses for the defence. However, they were never called upon to testify and the court, after arguments by the lawyers, dismissed the charges as baseless and wrong and withdrew the ban on the publication of *Adab-e Latif* with immediate effect. This incident had far-reaching effects on the future of the publication, with its readership increasing exponentially. Even after he moved to Lahore to teach at the Hailey College of Commerce, Faiz maintained contact with *Adab-e Latif*, visiting its offices in Amritsar every so often.

'Doctor' Faiz: Modern Urdu poetry 1857–1939

One aspect of Faiz's life that is not well known is that in 1939, Faiz planned to go to Cambridge University in England to pursue his

PhD. He had gained admission in the PhD programme and had even gone so far as to book an ocean passage. Unfortunately, he was unable to follow through since the Second World War broke out around the same time and it was no longer possible to travel by sea. Faiz, therefore, had to be content to stay in Lahore and teach at the Hailey College of Commerce. As an alternative, he prepared an outline of a PhD thesis with the title 'Jadeed Urdu Sha'airi—1857–1939' (Modern Urdu Poetry 1857–1939) and submitted it to Punjab University in Lahore on 3 November 1939. His outline had fifteen chapters, which examined the trends and ideas in Urdu poetry after the fall of the Mughal Empire. The unique thing about it was that instead of focusing on just poets and their lives, it proposed to examine the historical, political, social, cultural and artistic context of each era of Urdu poetry. Faiz pointed out that there had never been a scientific study of Urdu literature, especially modern Urdu literature. The outline in itself makes for very interesting reading.[13]

The records show that Faiz's proposal and outline were placed before the university's Advanced Board of Studies of Persian and Arabic on 22 February 1940. The board's opinion was that the subject was very broad and that Faiz should contact a lecturer in the Urdu department to refine his outline. On 9 March 1940, the academic council affirmed the board's decision. Faiz was informed of this in April and it is unclear whether he pursued it any further. It is likely that he never got around to it since his life took another unexpected turn. Soon after, he left teaching, joined the Indian army and moved to Delhi.

Notes

1. Faiz Ahmed Faiz, *Mah-o Saal-e Aashnai* (Karachi: Maktaba Daniyal, 2008), p. 11.
2. Ludmila Vasilieva, *Parvarish-e Lauh-o-Qalam: Faiz Hayat aur Takhleeqat* (Karachi: Oxford University Press, 2006), p. 41.
3. Carlo Coppola, *Urdu Poetry: 1935–1970, The Progressive Episode* (Karachi: Oxford University Press, forthcoming).
4. Syed Sajjad Zaheer, *Roshnaai* (New Delhi: Seema Publications, 1985), p. 44.
5. Another name for khadi—handspun cloth.

6. 'Jigar Moradabadi', the nom de plume of Ali Sikander (1890–1960), a celebrated poet and ghazal writer of the twentieth century. Received India's prestigious Sahitya Akademi Award in 1958 for his poetry collection *Atish-e Gul*.
7. Khadija Begum, 'Yaadon se muattar', in Mirza Zafarul Hasan (comp.), *Khoon-e Dil ki Kasheed* (Karachi: Maktaba Asloob, 1983), p. 51.
8. Faiz, *Mah-o Saal-e Aashnai*, pp. 11, 12.
9. Faiz Ahmed Faiz, 'Guftagoo—Faiz Ahmed Faiz', *Dunyazad*, no. 35 (Karachi: Scheherzade Publications, 2012), p. 52.
10. Ali Husain Mir and Raza Mir, *Anthems of Resistance* (New Delhi: Roli Books, 2006), p. 1.
11. Ahmed Ali, 'A Night of Winter Rains', *Annual of Urdu Studies*, no. 22, 2007, pp. 240–6 (available at http://www.urdustudies.com/pdf/22/16AhmedAli.pdf).
12. Syed Sajjad Zaheer, *The Light*, trans. Amina Azfar (Karachi: Oxford University Press, 2006), p. 25.
13. Abdur Rauf Malik, *Faiz Shanasi* (Karachi: Pakistan Study Center, Karachi University, 2011), pp. 131–6.

7

A Love That Lights Up the Sky

'Of fragrance and colour, beauty and goodness
The metaphors all began and ended in you.'[1]
—Faiz Ahmed Faiz

The woman who would become known the world over as 'Mrs Faiz' was born Alys Catherine Ivy George into a family of booksellers in 1913. Her mother, Alice Garton Crucifix, married her father, Geoffrey Osmond George, in 1910. About her name, Alys would later joke that in those days, such unwieldy names were the fashion. Geoffrey George was 'a witty and talented Londoner, under whose management, the family business of newsagents prospered famously'[2]. The Georges had five children in all: the oldest son, Geoffrey, was followed by Alys's older sister, Christabel, another son, Teddy, Alys and the youngest son, Peter. The matriarch of this household, Alice Crucifix, was, by all accounts, a lively and vivacious woman who was deeply interested in the performing arts. In fact, she had a keen interest in acting, something considered quite scandalous then for young girls from 'decent' households. A story from her younger days demonstrates this quite well. Shakespeare's *The Tempest* was being staged in London's famous Old Vic theatre. Alice and her best friend, Nellie, both single at the time, decided they wanted to act in it and went to the theatre. Upon being told that their names were 'Alice Garton Crucifix' and 'Nellie Bonaface', the manager naturally assumed that they were hiding their real names. After some convincing though, he agreed to give them parts in the play. When they asked what parts they would play, they were told 'waves'. They came home happily and on the day of the performance, dressed in their best clothes. They were shown a blue rug on the theatre floor and asked to crawl underneath it and move their arms and legs to give the impression of waves of the sea. After the show, caked in dust and filth, they returned home only to be roundly reprimanded for their impudence.

Alice Crucifix maintained her love of performing though, and years later, one of her granddaughters, Salma Mahmud would recall her 'beautiful singing voice' and another, Salima Hashmi would remember her thus:

> She was quite a rebel, very beautiful and full of spunk. When she came here [Pre-partition India], she was the most wonderful entertainer. She came here with a sea-trunk, they came by sea, and it was full of things like wigs and spectacles and false noses and they brought Punch and Judy glove puppets and they would set this up and all of us grandchildren would sit down and they would perform for us and it was, like, grandma was the best thing that had happened in our lives! Very entertaining, she would sing and she would prance around, fantastic, most unlike Bebe-ji [Faiz's mother]. One time, Auntie Molka[3] invited granny over to teach her students how to make glove puppets in the Punjab University Fine Arts Department. And she was wonderful with her hands. She would make Cossack dolls out of skeins of wool, she made me one of those one time.[4]

By the time Alys was born, the family, which had seen better times, lived in humble surroundings on Hoe Street in East London where her father ran a newsstand. They lived above the shop and Alys's grandmother lived with them. In later years, Alys would recall that she had to sleep in the same bed as her elderly, cantankerous grandmother, of whom she was terrified because of her ill temper. Alys studied till matriculation and was 'brilliant at Mathematics and French; she got the prestigious Mathematics prize for the entire city of London in her Matriculation.'[5] It was no longer possible though, after her matriculation, for Alys to study further due to her family's financial condition and so she did a stenographer's course and went to work. By this time, the 'Freedom for India' movement had started and both Alys and Christabel became supporters and members of the 'India League', with Alys actually going to work as a secretary for V.K. Krishna Menon.[6] She would later describe him as 'bad tempered', an impression that was not confined to her alone. Menon has been described as eloquent, brilliant, and forceful, but also highly abrasive, inspiring both widespread adulation and fervent detraction in both India and the West.

She had already joined the Communist Party of Great Britain at sixteen. 'She was passing by a hall and she heard this thunderous speech, she went in and heard Harry Pollitt[7] declaiming and she signed up.'[8]

According to her younger brother, Peter, Alys was always the rebellious one. Unbeknownst to parents and family, she secretly distributed the Communist Party's newspaper the *Daily Worker*, slipping it inside the pages of dailies. She also participated in amateur dramatics on stage and, with Christabel, she joined some Greek dancing groups in Hyde Park inspired by the brilliant, flamboyant dancer, Isadora Duncan. It was while working with the India League that Alys and Chris became friends with students and expatriate Indians living in and around London, some of whom would later become the driving forces of the All-India Progressive Writers' Association. Their circle included Mohammad Deen Taseer, whom Chris eventually married. Others in the group included Syed Sajjad Zaheer, Jyotirmaya Ghosh, Mulk Raj Anand, Ralph Fox and Rajni Palme Dutt, besides Mohan Kumaramangalam, Rajni Patel (the grandfather of Bollywood siblings Ameesha and Ashmit Patel) and Somnath Chib. The eminent Marxist historian, Victor (V.G.) Kiernan, who later lived for many years in Lahore and whose English translations of the poetry of Iqbal and Faiz are still highly regarded, was also part of this circle.

'The shadow that chills my view'

Heart of the heartless world
Dear Heart, the very thought of you
Is the pain at my side,
The shadow that chills my view

—John Cornford to Margot Heinemann

The decade of the 1930s was a turbulent one. The worldwide economic depression that had started with the Wall Street crash of 1929 had spread to the rest of the world. In response to the economic distress experienced by most people (because of rampant unemployment, inflation and the rapid breakdown of trade and commerce), fascism was on the rise in Europe, exemplified by

Adolf Hitler in Germany, Benito Mussolini in Italy and General Franco in Spain. The 1930s was a decade in which 'the individual felt a terrible burden of responsibility, both in the West as well as in British India'[9].

This sense of responsibility was, as usual, most eloquently expressed by the era's poets, notably John Cornford, the English poet who was one of a large number of brave, idealistic volunteers who went to Spain to fight on the side of the Republicans against the fascist armies of General Franco and who was killed, along with thousands of others, at the age of twenty-one. One of his contemporaries, the poet Stephen Spender, expressed his sentiments in the timeless poem 'Two Armies' (1937):

> No one is given leave
> On either side, except the dead and wounded…

In 1934, M.D. Taseer arrived at Pembroke College, Cambridge, for his PhD in English literature. He was part of the group that wrote the first draft of what became the manifesto of the All-India Progressive Writers' Association (although he was to later distance himself forcefully from the organization) and it was at Cambridge that he first met Christabel. They fell in love and Christabel's parents happily consented to the marriage. Taseer finished his studies and returned to India and once he found employment, in September 1936, Christabel came to India as well. Allama Iqbal, Taseer's teacher and mentor, who had advised Taseer to choose a European wife, had spent three months carefully drafting the ideal marriage deed for the couple. It contained two unusual clauses. The first, which is allowed in Islam, was that the husband delegated his right of divorce to his wife. The second stated that Taseer would not contract any other marriage during the continuance of his marriage to Christabel. Iqbal, though he was very ill, also acted as qazi for the marriage. Later, Faiz and Alys's marriage contract would be written along the same lines, and these clauses would come to be incorporated into Pakistan's Muslim Family Laws Ordinance.

By 1938, Christabel and Taseer had had their first child, a girl they named Salma. Alys came to India to visit Christabel and her family. By this time, Taseer was principal of MAO College,

Amritsar, where Faiz was lecturer. Being a long-time supporter of the Communist Party of Great Britain, Alys was as passionate about India's independence as any Indian. Staying with her sister at the Taseer house, she met many of Taseer's circle of friends, including Faiz. Eventually, she became acquainted with the very quiet Faiz, whose voice she would only hear when he would be asked to recite some of his poetry. They were polar opposites in temperament and, years later, Alys would say that's why she liked him; he was so quiet. She wrote: 'And there was Faiz, a teacher in MAO college who came regularly [to Taseer's house], was so silent, reciting poetry when called upon and claiming my early attention. We became good friends, walking in the evening, driving in Taseer's Victoria carriage to the gardens, to drink cool well water. We talked of all manner of things and I found he was not taciturn, but shy, with a becoming sense of humor. Our friendship grew into something special.'[10] Physically as well as in temperament, they could not have been more different. Alys was tall, with golden hair and blue eyes, the quintessential British woman. Once, while visiting Sufi Tabassum's house in Lahore with Faiz, a neighbourhood child wandered into the room where Alys was sitting, stared at her for a while, then ran back to his home yelling, 'Ammi, Ammi, there is a girl sitting in Sufi sahib's home, white, really white, like Allah mian [God]!'[11] Faiz, on the other hand was, like most people from north-western India, of average height (standing next to Alys, he looked short), with dark hair, dark eyes and a tanned complexion, as befits someone whose ancestors were Turkish or Afghan. Their temperaments, too, were polar opposites. Alys was a typical, hot-headed, 'Left' activist. She had strong opinions about everything, would open up easily and not mince her words, which endeared her to most people. She was also not shy about expressing her views. Faiz, on the other hand, preferred to sit silently in his circle of friends and listen, rather than talk. His reticence and reluctance to express his opinion remained a source of amusement amongst his friends most of his life. One reviewer, commenting on Faiz's first collection of poetry, couldn't resist writing, 'The Ghazal is not bad. It is balanced, eloquent and, unlike Faiz himself, the verses actually say something'![12]

It would be hard to find anyone in Faiz's close circle of friends who ever heard an angry word from his lips. Alys, though, had no compunction in calling a spade a spade. Even many years after being married, this quality in Alys would sometimes bother Faiz. In one letter, he wrote, 'Oh, yes, and it would be better if you avoided chiding people a bit. Being upset or angry with them is understandable but fruitless.'[13]

What they both fervently believed in was freedom, equality and justice. Her older daughter Salima recalls:

> She [Alys] used to get very very angry when she saw injustice or cruelty; it used to drive her nuts, she couldn't stand it; whether it was cruelty to human beings, animals, whatever. And she didn't care who was in front of her, she would really tell them off. And she had a flaming temper but as quickly as she would get angry, she would calm back down. And she had a terrific sense of humour and she was a wonderful mimic because she had that sense of drama. She specially liked to mimic pompous people and she would make Abba laugh and laugh.[14]

Her younger daughter Moneeza remembers her as a 'disciplinarian, very regimented in her ways, that's probably where I get it from; she wanted things done a certain way. That might have been her British upbringing, she had her strong likes and dislikes about people'.[15]

Alys believed in no compromise with what she believed was evil, while Faiz liked to ponder on the nature of evil first before coming to a decision. He remembered the teaching of the ancients, that it is only Love which can combat Evil. His verse:

> Be it the beloved's face, enemy's hand, or grief
> To all, and alike, as a lover I submitted[16]

could as well have summed up his life philosophy.

In a letter to Alys, he summarized an argument they had with each other:

> I enjoyed how vigorously you defended your combative philosophy. I know that this is how the world works. I also know that my philosophy of not casting the first stone can only produce poetry and that too, not very good poetry. The only

> difference is that in spite of disagreeing with you, I respect your point of view while you reject mine. And that is the way it should be since otherwise, it would negate your philosophy. But we are both helpless. I am as bound to help the wayward and the sinners as you are to dislike them. The best thing would be if we could combine our philosophies into an aggressive humanism.[17]

When Alys came to India to stay with Christabel and Taseer, she was already engaged to someone in England. Salima remembers:

> She was such a lively person, the boys [in England] used to be mad about her. She was engaged when she came here [to India]; to this chap called Stanley, we used to have his photographs in our albums. They were engaged and she had just come here for a holiday and then she got stuck here because of the War [Second World War], otherwise she and Abbu were going to go back to England and study. So Stanley waited because he couldn't believe that she had jilted him. It was only when Granny and Grandpa [the Georges] went back to England [after visiting us] and told Stanley, 'Listen, she's happily married, she has two children, we've seen her ourselves that he moved on, poor chap [laughing].[18]

The effect of Alys's vivacious personality was also evident in her circle of friends at Taseer's house and led to some anxious moments for Faiz. For instance, when Faiz heard that one of the regular attendees at Taseer's house, the director of the Lahore Museum, a Hungarian man by the name of Dr Faubry had become interested in Alys, Faiz was distraught and peppered her with cautionary letters about how she was unfamiliar with the customs of the subcontinent, how she should not have any contact with this man, how it was considered undesirable for single young girls to have any contact with males, etc.[19]

Here, Faiz conveniently overlooked the fact that the same cautions would apply to Alys's meetings with Faiz himself.

In fact, M.D. Taseer was initially opposed to Faiz and Alys's growing friendship. According to Salima, 'They started courting and Uncle Taseer didn't like it at all. He was very possessive about Mummy, he didn't want any of these young men coming yapping around her; he didn't think my father [Faiz] was worthy of her so he totally frowned upon this liaison and of course Abba didn't tell his family so they used to meet secretly.'[20]

Describing her first few months in India later, Alys would simply say, 'For me Amritsar became Hindustan and Hindustan became Faiz.'[21]

They were in love and at first, they kept it a secret. They had not envisioned yet how they would spend their lives together. Alys said later, 'His family was very traditional, I doubted that they would approve. But we were in no rush either.'[22]

Cataclysm

While both of them were in no rush to get married, the model set by Taseer and Christabel must have been in the forefront of their minds. Once Taseer and Christabel got married, his family in India had no choice but to solemnize their marriage according to Muslim rites. Perhaps this was in Faiz's mind when he planned to proceed to England for further studies (with Alys). In later years, Faiz referred to his growing attachment to Alys in his typical perfunctory fashion: 'We met every day, we thought alike. My mother had not put any conditions on my choice of a spouse. We started liking each other and decided to get married. We were never madly in love like Laila–Majnun or Shireen–Farhad, we were just two normal young people.'[23]

The reality was somewhat different. In addition to Taseer's initial opposition to the match, says Salima, 'When Bebe-ji [Faiz's mother] found out, she had a fit, in her own quiet way. She tried to show Abba lots of 'suitable' girls [to marry] and once she went to Gurdaspur and decided to say that she was seriously ill and Abba had to go to Gurdaspur and she pleaded with him that it was her life's last wish to have him marry so and so and Abba just quietly said, "you'll be fine, you'll recover", because he could be really obstinate too and so she recovered [laughing]. It took them about three years to convince everyone, from about 1938 till 1941.'[24]

In the latter half of 1939, Faiz applied for admission to Cambridge University and was accepted. He stared preparing for his departure, booked his passage on an Italian ship and bought his train ticket to Bombay from where the ship was due to sail. The ship was due to sail for England on 11 September 1939. On 1

September came the news that the Second World War had broken out. All national borders were sealed. There was no question of anyone leaving.

The British announced that India had entered the war against Germany without consulting any of the Indian political parties. This led to widespread protests all over the country which soon assumed the shape of a national anti-War movement. No one wanted war and, more importantly, the Raj had, as usual, not bothered to take the sentiments of Indians into consideration before thrusting them into the War. Protests and demonstrations became commonplace, often organized in the initial phases of the War by Left-wing parties. Inflation skyrocketed with hoarding of food and essential items and, in addition to anti-War protests, anti-imperialist slogans began to be raised as well. The British responded brutally with widespread arrests of political leaders and trade-union activists, including many whom Faiz knew personally.

Because of the War, Alys had to postpone her plans to return to England. Her parents, as well as Taseer and Christabel, also wanted her to stay in India for a while and, of course, so did Faiz. Fortunately, she also found employment in Amritsar's Rosemary Inter-Girls College where she would teach English and French. A short while later, Taseer was offered the prestigious job of principal of a college in Srinagar and shifted there with his family. Alys moved into the Rosemary college hostel. Faiz had also shifted into his own residence from the teachers' hostel and they started meeting regularly.

Faiz, though, was already being watched for his Left-wing ideas and activities to raise awareness among factory workers and labourers. In Amritsar, the police and army started house-to-house searches for those who had gone underground as well as to seize 'dangerous' publications which inflamed the population against the British, including socialist literature. Since the Soviet Union and the British Empire had not yet united against Hitler, the communists were still Enemy No. 1. Life in Amritsar became difficult for Faiz and, in 1940, he decided to move to nearby Lahore where his mother, relatives and close friends lived. He had offers of employment at several places, including All India Radio and the BBC in New Delhi. Faiz, however, had no interest in serving the Raj in an official capacity (and New Delhi would have been far from where Alys was). Instead, he decided to accept the offer of a lectureship in English at Lahore's Hailey College.

Being in love with Alys had given new life to Faiz's poetry. They wrote to each other often and occasionally met. Alys would come to Lahore on Sundays and stay at the house of Sufi Tabassum. She had started learning Urdu. Faiz would sit with her and try to explain a poem he had recently written or, if he was feeling particularly enthusiastic, attempt to explain the creative impulse behind the poem. Many years later, after Faiz's death, in a conversation with the poet Amrita Pritam, Alys would say, 'The truth is that I have never been able to appreciate the depth of Faiz' poetry. Learning a new language is one thing, but to understand a whole culture, a whole civilization is something else.'[25]

Till death do us part

Faiz's mother and his sisters were eager for him to marry into an affluent household but Faiz had made up his mind. This was a hard time for the family. Most of the family lands had been sold and the rest were stuck in litigation. Some grains and foodstuffs would come from the village but, other than that, Faiz's modest salary and that of his brother, Tufail, now a civil judge, was the family's sole sustenance. Faiz had explained all this to Alys beforehand. She knew that she was marrying not only Faiz but his entire family, most of whom depended on him for their survival.

At last, after a long wait, Faiz's mother relented and Faiz informed Alys that if Taseer and Christabel agreed, they could have a simple marriage the same year. Alys was delighted, as were Christabel and her husband, since this meant that both sisters could stay on in India. By this time, M.D. Taseer, too, had accepted their relationship, persuaded, in part, by his wife. Faiz also informed Alys that there was nothing much to be done from his side of the family. His older brother and some friends would come to Srinagar where Taseer could take care of the legal formalities. All Alys had to do was to accompany them back to Lahore after the marriage where there would be a formal ceremony arranged by his mother and sisters. Alys's only insistence was that he (Faiz) would have to bring a wedding ring. By mutual consent, 28 October 1941 was fixed as the wedding date.

Just because Faiz's family had consented did not mean that all would eventually be well. Alys was well aware of the challenges ahead. She wrote years later:

> I remember an evening in Srinagar, a few days before my marriage. Waiting for the sun to set...I remember a heartsickness almost stopped the breath in my throat. I was leaving so much behind. There had been so much opposition to our marriage, so many warnings, so many forebodings held out, that one wondered time and time again whether it would work out or not. There was no turning back now. Would this new country accept me? Could I live in this world of contrasts, poverty and riches? In the heat and dust of Punjab's summer? A poor man's wife? I could find no answer. Only the passing years would reveal it.[26]

As already mentioned, Taseer and Christabel's marriage contract, drawn up by Allama Iqbal, was used as the model for Faiz and Alys's nikah (marriage contract) as well. The document stipulated that Alys had the right of divorce as well and prohibited Faiz from marrying again while Alys was alive. In addition, providing for Alys was entirely Faiz's responsibility while any income that Alys earned was solely her own property. These conditions were put in to ensure that Alys, thousands of miles away from her home, her own culture and family, was well protected and taken care of.

At last, the big day arrived. Once again, Alys writes: At last the marriage party arrived, tired and dusty. Inayat, Faiz' younger brother whom I grew to love, Naeem, a communist worker and Faiz. The first thing Faiz did was to show me the wedding ring. I slipped it on. A perfect fit. How did you know? I asked. He slipped it onto his own finger. Another perfect fit. The eternity ring, I said. Faiz laughed.[27]

Faiz had borrowed Rs 300 from his friend Mian Iftikharuddin to buy the ring.

Sheikh Abdullah, the 'Lion of Kashmir' and one of its most illustrious politicians, acted as qazi and performed the nikah rituals. The happy couple honeymooned for a couple of days in Srinagar and then headed back to Lahore where Faiz's family was waiting to welcome them. Faiz, Alys and Faiz's two friends, the poets Josh and Majaz, bought train tickets to Lahore. As planned, when the train stopped at Rawalpindi, Alys had to change into her bridal dress because the family was waiting to welcome them at Lahore. In the women's waiting room at Rawalpindi Railway Station, the women were astonished to see a 'gori' in traditional Indian bridal dress and a couple of the younger women helped her with her make-up. They were all surprised at this strange bride with no jewellery, no dangling earrings and, most of all, her shoes, 'They weren't wedding shoes at all, as the ladies pointed out!'[28]

As planned, the family received them in Lahore and took them home. 'I was seated on a stool, surrounded by nieces and nephews, cousins and their daughters, sisters in law, half-sisters, all pushing, laughing, screaming, trying to peep at my face under my veil, gazing at those foreign blue eyes.'[29]

In one ceremony, Faiz's mother placed the Quran in her hands, blessed her and named her 'Kulsoom'.

Faiz and Alys were about to begin their new life together and not in her wildest dreams could Alys have known what was to follow. Daughter Salima recalls:

> All the children at my school loved to come to parties at our house because Mummy organized the best parties and she loved to cook. She was really bubbly and the house was always immaculate. All of that home making really stalled when Abba went to jail [in 1951] because then all of her energies were focused on working, making ends meet and taking care of us. She liked to cook English dishes like Irish stew and Shepherd's pie and various kinds of puddings. She longed for English food, which was not available of course.[30]

Moneeza remembers: 'She was a very hard worker, I remember that from my childhood. She worked very very hard all her life. She worked outside the house from the beginning. She was a writer and a journalist; I think that was her strength. She wrote two books; she had a flair for writing. She used to read a lot, right until her last days and she was an avid letter writer.'[31]

In addition, Alys set an example for many women with her hard work. She worked for the first Puppet Theatre in the Lahore Arts Council, the Children's Aid society, the TB Association of

Pakistan and was the moving force behind all of these organizations. She was Pakistan's first woman journalist. She started the first women's and children's page in a Pakistani newspaper—a column in *Pakistan Times* by the name of 'Apa Jaan'.

Once she left England, she did not return until twenty years later and then only for sporadic visits. However, in all the recollections of those near and dear to her, Alys's longing for the land of her birth is evident. Salima recalls:

> Her favourite perfume was French Fern soap, which she used to say reminded her of her girlhood and the other was a perfume called April Violets. Violets don't grow in the subcontinent, you see. She always used to talk about the smell of violets and none of us had a clue, of course. Once, we were in Nathiagali (in Pakistan's northern mountains) and under a tree, there were these wild violets growing and I said to her: 'Look Mummy, these are violets', and I still remember her mouth dropped and she went and smelled them and said, 'Yes, these are violets.' She missed daffodils and all those English things that she had left behind.[32]

And in spite of all her love for Faiz, her children and by extension for India and later Pakistan, she told Salima not to do what she herself had done. 'I must have been about sixteen and she said to me: "Never marry outside your culture." I asked her, "Why? You did it!" She said, "Yes, but I would not want you to go through what I went through".'[33]

Faiz greatly appreciated Alys's devotion to him and her family and understood the sacrifices she had made for them. A lesser woman might have crumbled in the face of all that was to come in their lives.

But in October 1941, all that was still in the future.

Notes

1. Translation by this author.
2. Salma Mahmud, *The Wings of Time* (New Delhi: Har Anand Publications, 2012), p. 65.
3. Anna Molka Ahmed (1917–1994), pioneering Pakistani artist born in London.
4. Salima Hashmi, personal recollection.

5. Ibid.
6. V.K. Krishna Menon (1896–1974), Indian nationalist, diplomat and later India's defence minister, described once as the 'second most powerful man in India after Nehru'.
7. Harry Pollitt (1890–1960), general secretary of the Communist Party of Great Britain for twenty years.
8. Salima Hashmi, personal recollection.
9. Mahmud, *The Wings of Time*, p. 68.
10. Alys Faiz, *Over My Shoulder* (Lahore: Frontier Post Publications, 1993), p. 24.
11. Mirza Zafarul Hasan, *Umr-e Guzishta ki Kitaab* (Karachi: Idara Yaadgar-e Ghalib, 1978), p. 69.
12. Shahid Mahli, *Mayaar*, Faiz number (New Delhi: Mayaar publications, 1987), p. 8.
13. Faiz Ahmed Faiz, *Saleebain Mere Dareechay Main* (Karachi: Maktaba Daniyal, 2011), p. 179.
14. Salima Hashmi, personal recollection.
15. Moneeza Hashmi, personal recollection.
16. Faiz Ahmed Faiz, *Nuskha hai Wafa* (Lahore: Maktaba-e Karvaan, 1985), p. 541. Translation by this author.
17. Alys Faiz, *Dear Heart: To Faiz in Prison 1951-1955* (Lahore: Ferozesons Ltd., 1985), pp. xiii, xiv.
18. Salima Hashmi, personal recollection.
19. Hasan, *Umr-e Guzishta ki Kitaab*, p. 68.
20. Salima Hashmi, personal recollection.
21. Khaleeq Anjum (ed.), *Faiz Ahmed Faiz: Tanqeedi Jaeza* (New Delhi: Anjuman Taraqqi-e Urdu [Hind], 1985), p. 293.
22. Alys Faiz, *Over My Shoulder*, p. 24.
23. Hasan, *Umr-e Guzishta ki Kitaab*, p. 60.
24. Salima Hashmi, personal recollection.
25. Anjum, *Faiz Ahmed Faiz: Tanqeedi Jaeza*, p. 293.
26. Alys Faiz, *Over My Shoulder*, p. 27.
27. Ibid.
28. Ibid., p. 29.
29. Ibid.
30. Salima Hashmi, personal recollection.
31. Moneeza Hashmi, personal recollection.
32. Salima Hashmi, personal recollection.
33. Ibid.

8
The Lamenting Image

Last night your faded memory filled my heart
Like spring's calm advent in the wilderness
Like the soft desert footfalls of the breeze
Like peace somehow coming to one in sickness.[1]

—Faiz Ahmed Faiz

In late 1941, Faiz and Alys returned to Lahore. Faiz was delighted to find that a copy of his first collection of poems had been delivered from his publisher. It was titled *Naqsh-e Faryadi* (The Image of One who Laments). The slim volume of poems became an instant hit both among ordinary poetry readers as well as critics, who singled out 'Faiz's "creative use of words", "energy" and "the uniqueness and freshness of (the collection's) imagery".'[2]

Since its first publication in 1941, *Naqsh-e Faryadi* has remained a perennial favourite of poetry lovers. Many of its poems have been set to music and sung by the biggest names of the subcontinent.

Today, close to eighty years later, it is obvious that in this first collection itself, Faiz created the particular poetic style which was to become his hallmark. It was in *Naqsh-e Faryadi* that Faiz created the language and the diction for which he became famous and because of which he is 'generally perceived as the hinge between classical and modern ghazal'[3].

It is often said that a poet's genius becomes evident early on in his career whereas a prose writer's art matures with age. This is certainly true of both Faiz and the man he considered 'the last and greatest of the classical poets of the Urdu language', Mirza Asadullah Khan Ghalib (1797–1869). He once wrote that no one can claim to have read enough of Ghalib, such is the depth and intensity of his poetry. Faiz borrowed the title of his first collection of poems from the very first verse of Ghalib's 'diwan', his collected works. Ghalib's diwan begins, as tradition dictates, with a 'hamd', an ode to the Almighty:

'Naqsh faryadi hai kis ki shokhi-e tahrir ka
Kaghazi hai pairhan har paikar'e tasweer ka'

About whose mischievousness of writing is the image complaining
[Made] of paper is the robe of every figure of the picture[4]

Writing in 1865, this is how Ghalib himself explained the verse:

> First listen to the meaning of the meaningless verses. As for *naqsh faryadi*: In Iran there is the custom that the seeker of justice [*dad-khvah*], putting on paper garments, goes before the ruler—as in the case of lighting a torch in the day, or carrying a blood-soaked cloth on a bamboo pole [to protest an injustice]. Thus the poet reflects, of whose mischievousness of writing is the image a plaintiff? —since the aspect of a picture is that its garment is of paper. That is to say, although existence may be like that of pictures, merely notional, it is a cause of grief and sorrow and suffering.[5]

It should be pointed out here that it is difficult, if not impossible, to adequately translate the term 'naqsh-e faryadi' into another language. In Russian, the title has been translated as 'forlorn images', and by noted Faiz translator, Victor Kiernan, as 'remonstrance'. Be that as it may, by choosing this title, Faiz paid tribute to his great predecessor and situated his poetry as a continuation of the same venerable tradition.

In order to understand the impact of a great poet on his era, it is necessary to also understand the age in which the poet lives. According to Faiz's friend and literary scholar Ludmila Vasilieva:

> A truly great poet is the product of his circumstances, the need of the times. What makes a great poet is not exactly something which can be quantified or categorized. It is like Iqbal says,
>
> 'Bari mushkil se hota hai chaman mein deedawer paida' [With great difficulty is a discerning eye born[6]].
>
> A great poet, a true seer, is a representative of his times. He is born when the time is exactly ripe for him to come forward and stand in for his era through his poetry. Faiz was a poet of few words. He has not written a lot but just the same, there is not a single chapter in the history of the subcontinent that has not been reflected in Faiz's poetry. Before the turmoil surrounding 1947, his poetry spoke of love, of romance.

> Then came his famous
>
> 'Mujh se pehli se muhabbat merey mehboob na maang' [Do not ask of me, my darling, that love of old].
>
> After 1947, he wrote of his country, of the world and everything he wrote clicked instantly with the masses. He was sparing in his words, but how well he spoke them! The "Inqilaab" chanting, thundering firebrands departed with Josh (Malihabadi). Faiz's call for the truth is much more dulcet and soothing and has transcended far greater boundaries...The appeal of Faiz's words was such that even his staunch enemies used to recite his verses and sway to the rhythm of his words in the privacy of their own houses. I believe that is the truest test of a great poet.
>
> All the truly great poets rise from the troubles that embroil their people and their times. Take the Soviet Union. The atrocities of the Tsarist regime produced the likes of Pushkin and Lermontov. In Pakistan, you had Faiz. Going back further in history, even Ghalib was the product of his circumstances, since that was a time when the old world order was crumbling in on itself to usher in a new world.[7]

Ghalib wrote:

> Consumed by the agony of remembrance
> The remembrance of night's festive company
> The one remaining candle flickers and dies.[8]

'The flickering candle,' wrote Faiz, 'battling to the last breath [was] the poet himself [i.e. Ghalib]...the last articulate spectator of the glory that has departed. [Ghalib] envisions the passing away of an age, a civilization and a way of life [and] an experience timeless and universal—the experience of the evanescence of time.'[9]

Just as Ghalib became the mirror of the tumultuous changes occurring in India with the decline and fall of the Mughal empire and the ascendancy of the British, Faiz became the voice of his era with the rise of socialism and the cataclysms of the First and Second World Wars and all they entailed.

About Ghalib, Faiz said in a speech, referring to the importance of poetry and the responsibilities of a poet: The mark of great poetry and that of a great poet is this: what is the expanse of his vision in relation to the expanse of his era and how much of the pain of the world and the pain of humanity has he included in his art. The more profound his pain, the greater will be his art. Ghalib fulfils this condition. He is, no doubt, a great poet.[10]

Like Ghalib, Faiz does not belabour the harsh realities of life. He prefers to allude to them through the metaphors and symbols of classical Urdu poetry. The particular artistic and linguistic qualities evident in Faiz's first collection of poetry marked him out as someone special and even today, *Naqsh-e Faryadi* is the benchmark against which all his later work is judged.

The foreword to *Naqsh-e Faryadi* was written by a contemporary of Faiz's, N.M. Rashed, a man who was Faiz's senior at Government College, Lahore, by a couple of years and whom Faiz once called malik-us shoara (king of poets). Rashed, the fierce individualist and avowed 'anti-progressive', was the first person to correctly identify the central trait of Faiz's poetry, a quality which was later universally recognized. He wrote: This is a collection of "ghazals" and "nazms" by a poet standing at the intersection of romance and realism.[11]

Rashed goes on, 'His [Faiz's] nature impels him towards love but he cannot stop himself from asking his reader to cast a glance on the nakedness and bitterness of life through the narrow window of reality.'[12] A foreword is traditionally used to praise and appreciate a writer's art, but Rashed cannot hold himself back from demonstrating his disapproval of the Progressive Writers' Association. He also accuses Faiz of being somewhat dreary in the use of his language and poetic imagery. However, even Rashed, renowned for his use of vivid imagery and experimentation in poetry, admits that one secret to Faiz's success is that 'he uses only words that, together, strum the strings of experience in an intense and durable way'.[13]

As Vasilieva notes, Rashed, in his use of the term 'the secret of Faiz' correctly identifies the central quality of his poetry: its mystery. Here, it is worth remembering the words of famed Russian modernist poet Anna Akhmatova (1889–1966), who commented about a writer with supreme command over language: 'He's a good poet but there is no mystery in his verses.'[14]

Naqsh-e Faryadi was reprinted numerous times. In editions published after 1952, both the preface, written by Faiz himself, as well as the foreword, by N.M. Rashed, were excluded for unknown reasons. One commentator has surmised that the change was for purely commercial reasons, to reduce the size of the book.

Naqsh-e Faryadi contains a total of thirty-two 'nazms', fifteen 'ghazals' and four 'qitas' (verse sets). In his later writings as well, Faiz favoured these genres and, in fact, used them almost exclusively. In the fifty years or more that he wrote poetry, he wrote just a handful of marsiyas (elegies) and qawwalis (devotional poems) and even those can be considered poems, based on their style and diction.

Faiz came to be known as a poet who wrote relatively brief poems. Even his longest poems are no longer than two or three pages and this could, perhaps, also be considered a reflection of his personality. He was famous for his reticence and quietude. He could sit for hours in a group of friends listening, without saying a word, responding to questions with just a smile or perhaps a yes or no.

Faiz himself divided his first collection into two parts. In his essay, 'The two epochs of the creation of *Naqsh-e Faryadi*', he wrote: 'I feel that from 1920 to 1930 and then from 1930 to 1940, these two eras are totally different from each other, in terms of literature, political conditions and the attitudes and emotions of people. The poems of the first half of *Naqsh-e Faryadi* were written between 1928 and 1934, my student days. Most of these were influenced by the first era (of the 1920s to 1930s). The second half contains poems written after 1935 when I was teaching and most of them were written in Amritsar and these relate to the second era (of the 1930s to 1940s).'[15]

The first half of *Naqsh-e Faryadi* contains mostly love poems, reflecting the typical preoccupations of a young person. As Faiz later wrote, they are the musings of a 'carefree youth'. He wrote further 'first of all, this was a time of leisure, of financial security and freedom from worries or cares.'[16]

Naqsh-e Faryadi begins with perhaps Faiz's most well-known and loved verse set 'Last night'. Many critics have termed this qita'a critical in understanding and appreciating Faiz's poetry. The images and metaphors used in this set are common enough in Urdu poetry, but the way Faiz has juxtaposed them to each other is remarkable: 'wilderness' and 'spring'; 'desert' and 'breeze'; 'sickness' and 'peace'.

Vasilieva writes that despite the ordinariness of the metaphors (since they have been, and continue to be, widely used in Urdu poetry), Faiz's inventive use lent them a new freshness.

What is also notable about this, one of Faiz's earliest creative endeavours, is the instinctive use of sentiments that immediately burrow deep into a reader's heart to resonate with his or her own experience.

Poet, novelist and literary critic Zulfikar Ghose, writing on another subject, has accurately captured the sentiments aroused in a reader's heart upon reading a verse set like 'Last night'. He refers to 'that chaotic wilderness of the inner self in which the human being is both a pilgrim journeying towards a hoped-for redemption and a lonely lost soul in a jungle of confusion and hopelessness'.

Ghose goes on to beautifully describe why a verse set like 'Last night' is so captivating for the ordinary reader. He refers to 'the restlessness of the human spirit that is constantly searching for that new abode, that new friendship and above all that ideal love which will be the soul's consummation...but finding that search forever frustrated...there is no consolation for the tormented self'.[17]

Faiz's verses offer this restlessness some balm and consolation, even if it is temporary. Faiz himself put it more simply: 'The depth of your perception of the outside world determines the depth of your inner wisdom. The important thing is to what degree your own personal experience is shared by people at large. This is not a new thought. As Ghalib said, "*Main nay yeh jaana ke goya yeh bhi meray dil main hai*" [I discovered that this too, is in my own heart (as well)[18]]. What you say will only reach another [person] if it is in their heart as well.'[19]

The romantic poems of the first half of *Naqsh-e Faryadi* are clearly influenced by the English Romantic poets. Faiz acknowledged this, citing both the classical English Romantic poets such as Keats and Shelley, as well as more contemporary ones like Houseman as major influences on his early poetry. Amongst the Indian poets of the times, the quintessential romantic was Akhtar Shirani, who was also one of the early influences on Faiz, along with Hasrat Mohani.

An example of these early romantic poems by Faiz is 'Surood-e shabana' (literally, Music by night)

Midnight, Moon, Oblivion
The sum of things an emptiness
Desire hushed into stillness
Listless the fellowship of the stars
A cataract of silence streaming;
Everywhere, self-forgetting reigns.[20]

As Vasilieva has pointed out, this poem is unique in that all the verses contain nouns and in contrast to the established rules of Urdu poetical grammar, there are no connecting verbs between the verses. This style of writing, which Faiz adopted early on in his writing is common in European poetry (which Faiz had read extensively), but was quite an innovation in the canon of Urdu poetry in 1940. The verses give an obvious impression of melancholy, which again is typical of the English Romantic poets. Later, Faiz moulded these sentiments to his own particular style.

Years later, when he was a renowned poet, Faiz was asked about how he managed to find the balance between the 'self' and the 'outside'; and the fact that there was, in his poetry, both an aesthetic point of view based on the influence of the English Romantic poets and Akhtar Shirani, etc., and also a purposeful point of view which came after the arrival of the Progressive Writers' Movement. In response, Faiz said:

> Yes, I did make a formula [to balance both points of view]. Actually when I started writing, I wasn't able to comprehend the technique. At that time I felt that it was necessary to write about both these things so I was patching up one subject with the other. It was only with time I understood the possibility of political lyricism, that one can voice political opinions in the colors of poetry and ghazal, without abandoning one's habit, vocabulary, and style...[eventually] I resolved this dichotomy, and instead of doing half this and half that, I figured out the right way to go about it.[21]

The second part of *Naqsh-e Faryadi* contains poems which quite obviously demonstrate Faiz's progression from 'self' to the larger concerns of the world outside. About this transition, he said:

> The Progressive Writers Movement helped cultivate my mind. I have written about this in the preface [Introduction to his second

> volume of poems *Dast-e-Saba* (The Hand of the Morning Breeze)] that first a man writes by inspecting his own self about his emotions. As his field of vision broadens, he realizes that man's self in an insignificant thing and not worth writing about. What should be looked at is the experience of an individual belonging to humanity or belonging to a nation.[22]

These poems, written after Faiz became an active member of the All-India Progressive Writers' Association, and after his 'field of vision broadened' beyond his own self, became instantly, and in some cases hugely, popular. Of these, perhaps the most loved is 'Mujh se pehli si muhabbat meri mehboob na maang' translated by Victor Kiernan as 'Love, Do Not Ask'

> Love, do not ask me for that love again,
> Once I thought life, because you lived, a prize
> Your beauty gave the earth everlasting spring
> If I won you, I would be master of my fate.
>
> This was not how it was but merely how I wished it to be
> The world knows other torments than of love,
> And other happiness than a fond embrace.[23]

Another poem, 'Bol' (Speak), was written much later and became the anthem of the Progressive Writers. It is still recited regularly at political gatherings (of all ideological persuasions):

> Speak, your lips are free
> Speak, your tongue is still your own
> Your gaunt body is yours
> Speak, your life is still your own.
> Look, in the blacksmith's forge,
> The furious flames, the red-hot iron
> Padlocks open their jaws
> Every chain's embrace widens
> Speak, this brief time is enough
> Before the death of body and tongue
> Speak, the truth lives
> Speak, say what you must![24]

About another poem, 'Raqib se' (To the rival), noted poet Raghupati Sahay, better known as Firaq Gorakhpuri, raved, 'It is not a poem, it is the unified evening…of heaven and hell. Shakespeare, Goethe, Kalidas and Sa'adi; even they could not have said anything better to the rival.'[25]

Yet another one, 'Tanhai' (Solitude), also earned gushing praise from critics. Even N.M. Rashed, who had hitherto been guarded in his praise, spoke of the astonishing and heart-warming beauty of this poem.

> 'Someone has come, forlorn heart, no, no one is there;
> Perhaps a traveller, he will go elsewhere.
> The night declines, the cloud of stars scatters
> Sleepy lamps flicker inside halls
> Every highway is asleep, tired of waiting
> An alien dust has blurred every footstep's trace
> Extinguish these candles, remove wine and flask and cup
> Lock your sleepless doors,
> No one will come this way now.[26]

The remarkable thing about poems like these was that even noted literary critics, famous for their nit-picking, were effusive in their praise. Dr Wazir Agha declared:

> I started studying the poem and the first verse transfixed me. As I read on, a strange mysterious sensation arose out of the poem and gripped me in its magical halo. When I finished reading, I felt as if I had changed completely from the person I was before I read the poem. Inside me, something had shattered and something else had grown in its place. No poem I had ever read had affected me like this. For days, the poem was all I could think about. Perhaps the reason was that in those days, I was going through hard times and I could understand the unspoken agony of loneliness.[27]

Vasilieva makes an interesting interpretation of this particular poem:

> On the surface, the poem describes the apex of loneliness with no reward for waiting, but on closer inspection, the entire atmosphere of the poem is suffused with life. Take the language. How many of the verses contain verbs which signify movement, itself a symbol of life and action. Someone's coming or not

> coming, a traveler's going somewhere else, the night is declining, the stars' cloud scattering, the lamps flickering, the highways sleeping...and when the night is ending, obviously day break is near with its promise of new hope and yet another wait (obviously, such an interpretation is in favor of progressive thought!).[28]

Despite the accolades that *Naqsh-e Faryadi* received, Faiz, in his usual self-effacing style, wrote that he was not too satisfied with the collection and that perhaps just a handful of poems in it were 'bearable'.

It would be more than ten years, though, before his next collection would come out and they would be years of tumult and upheaval.

Notes

1. Translation by V.G. Kiernan.
2. Shahid Mahli, *Mayaar*, Faiz number (New Delhi: Mayaar publications, 1987), p. 51.
3. Frances W. Pritchett, 'The sky, the road, the glass of wine: On translating Faiz', *Annual of Urdu Studies*, no. 15, 2000, pp. 57–75. Available at www.urdustudies.com/pdf/15/07pritchett.pdfý
4. Translation by this author.
5. Khaliq Anjum (ed.) *Ghalib ke Khutoot* (New Delhi: Ghalib Institute), vol. II, p. 837.
6. Translation by this author.
7. Ludmila Vasilieva, 2013, unpublished interview with the author.
8. Translation by Faiz Ahmed Faiz.
9. Faiz Ahmed Faiz, *Culture and Identity* (Karachi: Oxford University Press, 2005), p. 156.
10. Faiz Ahmed Faiz, *Mataa-e Lauh-o Qalam* (Karachi: Maktaba-e Daniyal, 1973), p. 70.
11. Faiz Ahmed Faiz, *Naqsh-e Faryadi* (New Edition with foreword by N.M. Rashed) (Lahore: Maktaba Urdu, 1941), p. 8.
12. Ibid.
13. Ibid., p.14.
14. Ludmila Vasilieva, *Parvarish-e Lauh-o-Qalam: Faiz Hayat aur Takhleeqat* (Karachi: Oxford University Press, 2006), p. 107.
15. Faiz, *Mataa-e Lauh-o Qalam*, p. 47.
16. Ibid.

17. Zulfikar Ghose, 'Alvaro Mutis: Novelist in the crow's nest', *Dawn*, Books and Authors, 9 March 2014.
18. Translation by this author.
19. Faiz Ahmed Faiz, 'Guftagoo—Faiz Ahmed Faiz', *Dunyazad*, no. 35 (Karachi: Scheherzade Publications, 2012), p. 73.
20. Translated by V.G. Kiernan.
21. Ibid., p. 54.
22. Ibid.
23. Translation by this author.
24. Translation by this author.
25. Sehba Lakhnavi, Kashish Siddiqui (comps), *Afkar*, Faiz number (Karachi: Maktaba Afkar, 1965), p. 498.
26. Translation by this author.
27. Wazir Agha, 'Faiz aur unnki shaa'eri', *Mayaar*, Faiz number (Delhi: Mayaar Publications, 1987), pp. 50–1.
28. Vasilieva, *Parvarish-e Lauh-o-Qalam: Faiz Hayat aur Takhleeqat*, pp. 135, 136.

9

The Iron Corpse of Night

Cry 'Havoc' and let slip the dogs of war

—William Shakespeare

It was the start of the 1940s. Faiz had been teaching at Lahore's Hailey College of Commerce for two years. He was now a poet of repute. His first collection of poems, *Naqsh-e Faryadi*, had achieved wide popularity. The first edition was sold out in months. The activities of the All-India Progressive Writers' Association (AIPWA) were also proceeding apace. Many writers from the Punjab who had been associated with AIPWA, including Saadat Hasan Manto, Ahmad Nadeem Qasmi, Krishen Chander, Sahir Ludhianvi, Ghulam Abbas, Meerza Adeeb and Rajinder Singh Bedi, had achieved recognition in both literary circles as well as with the general public.

Faiz and Alys had started their new life together and Alys was trying hard to become a part of her new family. She and Faiz's mother were gradually getting to know each other and Alys had even learnt a few words of Urdu and Punjabi. In addition to teaching at Hailey College, Faiz also took classes at Oriental College to earn some extra money, since his expenses had gone up after marriage. Occasionally, he would get an assignment on radio as well. Alys wanted to start working right away but Faiz advised her to wait, both because his mother may have objected and also because they had moved to a house in the suburbs, far away from Lahore's centre, and it would have been difficult for Alys to commute back and forth to a job.

Despite Faiz's domestic tranquillity though, and the success of his first published collection, there was no escaping the turmoil taking place in the world outside, foremost being the upheaval in Europe. Hitler and his Nazi armies had attacked Poland in 1939 and within months had overrun and occupied large parts of Europe, including France. By mid-1940, the Nazi armies were knocking on the doors of Britain itself, with an invasion seemingly imminent.

Starting with the war in 1939, Faiz and his fellow nationalists in India were in a difficult situation. There were no two opinions about the brutality of fascist Germany, but it was difficult, if not impossible, to join hands with the hated British Raj. What made it even more difficult were the terms of the Hitler–Stalin pact concluded in 1939, according to which the Soviet Union, the world's only communist state and a beacon of hope for all Left-wing forces around the world, was officially an ally of Nazi Germany. The question that faced all Indian patriots was: where did their loyalties lie?

In 1941, after subjugating Europe, Nazi Germany as expected, turned East. Hitler had always coveted the riches of the Soviet Union, from the 'bread basket' of the Ukraine to the oil fields of the Caucasus. In addition, the Soviet Republic was the only government in the world that claimed to speak for ordinary workers and peasants. That was reason enough for it to be hated by both the German and the Allied imperialists. One of the reasons that Stalin had concluded the non-aggression pact with Nazi Germany in 1939 was because of the games played by the British and the Fascist forces. Their common desire was to see the Soviet Union destroyed. Stalin hoped that the pact with Nazi Germany would buy him some time. In June 1941, the invasion of the Soviet Union, codenamed Operation Barbarossa, began. It was the largest military assault in the history of warfare. Over the course of the War, 95 per cent of German casualties and 65 per cent of Allied casualties would occur on the Eastern front. The Soviet Union would suffer the greatest number of casualties with over 20 million people killed, and by the end of the War, it would be the Soviet Union's Red Army which would break the back of Hitler's armies and liberate Berlin from the Nazis.

Faiz wrote about those times in his memoirs:

> In those days, people like us, who had been busy writing against Fascism as well as struggling against the British Raj were caught in a strange sort of mental confusion. But the Japanese militarists and the Nazi aggressors soon made it easy for us. On this side, the Japanese armies rolled over East and South Asia and were soon knocking on the doors of India and over there, the Fascists laid waste to Europe and were soon circling the Soviet Union.

> And then, a third picture emerged; the sight of the bloody battlefields of the Soviet Union. I observed closely how the Fascist onslaught swelled from three sides; from the East in Burma, from North Africa in the West and from Southern Russia in the North. And when our land, too, came in the sights of this invasion, I joined the Army.[1]

Once Hitler's armies attacked the Soviet Union, the British offered their assistance to the Soviets in July 1941. As a result of this agreement, the British and the Soviet Union officially became allies in the War and the British Indian government decided to loosen its restrictions on progressive and Left-leaning groups in India as well. In fact, members of the Communist Party of India, trade unions and other Left-wing groups were encouraged to join the War effort and help mobilize public opinion against the Nazis.

In an interview, in response to later objections that he should never have joined the British Army, Faiz said:

> Before the second world war, when the Fascist movements under the leadership of Hitler and Mussolini gathered strength, all conscientious intellectuals around the world including the Progressives of India united against it. But the British and American Imperialists, instead of opposing the gathering storm, were urging the Fascists on [against the Soviet Union]. One by one, the Fascist monster started devouring weaker nations: Ethiopia, Spain, Austria, Czechoslovakia, once these were destroyed, the Imperialists hoped that the onslaught would turn against the Soviet Union. In the beginning, this war was between two Imperialist powers [the British and the Germans] and we had nothing to do with it. But the Fascist forces rolled through Europe and Africa to the borders of Egypt and in the Soviet Union, up till the Caucusus. And on this side, the Japanese Fascists conquered Burma and reached the very gates of India and so now, the war was no longer a fight between two far off opponents. The flames were now licking at our doorstep and remaining neutral seemed impossible. We had to fight to defend our homeland and human civilization from destruction. I, and many like-minded people, joined the (British) Army. In those days, there were many short-sighted people including Congress leaders who were under the illusion that the Japanese forces would liberate them from the British and wanted to oppose the Allies instead of supporting them.[2]

In 1942, on the advice of his old friend Majeed Malik who was already a major, Faiz applied to the army. Major Majeed Malik was in the army public relations department and this was the department that Faiz applied to as well. Upon his first meeting with the man in charge of the department, a jovial Irishman by the name of Colonel Beard, who was a journalist by profession, Faiz relates how the man looked at him and said, 'Look, I have your police report. It says you are an advanced communist. Are you?' Faiz replied, 'Are there retarded communists too?'[3]

Literary life in Delhi

Leaving behind his relatively peaceful teacher's life, he moved to Delhi to take up his new commission. Major Majeed Malik and his wife Amina insisted that he stay with them. After two months, Faiz found a small house and Alys joined him. Professor Patras Bokhari, who was heading All India Radio, lived close by. 'Gradually, most of the Progressive writers congregated in Delhi and our literary meetings started again.'[4] Delhi, in those days, was a hotbed of Urdu literary activity. In addition to Professor Bokhari, many other notable writers, poets and artists, both in and out of uniform, had made Delhi their home. These included Maulana Chiragh Hasan Hasrat, N.M. Rashed, Abdul Majeed Salik, M.D. Taseer and Hafeez Jullundhri. The activities of the AIPWA were at their peak and there would be gatherings every day where there would be arguments between Progressive writers and their opponents. One such meeting, in 1945 or 1946, held in the hall of the Delhi Municipal Corporation, serves to illustrate an important aspect of Faiz's personality. The opponents of the Association had prepared their assault carefully. Sajjad Zaheer and Faiz were chosen to represent the Progressives' point of view. Faiz walked in around the time the meeting started. He was still in army uniform. Seeing him dressed so, Sajjad Zaheer's heart sank and he whispered to Faiz, 'You could have at least changed your clothes,' to which Faiz replied, 'Everything is all right, nothing to worry about.'[5] The speeches started and the opponents of the Progressives went at them all guns blazing; they made fun of free verse, highlighted the language problems in Progressive literature, repeated the old charges of pornography and obscenity and generally made fun of everything associated with the Progressive movement, much to the amusement and merriment of the assembled crowd. When it was Faiz's turn to speak amid this chaos, Sajjad Zaheer remembers:

> Faiz started his speech and immediately got to the heart of the issue. He never bothered to reply to the objections and ridicule of the other speakers. Very cogently and calmly he proved that Progressive writing was nothing new. With the changes and evolution in society, literature had also changed and this process could not be stopped. The Progressive movement was inevitable but one should continue trying to refine it. There was no drama or sarcastic humor in Faiz's speech. It was fluent, well reasoned and non-confrontational. The assembled crowd listened respectfully and quietly. No one jeered or clapped.[6]

The fascist monster

In the army, Faiz was awarded the rank of captain and assigned to the department of broadcasting and public information. His duties included summarizing all the news received on wireless, writing commentaries and generally helping mould public opinion in favour of the War effort. He also monitored and reported to the English high command on the movements and activities of the Soviet Red Army on various fronts. According to one of his closest friends, Maryam ('Mira') Salganik: 'Twenty years after the war, when Faiz came to the Soviet Union for the first time, people would be amazed by his encyclopedic knowledge of the geography and military history of our country.'[7]

Once Faiz decided to join the fight against the Fascists alongside the British, he threw himself into his duties as wholeheartedly as he had elsewhere. His hard work and keen intelligence did not go unnoticed by his British superiors. In 1943 he was promoted to the rank of major and in 1944 to lieutenant colonel.

For Faiz, it was essential for all thinking people to resist the onslaught of fascism, an ideology that wore many masks and was not confined to any particular era, nation or place. Faiz understood that the bloodthirsty invasions of the Mongols or Tatars were a thing of the past. In the modern age, fascism was one form of capitalist oppression in which the aggressor took over the lands, resources and people of another region and used them for its own benefit, frequently denying the subjugated people even the right to live their lives in their own way. The First World War was a war between two empires that had grown over the previous 300 years and had come into conflict over their desire to devour each other's territories and resources. As a result, the map of the world, especially Europe, Asia and Africa, was radically redrawn. In every war, Faiz felt, a philosophical, religious or political slogan is coined to justify the slaughter. These slogans hide the real face of fascism as well as its bloodthirsty intentions. Mussolini in Italy and Hitler in Germany had reinvigorated their defeated nations after the First World War precisely by invoking the glory of their 'superior' race and this race's inevitable destiny of ruling the world. There was no question of dialogue or accommodation with other, 'inferior', races. Faiz was convinced that fascism had to be crushed before it destroyed everything that human civilization had achieved after hundreds of years of struggle and sacrifice.

This was why, when Germany and Italy were raining death and destruction on the cities of Soviet Russia, Faiz considered Gandhi-ji's 'Quit India' slogan neither democratic nor patriotic. One reason was that after the First World War, many groups in India, both Muslim and Hindu, had begun to find fascist ideology attractive since they had become convinced that the only way of ridding India of the British was by force. They were even prepared to find an accommodation with the fascists to achieve this goal. Faiz had recognized this tendency and in response to Gandhi-ji's slogan, he wrote his iconic 'To a political leader' (included in his collection *Dast-e-Saba*):

> Abhorrent to you is the all-enveloping darkness, yet
> You wish these hands be cut off
> And the day pulsing in the ambush of the East
> Be buried under the iron corpse of night![8]

In India, the Indian National Army (INA) of Subhas Chandra Bose, the Ahrar Party and the Khaksar Tehreek all carried the germ of fascism within them, and Faiz knew that unless society was cleansed of this germ, it would forever threaten human civilization with death and destruction.

Many of his friends enquired about the lack of any mention of fascism in his writings from this period, to which Faiz replied: 'The thing is, in those days, we were struggling against Fascism in actual practice and [I] never found time to write poetry [against Fascism] nor did I feel a need for it.'[9]

'Colonel Faiz' and the British army

Faiz's English superiors had been very impressed with his performance in the army. It would have been easy for him to continue serving in the army and achieve a high rank or to move to a prestigious government position, but he had already decided against it. First, as a sensitive, intelligent artist, he could already perceive the conspiracies being hatched by the British against the Soviet Union in anticipation of the War's end. In addition, the large-scale unrest beginning inside India and the army high command's response to it were distressing for him. Obviously, as an army officer, Faiz had to be involved in activities to suppress civil unrest amongst his fellow Indians.

One of the reasons for the unrest was the repatriation of soldiers and officers of the Azad Hind Fauj (INA) formed in collaboration with Nazi Germany and Japan to fight against the British imperialists. Initially formed in 1942, immediately after the fall of Singapore, it was revived under the leadership of Subhas Chandra Bose in 1943 and fought alongside the imperial Japanese forces against the British in the campaigns in Burma and South-east Asia. The end of the War saw a large number of the troops repatriated to India where some faced trials for treason which became a rallying point of the Indian Independence movement.

Given its association with imperial Japan and Nazi Germany, as well as its alleged complicity in War crimes in South-east Asia, the legacy of the INA is controversial. After the War, though, the so-called Red Fort trials of captured INA officers in India provoked massive public outcry. In the eyes of the common man, the soldiers were patriots. The unrest provoked by the trials was one cause of the massive Royal Indian Navy Mutiny, popularly known as the Bombay Mutiny, which had widespread public support and eventually involved 20,000 sailors, from Karachi to Calcutta. The only political party to support the sailors' action was the Communist Party of India, which later described the movement as a spontaneous nationalist uprising that had had the potential of preventing the partition of India had it not been politically betrayed by Congress and Muslim League politicians.

Obviously, average soldiers in the army were not immune to these sentiments either. The English were keen to defuse these rebellious sentiments and to cultivate loyalty to the British Raj in the soldiers. To this end, they created a separate section within the army by the name of the Inter-Services Moral Directorate (ISMD). This was created by order of the commander-in-chief of the British Army and Faiz was appointed deputy director to this department by special order. His official title was 'Chief Adviser ISMD'.

Remembering those days, Faiz recalled years later:

> The British had two problems on their hands: recruiting people for the Army and at the same time fighting this great movement against the British Raj. And I was amazed at the silly things they told the soldiers. For instance, they said 'You eat our salt[10] so you should be loyal, that's what your religion says' or they would say 'keep your regiment's flag high and maintain its honor'. I had thought the British were very cunning and clever but they seemed quite stupid. One day someone asked my opinion so I sent in a written opinion that both of these positions are incorrect. My superiors were quite upset. I told them, listen, this is not your salt, they are Indians, this is their own land and their own salt and secondly, the regimental flag is not the flag of independence, it won't impress them since the regiment is not involved in any national service. I gave my opinion: first, teach them what Fascism is, tell them what will happen if the Japanese Fascists conquer India. The death and destruction they will bring with them will be terrible to behold. Secondly, it is the duty and responsibility of every son of India to save her from this devastation.[11]

Faiz was asked how he proposed to implement this 'political' plan and he told them the army should do it the same way the communists do, by establishing a cell in every unit to teach the soldiers about fascism since most of the soldiers were not very literate. As the suggestion was controversial, it went to the commander-in-chief's office and then all the way to the viceroy. It was finally approved.

These 'Josh' groups, as they were called, were set up and proved hugely successful in motivating the soldiers. After the War, Faiz was decorated with the Member of the British Empire (MBE) award in 1946, in recognition of his meritorious services.

This was a source of some consternation amongst his friends, with some, especially his communist friends, protesting that he should have refused to accept this 'imperialist' award or given it back. As was his wont, Faiz ignored his detractors at the time but, years later, defended his decision vigorously in an interview: 'We had joined the Army to fight against fascism. The English authorities liked the advice I gave them and they acted upon the advice. As a reward, they said, we want to give you this award [the MBE] and I said, alright, I was very happy. I considered it a success in our struggle against Fascism. Why did I not return the award later? It is not traditional to return such awards. Military decorations are not returned.'[12]

In his five years with the army, Faiz remained extremely busy and got a chance to learn the ins and outs of the army as an institution and about the imperial character of the British government. Because he was so busy, he could find no time for poetry but being in charge of publicity on all fronts of the Indian army, he did learn the ropes of reporting and journalism, something that would come in handy later in his life, immediately after the War.

Salima and Moneeza: 'Buds, ready to blossom in the garden of tomorrow'

A little over a year after Faiz and Alys were married, their older daughter, Salima, was born in 1942 in Delhi. Alys stayed in Delhi for a few months and then came back to Lahore so Faiz's mother could help look after the child. It was neither practical nor desirable for Alys to stay on in Delhi since Faiz was often away to different cities and military instalments on official assignments. Christabel and Dr Taseer's family was stationed in Shimla, since Dr Taseer was working in the government's labour division at the time, and he too had to travel a lot. In those day, there were many other 'abandoned wives' (as they were called) living in Shimla whose husbands were in the army or government service. They were able to get food rations and items of daily use relatively easily and cheaply. Faiz would try to come back to Delhi every week. Alys would divide her time between Delhi, Shimla and Lahore. In 1946, Faiz's younger daughter Moneeza was born in Shimla. Alys wrote in her memoirs that the main reason she often left the girls in the care of Bebe-ji in Lahore was so they could learn the basics of housekeeping from her and would be spared the nomadic army lifestyle. Bebe-ji delighted in keeping the girls and this was a source of great satisfaction to Faiz.

Alys had performed in Shakespeare's *Hamlet* on All India Radio, Lahore. The radio staff at Delhi welcomed her warmly. She was a great asset since there were few women performing on radio who knew both English as well as something about broadcasting. She was therefore in great demand and could often be heard on radio discussing the social or economic problems of women and children. She would also broadcast programmes on the problems of women whose husbands, fathers or brothers had been killed in the War and would frequently visit the surrounding areas of the city to do welfare work among them.

The end of the War

The attack on the Soviet Union proved to be fatal for the fascists. The new Soviet Republic had suffered terribly in the civil war immediately following the revolution of 1917, when several armies from different countries, backed by the British and American imperialists, had attacked the country in order to crush the revolution. Following their defeat, the young Soviet Union lost its leading light. Lenin, the leader of the Bolshevik Party, who had earlier been weakened by an assassin's bullet, died of a stroke in 1924. After his death, a struggle for power ensued in the ranks of the Bolshevik Party, which eventually culminated in the rise to power of Joseph Stalin. As fascism was raising its ugly head in Europe with the coming to power of Hitler and his Nazi party, Stalin initiated the bloody purges of the 1930s, which would see many of the finest soldiers, scholars, artists and intellectuals of the revolution killed or exiled to the labour camps of Siberia. By the time the Nazis invaded, the Red Army had been weakened considerably because of Stalin's murderous purges. However, the ideals of the October Revolution still lingered and the Soviet leaders realized that such an enormous War effort could only be victorious if ordinary people participated as vigorously in it as the soldiers. Thus the War was presented to the Soviet people as 'The Great Patriotic War'. Every village and town that the Nazis conquered was retaken at great cost and eventually, in spite of their overwhelming initial superiority in numbers and equipment, the Nazi armies were beaten and pushed back all the way to Berlin itself. The Nazis' capital was also captured by the Red Army after fierce hand-to-hand combat. Allied forces arrived later but, by mutual consent, the Soviet government agreed to withdraw and administer East Berlin while the Allies (mainly the Americans) occupied West Berlin.

It was 1945 and the War was finally over.

Even before the fighting had stopped, the Allies (primarily Britain and the ascendant imperialist power, America) had started conspiring against the Soviet Union. Their fervent hope had been that Hitler and Stalin would destroy each other, leaving the field open for their empires to be taken over. The Soviets and the Red Army had spoiled their party. With the War now over, new conspiracies were under way to contain and eventually 'roll back' the communist 'menace'. This new turn in the strategy of the British army high command was obviously a source of concern for the Communist Party of India and all Left-wing organizations in India. It was now becoming harder and harder for Faiz to stay on in the army, especially since the Independence movement was also gathering steam. Even though the Allies had emerged victorious in the War, Britain had been fatally weakened and its dominion over its Empire was slipping. America, the newly ascendant superpower, had emerged unscathed and richer than ever after the War, and was eyeing Britain's colonies.

Faiz was posted at the time in the army's Northern Command headquarters in Rawalpindi, which included the North West Frontier Province (now 'Khyber-Pakhtunkhwa'), Sindh and Baluchistan. He writes of that time: 'Our superiors were not unaware of the situation. I and some other senior Indian officers were often invited to their conferences. We learned a few things which helped us understand the future plans of the British. First, that after the war, the British and the Americans were now preparing for the 'Northern danger' meaning the Soviet Union. Second that even if India became independent and was divided, the Army would not be divided and its command would remain in the hands of the British.'[13]

This was made clear when the viceroy, Lord Wavell, came to Rawalpindi in early 1946. At a dinner that Faiz attended, Wavell made it clear that in the event of a 'war in the north', it would not be possible to defend 'Pakistan' since there was no geographic depth in it; they would have to establish their line of defence somewhere else.

Faiz realized that the British were already planning, even before Independence, to make Pakistan a military outpost in their continuing conspiracies against the Soviet Union. Their primary goal was to topple the Soviet workers' government, which had been a thorn in their side since its establishment in 1917.

Faiz writes:

> When I heard these schemes, I was astonished at this duplicity. Just yesterday, the British and Americans had fought alongside the Soviets against Hitler, Mussolini and [Japanese Emperor] Tojo and here they were already conspiring against their allies and fellow soldiers. I was fed up. I decided that our war had entered a different phase. First of all, complete independence became an article of faith. We also decided that it was our duty to unmask these conspiracies against the Soviet Union. We could not be traitors to our nation, our principles and to International Socialism. It was time to leave the Army.[14]

A short time after he was appointed chief advisor to the Inter-Services Moral Directorate, Faiz took leave from the army and went to Lahore to see his friend and colleague in Government College, Professor Chatterjee, who was then director of the Punjab education department. Faiz writes:

> I said, 'The War is over, I want to come back, let me teach again.' Chatterjee was astonished and said, 'Faiz, what will you do if you leave the Army? How much do they pay you?' 'Two thousand five hundred rupees.' Chatterjee stood up and said, 'Bhai, who will pay you this much outside the Army? Even I don't make that much, it's impossible.' I tried to explain to

> Chatterjee that I didn't want two and half thousand a month. 'All I need is five hundred a month and I'll be all set.' Chatterjee was looking at me strangely. After a long pause he said, 'Bhai, if that's what you have decided and you want to test your luck, then come. The highest pay for a lecturer is three hundred rupees.'[15]

But it was impossible to make do with such a meagre salary, especially now with two young children to look after. However, Faiz was determined to quit the army and continued looking for work. One of his friends, who was a member of the Indian National Congress and also friends with Sardar Vallabhbhai Patel, had recommended Faiz's appointment in the political department of the Congress party several times. A date was set for Faiz to meet Patel. But it seems Faiz was not destined to be a politician. Just before his meeting with Sardar Patel, one of his old friends, Mian Iftikharuddin, who was also a publisher (Faiz had already worked for one of his publications, *Adab-e Latif*) called him from Lahore and informed him that he was starting a new English newspaper called *Pakistan Times* and wanted Faiz to be its editor-in-chief.

It was early 1947, six months before Independence (although most people were as yet unaware of this as well as the impending convulsion of Partition). Allama Iqbal's vision of a separate homeland for the Muslims of India, called 'Pakistan', which had received little attention at the time it was first presented in 1930, was now the central issue in the independence dialogues. Negotiations were ongoing between Congress and the Muslim League on 'Pakistan' and this was the reason that Mian Iftikharuddin decided to name his newspaper *Pakistan Times*.

Later talking about becoming a newspaperman, Faiz said:

> It wasn't intentional on my part [to join a newspaper]. Mian Iftikhar-ud-Din visited me one day from Delhi. I was in the army then. He urged me to leave the army, as the war was over, and go to Lahore. He told me that he wanted to bring out Pakistan Times and offered me the editorship. I protested that I knew nothing about being an editor. In fact, I had never even set foot in a newspaper office. *laughter* So how could I be an editor? I suggested that he should appoint someone else as the editor, hire me as his assistant and I will slowly learn the work.

> I myself suggested a few names. Colonel Majeed Malik was my senior in army, I gave his name. He was an old journalist and had started a newspaper in Lahore by the name of Outlook and had remained associated with it for a long time. Ultimately it was decided that some experienced person should help me for 10, 15 days, and that this would be sufficient time for me to learn the skills and then I can start on my own. The army public relations officer in Delhi at that time was Brigadier Desmond Young. He was also a famous writer, and wanted to leave the army. So we came together from Delhi. He worked with me for 2, 3 weeks and then declared that I knew everything and could work independently. Initially I was nervous, but after a week or so I realized that it wasn't such a big deal.[16]

Faiz resigned his commission in the army and accepted Mian Iftikharuddin's offer. He soon distinguished himself as a newspaper editor and *Pakistan Times* quickly became one of the most popular newspapers in Lahore. A short time later, its sister publication in Urdu, *Imroze*, also came out. Faiz was the editor of this paper as well and he hired his friend, noted writer and poet Maulana Chiragh Hasan Hasrat, to take charge of its day-to-day affairs.

The situation in the country was getting more and more volatile by the day. Demonstrations and protests against the Raj were now a daily occurrence and British plans to leave India were well advanced. 'Independence' was on everyone's lips. Alys stayed in Delhi with Salima and Moneeza for a short while and once Faiz found a suitable house in Lahore, they all moved there.

August 1947 was getting closer and with it, the 'night-bitten dawn' that Faiz would write about soon in his poetic masterpiece, 'Dawn of Independence'.

Years before, Allama Iqbal had written of the First World War: 'That is not the rosy dawn of a new age on the horizon of the West, but a torrent of blood.'[17] The same was about to be true for his own horizon of the East.

Notes

1. Faiz Ahmed Faiz, *Mah-o Saal-e Aashnai* (Karachi: Maktaba Daniyal, 2008), p. 17.
2. Dr Ayub Mirza, *Faiz Nama* (Lahore: Classic Publishers, 2003), p. 55.

3. Sheema Majeed (comp.), *Culture and Identity: Selected English Writings of Faiz* (Karachi: Oxford University Press, 2005), p. 10.
4. Ludmila Vasilieva, *Parvarish-e Lauh-o-Qalam: Faiz Hayat aur Takhleeqat* (Karachi: Oxford University Press, 2006), p. 139.
5. Ashfaq Hussain, *Faiz: Shakhsiat aur Fun* (Karachi: Pakistan Study Center, 2011), p. 54.
6. Sajjad Zaheer, 'Shakhs-o Aks', *Afkar*, Faiz number (Karachi: Maktaba Afkar, 1965), p. 171.
7. Maryam Salganik, *Selections from Faiz* (in Russian) (Moscow: Raduga Publishers, 1985), Epilogue, p. 284.
8. Translation by this author.
9. Dr Ayub Mirza, *Hum ke Thehre Ajnabi* (Islamabad: Dost Publications, 1996), p. 82.
10. Literal translation of an Urdu proverb, meaning someone who is employed for money and should thus be loyal.
11. Mirza, *Hum ke Thehre Ajnabi*, pp. 63–4.
12. Ibid., pp. 62–3.
13. Ibid., p. 76.
14. Ibid., p. 77.
15. Ibid., pp. 83, 84.
16. Faiz Ahmed Faiz, 'Guftagoo—Faiz Ahmed Faiz', *Dunyazad*, no. 35 (Karachi: Scheherzade Publications, 2012), p. 53.
17. V.G. Kiernan (trans.), *Poems from Iqbal* (Karachi: Oxford University Press, 2004), p. xxiv.

10
Independence

> Do men think that they will be left alone on saying,
> 'We believe', and that they will not be tested?
>
> —The Quran 29:2

Six years after the publication of his first collection of poetry, Faiz was fully immersed in the newspapers he was heading, *Pakistan Times* and *Imroze*. Because of the hard work that he had put into raising standards, both papers had achieved significant recognition and respect in journalistic circles. Editing two newspapers was time-consuming and he rarely found the time to write poetry, giving rise to speculation that he had decided to give up poetry and concentrate on a career in journalism. The occasional poems that were published here and there were as popular as ever, but it appeared that the muse of poetry had deserted Faiz.

Faiz was lucky, though, that in contrast to his dreamy disorganization, Alys was a good household manager and things were in good shape on the home front. They had rented a small house, which was rather rundown, but it was near the newspaper office so they had decided in its favour. Alys was now comfortable enough with Urdu to manage household chores on her own. She would visit her mother-in-law often and remained aware of Faiz's (and her) responsibilities towards his large family. In addition, she had assumed full responsibility of taking care of their two young daughters. Being widely read, and having taught in Indian schools for several years and hence aware of their problems, Alys would also occasionally contribute short pieces on educational matters to *Pakistan Times*. Later, when Faiz was behind bars for several years, this experience was to prove very useful. Alys became a full-time employee of the newspaper and was able to support the family with her income while Faiz was incarcerated.

In the spring of 1947, Alys's parents came to visit Lahore. It was their first visit to India. The War was over and they wanted to see their younger son-in-law and their two granddaughters whom they had never met. From Lahore, they were planning to go to Srinagar to see Christabel and her family, and Alys was eagerly looking forward to the trip. She tried to persuade Faiz to take a few days off work and accompany them, but to no avail.

A recollection related to her parents' visit that Alys recorded in her memoirs serves to illustrate the humble conditions in which both she and Faiz had chosen to live:

> The rented house in which we lived was old and run down, there were scorpions and other creatures living in the cracks of its walls and I had warned my parents to be careful and not sit near any large cracks in the wall and to not go to the bathroom barefoot.
>
> One time, my father was laying on the large bed playing with Meezoo (her younger daughter Moneeza). She was enjoying herself, laughing and rolling around from one end of the bed to the other. As she did a somersault on the bed, her laughter was drowned out by a loud sound. Right where she had been just an instant before, the heavy ceiling fan had fallen on the bed. We were all shaken and when we had recovered, it was decided that my parents would leave soon for Srinagar and the girls and I would join them in a few days.[1]

Even by the usual Indian standards, the summer of 1947 was unusually hot and unsettled. 'Partition' was now seeming inevitable. In Lahore, where Muslims were in a majority, there were daily processions with green flags and slogans of 'Azadi Zindabad' (Long Live Independence) and 'Pakistan Zindabad' (Long Live Pakistan).

Alys received news of partition, and the emergence of the new republic of Pakistan in Srinagar, which had become a part of Indian Kashmir while Sialkot, Lahore, and the family were now in Pakistan.

'Darkness'

Communal violence had already become commonplace in the months leading up to August 1947. There was real danger of massive bloodshed as Independence approached. This was made worse by the fact that Britain's treasury was empty after the massive destruction of the Second World War, making it increasingly difficult to maintain any semblance of governance in India.

On 15 July 1947, the Indian Independence Act 1947 of the Parliament of the United Kingdom stipulated that British rule in India would come to an end just one month later, on 15 August 1947. The Act also stipulated the partition of the provinces of British India into two new sovereign dominions: the Union of India and the Dominion of Pakistan.

The new border sliced through two of the most populous provinces of India: the Punjab and Bengal.

Punjab's population distribution was such that a line couldn't neatly be drawn to divide Hindus, Muslims and Sikhs. However, it was felt that a carefully drawn border could minimize the dislocation that people would experience.

But it was not to be.

Massive population exchanges occurred between the two newly formed states in the months immediately following partition. Once the lines were established, about 14.5 million people crossed the borders to what they hoped was the relative safety of 'their' religious majority.

In 'the sub-continent as a whole, some 14 million people left their homes and set out by every means possible—by air, train, and road, in cars and lorries, in buses and bullock carts, but most of all on foot—to seek refuge with their own kind'.[2]

It was the largest human migration in history. The newly formed governments of India and Pakistan were completely unequipped to deal with migration of such staggering magnitude, and massive violence occurred on both sides of the border. Many of the refugees were slaughtered, some starved or died of exhaustion or illness.

Estimates of the number of people who died range between 2,00,000 (official British estimate at the time) and two million, with the consensus being around one million.

The agony of Partition was mirrored in the famous dirge by renowned Punjabi writer and poet Amrita Pritam (1919–2005), 'Aj aakhan Waris Shah nun', addressed to the historic Punjabi poet Waris Shah (1722–1798), who had written the most popular version of the Punjabi folk love tragedy, 'Heer–Ranjha'. It appeals to

Waris Shah to rise from his grave, record the Punjab's anguish and turn over a new page in history.

Despite the rapidly deteriorating law-and-order situation, Faiz managed to make it to Srinagar. He did not want Alys and the children to travel alone, as the way back to Lahore led through some of the worst-affected areas. They went back to Lahore via Amritsar and then Rawalpindi and, fortunately, did not have to witness any of the carnage that was raging all around.

In those horrific days, Faiz made it a point to go in person to the most dangerous areas so that the most accurate reports could be filed. Foreign correspondents, who were reluctant to accompany the chief editor of *Pakistan Times* in some cases, would be amazed by his courage and fearlessness.

Faiz's editorials in *Pakistan Times* from those days were filled with rage and sorrow at the needless slaughter of innocents and full-throated appeals for humanity and empathy. In the 15 August 1947 editorial, he wrote:

> It is August 15 today. The dawn that brought this day into the world also restored to our people their long-lost freedom. Through many bleak decades of political serfdom, millions of us have waited and hoped for this dawn. It has arrived at last and yet, for us in the Punjab, it is not bright with laughter and buoyant with song. It is black with sorrow and red with blood. The reality of freedom, compared to the reality of the death and suffering around us, appears insubstantial and far away. While, in the West, the new edifice of Pakistan is emerging above its foundations, in the fire ravaged countryside of the East, the ancient homesteads of our less fortunate brothers are crumbling into ashes: while we are entering into our heritage, they are being turned out of theirs.[3]

In the same vein, in a letter to Alys while she and the girls were still in Srinagar, a saddened Faiz had written: 'The Muslims have got their Pakistan, the Hindus and Sikhs their divided Punjab and Bengal but I have yet to meet a person, Muslim, Hindu or Sikh who feels enthusiastic about the future. I can't think of any country whose people felt so miserable on the eve of their freedom and liberation.'

'Subh-e azadi'

As the horror of partition gradually receded over the ensuing months, peace returned and poets picked up their pens once again. All of them wanted to express in their own words, the sentiments of their fellow Pakistanis. Most of these poems proved transitory but in the ones that have been preserved, there is a reflection of the hope and optimism which most citizens of the new land were feeling. At last, they were free of the hated British Raj and the Muslims of the subcontinent had a land to call their own.

It was Faiz, however, from whose pen sprang one of the earliest, and most memorable, tributes to this bloody chapter in the history of the subcontinent. This is how one author later described it:

> On June 3, 1947, the partition of the subcontinent was announced. A few days later, summer vacations started...[We] came to Srinagar in August. Across the river from our houseboat was a large mansion, 'Harmony', where Dr. MD Taseer and Faiz's family were staying. Two or three days after August 14, Faiz sahib arrived there. I met him the next day at Taseer sahib's house. Faiz, who always used to be somewhat hesitant in front of his elders, especially Taseer sahib and Bokhari sahib, remarked that he had started a poem in Lahore and finished it by the time he got to Srinagar. At Taseer sahib's request, he recited it for us.[4]

The poem was titled 'Subh-e azadi' (Dawn of independence) and it was to become one of the enduring pieces of writing on the partition:

Ye daagh ujala, ye shab gazeeda seher
Wo intezaar tha jiska ye wo seher tau nahi
Ye wo seher tau nahin, jis ki arzu le kar
Chaley thay yaar ke mil jaye gi kahin na kahin
Falak ke dasht mein taaron ki aakhri manzil
Kahin tau hoga shab-e sust mauj ka saahil
Kahin tau ja ke rukay ga safeena-e gham-e dil.

This stained light, this night-bitten dawn;
This is not that long awaited day break;
This is not the dawn in whose longing,
We set out believing we would find, somewhere,

In heaven's wide void,
The stars' final resting place;
Somewhere the shore of night's slow-washing tide;
Somewhere, an anchor for the ship of heartache.

Faiz ended the poem with these lines:

Abhi giraani-e shab mein kami nahin aai
Nijaat deeda o dil ki ghadi nahin aai
Chaley chalo ke wo manzil abhi nahin aai.

Night's heaviness is unlessened;
The hour of the heart and spirit's deliverance has not yet
arrived;
Let us go on, that goal has not yet arrived.[5]

The people in Faiz's circle of friends who first heard the poem were 'transfixed, especially Dr Nazir Ahmad [Faiz's old friend, later principal of Government College, Lahore], who kept repeating the poem after Faiz finished reciting it. In between, Taseer sahib also requested Faiz to repeat some verses two or three times'.[6]

The poem, as was usual with Faiz's poetry, did not go unnoticed by the general public either. However, the reaction was decidedly mixed. In fact, Faiz, by gently combining lyricism with political comment and expressing his sorrow about what had happened (and perhaps his apprehension about what was to come), raised hackles on both sides of the political divide. Those on the right scorned the poem for not celebrating independence enthusiastically. This, according to them, was not the time to cry over the anguish of ordinary people but to be happy that freedom had finally arrived.

Those on the Left were not too happy either. Faiz's friend and Marxist historian Syed Sibt-e Hasan wrote:

> Both those on the Right and the Left protested [about the poem]. Those on the right said outright that it was a betrayal of the cause of Independence and that Faiz was against Pakistan. His enemies were also upset that he had not criticized the Radcliffe award outright in the poem. They could never understand the depth of the metaphors 'stained light' and 'night bitten dawn'.
>
> The critics on the Left said the poem was too vague, claiming

> that if the title was removed, it would be impossible to tell if the poem was about Independence. They also protested that the romantic symbols had lessened the impact of the poem. These people are happy to extend permission to Mirza Ghalib to describe the truth in terms of wine and cup but are unwilling to extend the same to Faiz sahib.[7]

Faiz's friend and fellow Progressive poet, Ali Sardar Jafri, called the poem 'half truth' and wrote that a poem like this could be written by both a member of an Islamist or a Hindu religious organization, that if Faiz felt that independence (and its ensuing partition) was a negation of the aspirations of common people, he should have been more forceful in his denunciation of it, etc.

Defending Faiz, Professor Fateh Mohammad Malik wrote: It is surprising that those who were criticizing Faiz never managed to see in it his deep, undying love for his land, especially at a time when the wounds of the Radcliffe Award (Partition) were still raw, when our (Pakistan's) leaders were bemoaning the cunning and betrayal of the British about this 'moth-eaten' Pakistan.[8]

'Subh-e azadi' was written on the occasion of Pakistan's first birthday and Faiz, in his own unique way, highlighted the problems facing the new nation. From 1947 till his death in 1984, Faiz composed a total of eleven more poems to celebrate either Pakistan's Independence Day or Republic Day. In all of these poems, Faiz spoke lovingly and sadly about his land and its long-suffering people, their hopes and fears, their joys and sorrows, their dreams and disappointments. There is also, in these poems, both an expression of solidarity with his land and its people and also a challenge of the oppressed against their oppressors. The beauty of these poems (and Faiz's poetry) is their melody and their message of hope, although many of them also reflect the agony of the poet in the face of life's painful realities. Agha Nasir has noted, 'These poems were written at different times and are composed in different styles and different metres but if we read them together, their internal rhythm makes them appear like a single long poem.'[9]

'Writers, where do you stand?'

Faiz started his career as a teacher and described teaching as the most fulfilling thing he had ever done. In addition to his poetry, though, it was as a journalist and newspaper editor that he achieved greater renown. His first experience at journalism was early on in his career, around 1938. The activities of the AIPWA were at their peak and there was a huge volume of Progressive literature being produced, both prose and poetry. The literary quality of some of these works was dubious; nevertheless, the movement had provided a vast new platform for writers and ideas. As Faiz would later point out repeatedly, Progressive ideas had not fallen out of the sky (nor were they, as opponents of the Association alleged, 'communist' or 'subversive' ideas). Progressive ideology was simply a reflection of the existing social conditions in India at the time. There was a need for new publications to accommodate all of the work that was being produced. The literary magazine *Adab-e Latif* was founded for the same reason by Chaudhry Bashir Ahmad, with its official policy being the publication and promotion of Progressive literature. Faiz was offered the editorship of the journal, which he accepted upon the encouragement of friends.

One important reason that Faiz accepted the offer was to highlight those writings that best represented the ideals and aspirations of the Progressive movement since, as mentioned earlier, there was a huge quantity of works being produced under the 'Progressive' label, many of them of dubious quality. Faiz immediately set to work trying to elicit the best writings for the journal from both new authors as well as established writers. As a result of the quality of writings published in it as well as its presentation, *Adb-e Latif* soon acquired a wide readership and a reputation as one of the leading Urdu journals in the country. With Faiz at its helm, there was hardly any important Urdu writer of the time whose work, whether prose, poetry, drama, short story or essays, was not published in *Adb-e Latif*. Faiz also started a series in the journal, highlighting classics of international literature.

Progressives and pornography

As already mentioned, Faiz's time at *Adb-e Latif* was brief but eventful. In the 1941 annual issue of the journal were published a bunch of writings that caused a commotion. These included Saadat Hasan Manto's 'Kaali Shalwar' about a prostitute and her pimp who move to the big city to find livelihood, Ismat Chughtai's

'Lihaaf', one of the first Urdu writings to deal with the subject of female homosexuality and Mumtaz Mufti's 'Badmaash'. There was an immediate outcry and not only was *Adab-e Latif* banned, Manto and Chughtai were both charged in court with pornography. Instead of apologizing and excusing himself from the matter, Faiz decided to fight the case in court. In his testimony to the court, he declared that the writings for which *Adab-e Latif* had been banned were most decidedly not pornographic.

Years later, talking to his friend Dr Ayub Mirza, he described the trials of Chughtai and Manto:

> It was around 1940. 'Lihaaf' was published in 'Adb-e Latif' and it was like an atomic bomb went off in Hindustan's literary world. 'Adb-e Latif' was hauled in court for pornography. Manto's cases happened much later. He was my student in Amritsar but he never came to class, he was the mischievous sort. He was only a month or two younger than me. He was intelligent but wouldn't listen to anyone. He respected me though, and considered me his teacher. I gave him some short stories by Gorky to translate, then some more and he became a writer. He wrote some exquisite short stories but after 1950, he lost his way. The film people would give him a bottle of liquor and have him write whatever they wanted. Every time he was taken to court, I would be one of the defense witnesses. He was arrested four times; for 'Kaali Shalwar' ('Black Trouser'), 'Thanda Gosht' ('Cold Meat'), 'Khol Do' ('Open It') and 'Dhuan' ('Smoke'). The first three times, we managed to get him off. The fourth time, I was in jail as well as a 'guest' of the government and he was jailed.[10]

In later years, both Manto and Ismat Chughtai would be attacked not just by religious conservatives and the government, but by Progressives as well, for their fiercely independent outlook. Faiz was opposed to this 'literary extremism' and wrote: 'Some people [amongst the Progressives] veered towards extremism in their emotionality and as a result, people who were with us, whom we should have kept with us as we moved the [Progressive] movement forward, we excluded from our circle, thus restricting it. This was obviously wrong…As a result, writers such as Manto, Ismat and Quratulain Haider were excluded from our group which I was against.'[11]

In his plea to the court, Faiz requested that since the charges against both the journal and the authors were unfounded and baseless, the ban on *Adab-e Latif*'s publication be lifted forthwith and both Manto and Ismat Chughtai honourably acquitted in the case. Faiz also demanded that the court provide restitution for the damage done to their reputations because of the slanderous campaign conducted against them. Faiz prepared a detailed list of witnesses, which included both well-known jurists as well as authors of repute to appear for the defence in order to shed light on various aspects of the literary works under attack.

The case never got that far. The court listened to the arguments of the lawyers and dismissed the trial as unsubstantiated and misguided and immediately restored *Adab-e Latif*'s publication. The trial caused the readership of *Adab-e Latif* to grow substantially. Faiz's time at *Adab-e Latif* was brief and he soon moved to Lahore to start teaching English literature at Lahore's Hailey College of Commerce.

Progressive Papers Limited and **Pakistan Times**

By the end of 1946, plans for the division of India into Muslim-and non-Muslim-majority areas were well advanced. The Communist Party of India had also finally threw its weight behind the demand for Pakistan, terming it a matter of national self-determination. Discussions were being held in Party meetings on how to prepare for the most important matter at hand: protection of the minorities living in the areas proposed to be included in the new nation of Pakistan.

Oddly enough, the Muslim League, the party which had promulgated and worked hard on the demand for a separate homeland for the Muslims of India had no organizational networks in the areas designated as Muslim-majority areas. The landlords, tribal sardars, religious 'peers' and business owners in those areas were all supportive of the Muslim League but there was a pressing need for a newspaper which would serve as the voice of the League in these areas, especially in the English-language press. Accordingly, the provincial council of the Punjab advised its affluent supporters to invest in such a project. In May 1946, a company by the name of Progressive Papers Limited was registered under the Companies Act, 1935. The directors of the company included some of the most prominent and affluent men of the times, including the president of the Punjab Muslim League. Most of the shares in the company rested with Mian Iftikharuddin, then member of the Punjab Legislative Assembly, and, by consensus, he was elected its managing director. The stated purpose of the company was to promote journalism that reflected the aspirations and needs of the new nation in light of the principles of the Muslim League.

Until this time, the English-language newspapers being published in the Western part of Pakistan—among them *The Civil and Military Gazette* and *The Tribune* from Lahore and *The Daily Gazette* from Karachi—all belonged to non-Muslims and none of them was considered suitable to be tasked with being the official organ of the Muslim League. There were also other newspapers sympathetic to the cause of 'Pakistan' and the Muslim League, such as the daily *Dawn* being published from Delhi and *The Morning News* and *Star of India* from Calcutta but they, too, were considered unsuitable owing to geographical distance.

The announcement of the setting up of *Pakistan Times* then was a welcome development. Faiz accepted Mian Iftikharuddin's offer to be its first editor–in- chief after some initial hesitation (as already discussed). No doubt the salary being offered, Rs 1,000 a month, also helped him make up his mind.

On Faiz's insistence, Mian Iftikharuddin had hired a Brigadier Desmond Young to help him (Faiz) learn the ropes of running a newspaper. The brigadier would later become better known for his book *Rommel*, about one of Hitler's shrewdest and most successful soldiers, Field Marshal Erwin Rommel, also known as the 'Desert Fox' for his exploits in the North African campaign of the Second World War. The book was later made into a popular movie, *The Desert Fox*, starring James Mason as Rommel. Young had fought against Rommel's forces in North Africa before his promotion to brigadier and his appointment as director of public relations in the army headquarters, India. He wanted to retire from the army and return to England, but Mian Iftikharuddin persuaded him to stay on for a few months to help train Faiz and his staff at the new publication. This included people who would later go on to achieve renown in Pakistani journalism, including Mazhar Ali Khan, son-in-law of famed Indian politician and statesman, Sardar Sikander Hayat Khan, and Safdar Mir, who would later adopt the pen name 'Zeno', after the pre-Socratic Greek philosopher. Faiz was always on the lookout for bright and talented young writers who were courageous in their writings and displayed some freshness of thought. The only restriction from Faiz's side was that no one would be accepted onto the staff solely on the basis of his 'connections' with someone important. To Mian Iftikharuddin's credit, neither he nor the other shareholders of the company ever interfered in Faiz's decisions.[12]

The founding of the *Pakistan Times* a few months before the formation of Pakistan had galvanized activists of the Muslim League and especially Muslims of the Punjab. The enthusiasm of the staff was palpable. Everyone would arrive early at the office and stay till late at night. There would be long discussions on policy and planning for the new nation. Even though the new paper was not the official mouthpiece of the Muslim League, all of its sponsors and directors were part of the party's hierarchy and the purpose of the creation of Progressive Papers Limited was to propagate the ideals and aims of the party. After the announcement of the Cabinet Mission Plan of 1946, the creation of Pakistan appeared inevitable but, as the wheel of history spun rapidly, even the founding fathers of Pakistan could have had little idea about what was to come.

'And never the twain shall meet'

It was perhaps not coincidental that the movement for the creation of Pakistan had been carried out most vigorously in Muslim-minority areas which could not be a part of the future Pakistan. It was natural for Muslims in these areas to feel under siege (economically and psychologically) from non-Muslim communities. The Muslim-majority areas did share a common religion but their similarities ended there. On the ground, their languages, cultures, traditions, ways of living, all differed drastically from each other. Even more importantly, the area with the largest number of Muslims, East Bengal, was separated from the other proposed provinces of Pakistan (Punjab, Sindh,

Balochistan and the North West Frontier Province [now Khyber-Pakhtunkhwa]) by a huge distance. In addition, both areas had little in common with each other. It could not have been otherwise. Naturally, the people of East Bengal had more in common with their fellow Bengalis in West Bengal (except that they practised different religions). The same was the case with the people of the Punjab, who had much more in common with each other than with their far-flung Muslim 'brothers' in Bengal. History has demonstrated conclusively that while religion can be a uniting force in a region, it cannot overcome the bonds of language, culture and tradition that have evolved over millennia.

This fact was conveniently overlooked in the excitement of independence and the people's burning desire to be rid of the hated British Raj. As a result, the new state of Pakistan faced huge, close to insurmountable, odds from the day of its birth, related to its existence and the organization of its various components. The organization and governance of the future state of Pakistan had not been discussed or planned in any meaningful way except for a few speeches of Jinnah and some resolutions of the Muslim League leadership. The points on which there was some agreement included that Pakistan would be a democracy and would be governed by the principle of equal voting rights for all adults; that all of Pakistan's Muslim-majority provinces were joining the new federation voluntarily; that Pakistan was coming into being as a result of a popular movement the purpose of which was to provide some protection to Muslims from political, economic and cultural domination by non-Muslim majorities and that therefore, a central motive for the creation of Pakistan was the welfare and progress of its people; that in Pakistan, people of all religions would be provided complete legal and constitutional protection to practise their faiths as they wished and that the state would guarantee the protection and freedom of all religious places of worship; that Pakistan was most emphatically not a theocratic or religious republic but a modern nation state willing to work alongside the nations of the world; that Pakistani society would be free of all exploitation, tyranny and oppression and would be administered on the basis of universal social justice and that the state would actively work to root out exploitation, oppression and economic injustice to bring its underdeveloped areas on a par with its more developed areas; that the ancient oppressive feudal system of governance would be organized along modern lines to raise agricultural production and wipe out famine, hunger and poverty; that every region of the new country would be given representation in the federation, at least according to its population, but that preference would be given to organizational abilities and talents regardless of provincial origin and that all languages and cultures in the region would be given equal representation and equal opportunities for development.

These points were repeated numerous times in Jinnah's speeches and represented as resolutions more than once in the Muslim League's general meetings. The editorial policy of *Pakistan Times* was, therefore, formulated along the same lines. After the Cabinet Mission Plan, there was general agreement on the outlines of the future Pakistan's economic policies but the award by the Border Commission again plunged the future into doubt. Partition, with its attendant violence, poisoned the landscape, especially in the Punjab and Bengal. Under these conditions, *Pakistan Times* had to play a role as peacemaker as well as unmask conspiracies and plots against peace and cooperation.

It was no easy task to get a brand new English newspaper running, but it was the need of the hour. Faiz, Mian Iftikharuddin and the entire staff worked day and night for two months, with Faiz narrating a story about it years later:

> It was the early days of *Pakistan Times*. Mian Iftikhar had imported a printing press from America and one day it stopped working. The American engineer who had been sent with the machine could not figure out what was wrong with it. Everyone was frustrated since we could not continue working without it. One of the old mechanics took me aside and said 'Sahib, I know what's wrong. If you will take the "gora" [white man] aside for tea or something, I can try to fix it. I stared at him in surprise but then made some excuse and took the engineer with me to my office saying, come, let's have some tea and you can then try again. We were drinking tea in my office when there was a loud clatter and then the machine started running at full speed. Even Mian Iftikharuddin was surprised but he praised the mechanic and gave him some reward.[13]

Faiz had decided early on that the running of the newspaper would be a collective responsibility. Every morning, there would be a one-hour meeting in which everyone would give their ideas about recent articles and compare them with the layouts, news and issues of other newspapers. One day, *Pakistan Times* failed to carry news of an important social function that had been covered by other papers. Faiz demanded an explanation and was told that the organizers of the function had not sent an invitation to the newsroom. Faiz responded, 'That's even worse. Do you need an invitation to gather news? The news is not going to come to you. You have to go after it.' Faiz used to say that 'the real success of a newspaper depends on its reporters who chase after the news on the streets, from one office to another, from one desk to the next'. On another occasion, before heading home, he asked the shift in-charge about the lead story for the day and was told that it was a story about Korea, to which he responded, 'Take a lead from a Pakistani story sometimes too. Your country is more deserving of your attention.' He was particularly insistent about the accuracy of published stories. He insisted that his staff verify each and every story to make sure that it had not been cooked up at a desk.[14]

Faiz brought his vast literary knowledge to *Pakistan Times* and this was evident in the titles of some his early editorials. On the 1951 visit of Prime Minister Liaquat Ali Khan to the Commonwealth, he wrote an editorial entitled 'Westward Ho!' after the novel by Charles Kingsley. On the prime minister returning empty-handed from the summit, Faiz wrote the editorial, 'Return of the Native' after the novel by Thomas Hardy.

Faiz and Alys moved several times after coming to Lahore in order to find decent housing for themselves and their two young daughters. Between work and moving, Faiz's poetic output dwindled to almost nothing in his years at *Pakistan Times*.

It would require another jolt, this time administered by the government of the new nation, to reawaken the poet inside Faiz.

Notes

1. Alys Faiz, *Over My Shoulder* (Lahore: The Frontier Post Publications, 1993), p. 39.
2. Sekhara Bandyopadhyaya, *From Plassey to Partition: A History of Modern India* (Delhi: Orient Blackswan, 2004), p. 260.

3. Faiz Ahmed Faiz, Editorial, *Pakistan Times*, 15 August 1947. Available at http://pdf.aj-pak.org/downloads/faiz_on_partition.pdf. Retrieved April 14, 2014.
4. Aftab Ahmad, *B'yaad e sohbat e naazuk khayaalan* (Karachi: Maktaba Daniyal, 1996), p. 47.
5. Translation by this author.
6. Syed Sibt-e-Hasan, *Sukhan dar Sukhan* (Karachi: Maktaba Daniyal, 2009), p. 24.
7. Ibid.
8. Fateh Mohammad Malik, *Faiz, Shai'ri aur Siyasat* (Lahore: Sang-e-Meel Publications,1991), pp. 52, 53.
9. Agha Nasir, *Hum Jeetay Jee Masroof Rahay* (Lahore: Sang-e-Meel Publications, 2011), p. 21.
10. Dr Ayub Mirza, *Hum ke Thehre Ajnabi* (Islamabad: Dost Publications, 1996), pp. 130–1.
11. Dr Ayub Mirza, *Faiz Nama* (Lahore: Classic Publishers, 2006), p. 100.
12. Sehba Lakhnavi, Kashish Siddiqui (comps) *Afkar*, Faiz number (Karachi: Maktaba Afkar, 1965), p. 200.
13. Mirza, *Hum ke Thehre Ajnabi*, p. 91.
14. Shakir Hussain, 'Faiz Sahib ke bad…ab kuch bhi naheen hai' by Hameed Akhtar. In *Teri Yaadon ke Naqoosh* (Lahore: Sang-e-Meel Publications, 2011), pp. 281–2.

11

Workers of the World, Unite!

> The workers have no country. We cannot take from them what they have not got.
>
> —Karl Marx and Friedrich Engels

In 1933, while Faiz was still a student at Government College, Lahore, his larger-than-life father, Sultan Muhammad Khan, died of a sudden heart attack on the eve of his sister's wedding. Even before Sultan Muhammad Khan was lowered into his grave, creditors started lining up outside the door and the family faced destitution or worse.

Years later, Faiz would recall: 'Before I finished my first degree, my father died and I suddenly discovered that from grandees and rich men of the town, we had become paupers. He had left some property—some landed property—but he had left debts bigger than the property.'[1] Elsewhere, Faiz would write that this was the first time he was faced with the question of wealth and poverty in a very personal way. Why are some people rich and others poor? For Faiz, it took the painful personal experience of being forcibly 'de-classed' from a comfortable middle-class existence to one in which he did not know where his next meal was coming from, to raise in his mind the question of the unequal division of wealth.

The larger social issues of the day played their part as well, and Faiz wrote about them in later years: 'That [his father's death] was one factor that had a great impact on myself and my family. [Then] suddenly, came the Great Depression. As a result, the prices of agricultural produce hit rock bottom. The country side became very impoverished and the little income we had from land also stopped. The Great Depression had a great impact politically and personally, not only on myself, but also on whole communities.'[2]

The radicalization caused by the worldwide Great Depression was one of the causes of the rise of Hitler and his fascist hordes in Nazi Germany. In the Indian subcontinent, it led to a sharp resurgence of the independence struggle. The All-India Progressive Writers' Association (AIPWA) too was a product of this radicalization. Faiz had, by this time, finished his education and taken up his first job as a Lecturer in English at Mohammadan Anglo-Oriental (MAO) College, Amritsar, whose vice-principal (there was no principal at the time) was Sahibzada Mahmooduzzafar. He and his energetic wife, Dr Rashid Jahan, were both committed Leftists. It was 'Mahmood' and 'Rashida' who introduced him to communist ideas, and it was under their tutelage that Faiz began to take a practical interest in the problems of workers and peasants. It was in Amritsar that he chose to commit himself to socialist ideals; it was a commitment which would take him from the halls of MAO College to the editor's desk at *Pakistan Times*, a jail cell in solitary confinement and finally and repeatedly to 'the land of Lenin and the October Revolution', where he would be feted and praised till the end of his life.

Faiz wrote years later about his introduction to socialist ideas and the land of Lenin:

> Several years later, another picture of Russia arose in my mind (I was unfamiliar with the name 'Soviet Union'). In University for my MA degree, I had to study English literature, particularly eighteenth and nineteenth century literature. In addition to English literature, I had to read some European literature as well. I was fond of reading anyway and used to read whatever I could find and that's how I was introduced to Russian classical literature. So I read Gogol, Pushkin, Dostoyevsky, Turgenev, Tolstoy, Chekov; all of them I read deeply and the world of old Russia emerged before my eyes. Oppressed and helpless peasants, lascivious and self-satisfied nobles, love struck young men and amorous sweethearts, penniless revolutionaries and opium-addicted intellectuals, dark mud huts and glittering palaces, dense jungles and vast empty plains, deserts and rivers, wars, love affairs, conspiracies, Natasha, Anna Karenina, Uncle Vanya, the Karamazov family, tyranny and its cure, oppression and rebellion, sadness and gaiety, good and evil, disgrace and honor, like a cinema screen, all these pictures began to arise.
>
> In college, a few classmates and I were absorbed in this world and would sit for hours discussing these classic books and their characters. But we were so engrossed in this old world

> that we never paid attention to the new Soviet world that was emerging after the revolution even though we were dimly aware of its existence. The reason for this was that by the end of the second decade of the twentieth century, Lenin, Socialism and revolution were being talked about in some circles. In our subcontinent, this was the peak of the terrorist movement and everyone was talking about the Chittagong Army case, the Kakori train robbery, Bhagat Singh, Azad and all those things. One of my friend, Khwaja Khurshid Anwar had even been involved with the Bhagat Singh movement.
>
> Then I finished my education and set about looking for work. This was the time of global profiteering and economic depression. Grain was being sold for a pittance and hungry peasants abandoned their ancestral lands and flocked to the cities in search of two square meals a day. Unemployment was rampant, jobs were scarce and respectable women had started selling themselves for food. Capitalists and financiers were the only ones who were thriving, sweeping up the self respect and honor of those in need, along with their property. Before this economic crisis, foreign rule and national independence had been in everyone's mind but this new situation brought to the forefront the problem of the division of the national wealth, poverty and wealth, workers and capitalists, peasants and landlords, submission and ruler ship; all conscientious people began pondering these issues. Kissan Sabhas were formed, workers' movements gathered steam and along with national independence, calls for socialism and social equality and justice also became louder.[3]

It was in Amritsar, too, that Faiz was introduced to a central tenet of Marxist thought: socialist internationalism; the idea that nations and national boundaries were artificial constructs and were often used to pit the workers of one nation against another in the interests of their ruling classes. When Marx and Engels had first put forward this idea in *The Communist Manifesto* in 1848, they were decades ahead of their time. Even in the first half of the twentieth century, it was a radical idea. In the current scenario of the increasing advent of 'globalization', exactly what Marx had predicted, the idea of workers and their work transcending national boundaries may not seem quite so profound, but in the 1930s, before telephones, TV and the internet, it must have sounded quite fantastic. For someone like Faiz, however, it made intuitive sense, as did other aspects of Marxism.

It was also in Amritsar that Mahmooduzzafar and Rashid Jahan introduced him to working on the ground to help poor factory workers and their families outside Amritsar. Soon after he started working in the workers' colonies outside Amritsar, he was made a member of the Amritsar Labour Federation, affiliated with the All India Trade Union Congress (AITUC). AITUC, run by the Communist Party, was the largest workers' body in the country and represented workers from all over India. This was Faiz's first taste of trade-union activities on behalf of workers and indicated his desire to do something practical 'rather than just theorizing'. He would continue to find ways later in life to remain practically active in all the causes that were dear to his heart.

The pen and the sword

Faiz's next experience with activism came after his stint in the army, with the setting up of *Pakistan Times* in 1947. He recalled later:

> After this comes 'Pakistan Times'. When the war ended I resigned from the army and came to Lahore. Then 'Pakistan Times' started. After some time we got freedom and Pakistan was created. There was such chaos that it was necessary that a man should do whatever he can, given the circumstances of the country. There was the work of organizing the newspapers and journalists. For that the Pakistan Newspaper Editors Conference was established. There was no trade union here, because all the trade union leaders had been non-Muslims who had migrated, so that work was also there. I worked in the trade union, but I couldn't bring myself to do any rallying and slogan-raising. I was just a worker.[4]

Notwithstanding Faiz's characteristic humility, it would be safe to say that he was the moving force behind journalistic trade unionism in the new nation of Pakistan. As already mentioned, he had been an active member of the Amritsar Labour Federation and the All India Trade Union Congress. However, other, more pressing, issues in the intervening years had not allowed him to remain as active in the trade-union movement as he would have liked. After the formation of Pakistan, he felt acutely that workers' movements had to play an active role in the politics of the new nation in order to defend the interests of workers and peasants. Faiz promoted their interests through *Pakistan Times* and its sister Urdu publication *Imroze*. He had already written numerous editorials on the problems of workers and peasants in the pages of both newspapers and, in fact, these two papers were the only ones that had actively raised the issues of poverty, workers' exploitation and destitution. His poem 'Subh-e azadi' (Dawn of independence) had already pointed out that independence from the hated British Raj meant nothing to ordinary people if it did not translate into independence from hunger, want and oppression. The poem was a stark reminder of the problems that the new nation could face in the near future if these issues were not resolved. But in spite of his misgivings, Faiz continued working hard at *Pakistan Times*. Partition had given rise to a new metaphor in the lexicon of the subcontinent. The new border between India and Pakistan was now being referred to as 'khoon ki lakeer' (line of blood) owing to the countless millions who had perished in the catastrophic division. On both sides of the Punjab, especially, this had sowed the seeds of fear and hatred. For Faiz, only a society based on social justice, equality and fraternity, which ordinary people on both sides of the border had been dreaming about, could heal this wound and wipe out the horrific memories of those grim days.

Faiz's hard work soon turned *Pakistan Times* and *Imroze* into newspapers that were widely read and respected. News and editorials from both newspapers, sometimes with a dissenting note, began to be quoted not just in government news releases but in international news as well. With this, Faiz began to be counted among the top newspaper editors and journalists in Pakistan. His focus remained the dire economic situation of the country and his newspapers were highly critical of flawed government policies. An editorial in *Imroze* had this to say: 'We can only buy what England allows us to buy and England herself can use our hard earned foreign exchange to buy whatever she wants. As a result, we are starved of resources which need to be used to establish our own factories and workplaces. The only way to rid ourselves of this situation is to rip off the yoke of the Sterling block from our necks and conduct all our financial transactions through the State Bank of Pakistan.'[5]

Faiz knew that the task of a free and independent press was not to uncritically toe the official line of the government. It was to point out its mistakes openly to encourage honest and productive public debate. This was, in his view, the only way of boosting participatory democracy so that the voice of the majority of people could be heard in official government circles.

Then, as now, the foremost problems facing the new government were the problems of the rural-majority population of the country. Like Faiz's own relatives, millions of poor peasants cultivated small plots of land and were obligated to hand over most of their produce to the legal owners of the land, the large landholders. This system was, and is, a huge obstacle in the development of more productive forms of agriculture. The production of grain was declining steadily and foodstuffs were becoming scarce. Profiteering in foodgrains by capitalists and traders was rampant. *Pakistan Times* and *Imroze*, with the support of all Left-wing publications and sections of the poor and middle classes, tried their best to pressure the government to end profiteering and ensure a steady supply of foodstuffs, to no avail. The new government signed a pact with the Government of the United States, in the name of friendship and humanity, to provide Pakistan with grain and other foodstuffs. Obviously, this was no real solution to the problem and only resulted in the policies and independence of the government becoming subservient to its new 'friend'. An editorial in *Imroze* said: 'We receive American aid in exchange for the respect and honor of our nation. America has given us grain to further its own imperialist agenda to use us as a weapon [against others].'[6]

Opinions like these were always based on facts and the newspaper quoted an American senator who said, referring to the huge amount of grain being produced in the USA: 'We will either have to feed the grain to animals or destroy it. It is better to give it to Pakistan. Pakistan can offer considerable help to the United States in realizing its plans in South Asia.'[7]

In keeping with Faiz's philosophy of doing something practical in addition to (as he called it) theorizing, he was also at the forefront of organizing trade-union activity in the field of journalism. In this, his experience in Amritsar was to prove very valuable. Initially, Faiz organized a newspaper Editors Committee and soon after, at his urging, the first All India Muslim League Editors Conference held its inaugural session in Delhi in 1947, addressed by Jinnah. Faiz and another intrepid journalist, Hameed Nizami, the founder of the Urdu newspaper *Nawai Waqt*, attended the conference together and thereafter, met and exchanged views frequently.

After the creation of Pakistan, Faiz helped set up and became the first convener of a Press Advisory Committee, which, after some intense lobbying, convinced the government that no action would be taken against any newspaper without consulting the committee first. Soon thereafter though, the Punjab government imposed press censorship to limit coverage of the riots and bloodshed taking place in the Punjab. Faiz and the committee opposed this step vigorously. This was to be a pattern that was repeated again and again. It had become clear to Faiz that the dream of independence was fast turning into a nightmare for the vast majority of the people of the new nation, who would see no end to their hunger, oppression and want. At one point, he wrote: 'Independence proved to be an illusion and the joy that came with it was thus also brief. Those who used to dream of political and social justice in a free Pakistan and used to write about it naturally influenced ordinary people. After independence, it was all proven to be a mirage, a lie.'[8]

Nevertheless, Faiz and his two newspapers set a new standard of journalism in Pakistan that remains unmatched to this day. Taking advantage of a unique combination of historical circumstances, Faiz and his staff became the voice of all those who wished to see an end to centuries of oppression and injustice and wanted to move towards a brighter future for themselves and their country. Years later, in response to a question about his views on journalism, he had this to say: 'Journalism had not yet become a business [in 1947]. Afterwards people discovered that it can be used to make money, so it became a business.'[9]

At the United Nations

Being an active member of the trades unions resulted in Faiz leading a delegation in 1948 to San Francisco for a meeting of the

International Labour Organization (ILO). This was the first time workers in Pakistan were being represented in an international forum. There was no national organization representing workers in Pakistan at the time. Faiz was leading the unofficial delegation and, according to the rules of the ILO, he was thus admitted to the conference, not as an official delegate, but as a workers' representative. This meant that he could participate in the conference but could not vote on any of the resolutions. Faiz argued vigorously during the conference for allowing Pakistani trade unions membership of the ILO but the existing rules did not permit it. Faiz's arguments, though, helped convince the ILO to pressure governments to formally recognize trade unions and send their elected representatives to international conferences.

The next year, in 1949, Faiz again led a delegation from the Pakistan Trade Unions Federation to the annual ILO conference, this time in Geneva. The conference passed a resolution to encourage all member countries of the United Nations to implement the ILO charter protecting worker rights in their countries. Faiz would report on the proceedings of the conferences to the Pakistan Trade Unions Federation when he would return home. During this time, communist parties in different countries had organized a collective platform, which was later named World Federation of Trades Unions. As a reaction to this development, labour unions in America attempted to create their own rival group, which the Leftists opposed vigorously and defeated. Years later though, with the weakening of socialist movements throughout the world, the ILO, like the rest of the UN, was taken over by the capitalist countries, led by the USA.

Office bearers and leaders of trade unions respected Faiz and ordinary people adored him. When Faiz was billed to speak at a gathering, people would bring their entire families to hear him because, as his compatriots remember, no one else could describe complicated labour issues as simply and comprehensively as Faiz.

Faiz and postal workers

Immediately after partition, most trade union leaders and experienced activists, being non-Muslims, had moved to India and workers organizations in the newly formed Pakistan were left rudderless. Workers in the cities had no one to look to for guidance. There was a pressing need to reorganize workers unions. Here, Faiz's previous experience proved invaluable. He initially started working with the union of railway workers, the largest workers union in the newly formed country. His friends used to tease him about his 'promotion' since he had worked before this with the tonga workers' union.

Around the same time, Faiz also accepted leadership of the postal workers' union since he never refused anyone if they asked for his help. He worked without a title or financial compensation from any of the unions. Faiz felt special sympathy for postal workers. He would often mention in his speeches that what postal workers received in wages was a pittance in comparison to the work they performed. He wanted Pakistani postal workers to receive the same benefits as their counterparts in advanced capitalist countries. Faiz believed that most people were unaware of the crucial role postal workers played in their lives. He had to work a lot harder for them than he did in the case of railway workers, since the railway workers' union was larger and much better organized.

He expressed his feelings about postal workers in his touching, incomplete poem 'Intesaab' (Dedication):

> To this day
> and
> The anguish of today
> The anguish of today, displeased with life's overflowing garden
> The wilderness of yellowing leaves, which is my homeland
> The carnival of pain which is my homeland
> To the forlorn lives of clerks
> To moth-eaten hearts and tongues
> For postmen
> For tongawallahs
> For rail workers
> To the starving stalwarts working in factories.[10]

Both postal workers and their officers admired and loved Faiz. Once, years later, Alys Faiz went to a post office and a postal worker struck up a conversation with her. She mentioned that she was Mrs Faiz. He was taken aback, 'Are you the wife of the famous poet Faiz sahib?' When she responded in the affirmative, the postman said, 'Begum sahiba, you are the wife not just of a great poet but a great man. Faiz sahib has been the president of our postal union. Is he still alive?' Alys smiled at his innocence and replied, 'May God grant him a long life.'[11]

Since he was so well known amongst postal workers, whenever anyone abroad would ask for his postal address, Faiz would say, 'Just address it to "Faiz Ahmed Faiz, Pakistan", it will get to me.'

Prime Minister Liaquat Ali Khan's government kept trade-union and all Left-wing activities under strict surveillance. This was a continuation of the pattern under the British Raj. Every trade-union leader and Leftist intellectual was followed and watched by members of the secret police. Faiz, of course, had been on the government's watch list since his Amritsar days, well before partition. Once, during a meeting of the postal workers' union in Peshawar, Faiz spotted a government spy outside his hotel. The conference continued for the whole day at a different venue. When the delegates returned to the hotel, the government sleuth was still tiredly following them. He stopped and waited at the hotel gate while they went in. When dinner was served, Faiz told the workers to invite him in since the poor man had been doing his duty all day without food or drink. When the man came in, he went up to Faiz and said, 'Thank you. I have been following you around all day without a break.' Faiz replied, 'It's all right, we are all doing our duty to the best of our abilities.'

This attitude was typical of Faiz and endeared him throughout his life to friend and foe alike. In his trade-union activities, his attitude was always conciliatory. He believed that there was nothing that could not be resolved through reasonable negotiation and compromise. One author writes, 'He would present the problems of the postal union very simply and sweetly. He would not indulge in long arguments, nor get angry or get side tracked. When he was defending the interests of the union, he would keep in mind the obvious limitations of the postal department, something often neglected by other union leaders.'[12]

Faiz was convinced that Pakistan was, and had to be, a part of the wider world and would be impacted by the changes taking place in it. The one thing which made him uneasy was the prospect of fresh wars and more bloodshed. This was the reason that he had joined the British army after much soul-searching. At the end of the War, the use of the atom bomb by the Americans in Hiroshima and Nagasaki had shocked the conscience of people all over the world and confronted mankind for the first time with the prospect of complete annihilation. Faiz was convinced that another world war would mean the end of civilization and, most likely, of humanity. He had decided that world peace was worth fighting for and it had become his life's purpose. He started participating in the Pakistan Aman [Peace] Committee and soon became its secretary. In 1948, he was appointed to the Executive Committee of the World Peace Council and remained in this position till 1970. Since these efforts at peace were being spearheaded by the Soviet Union and had widespread popular support in the aftermath of the Second World War, the Pakistani government viewed them—and Faiz—with suspicion.

In addition, the new Pakistani government was attempting to cultivate friendly relations with its future imperial master, the United States of America, and all newspaper editorials, columns and popular demonstrations targeted the USA under the guise of being 'anti-imperialist'. In order to muzzle Left-wing activities, the government promulgated a 'Safety Act' specifically to suppress the activities of the Pakistan Aman Committee, the Progressive Writers' Association, Railway Workers' Union and kisan (peasant) committees.

Faiz and his two newspapers were at the forefront of opposition to the Safety Act and being the editor of two influential newspapers, secretary of the Pakistan Aman Committee and vice-president of the Pakistani Trade Union Federation, Faiz was under close watch by government agencies. He never seemed to care though and carried on his work. Often, he would not see his two young daughters for weeks on end, leaving early in the morning and returning late at night.

Under these conditions, the muse of poetry could not keep up with him either. His poetic output had dried up and he would often complain to friends, 'As soon as a fresh verse arises in my mind, it's time to get up and go to the office!'[13]

Little did he realize that the next storm of his life was already brewing. His poetic muse would return with a vengeance; only this time, it would be when he was in a prison cell.

Notes

1. Faiz Ahmed Faiz, *Culture and Identity* (Karachi: Oxford University Press, 2005), p. 7.
2. Ibid.
3. Faiz Ahmed Faiz, *Mah o Saal e Aashnai*, (Karachi: Maktaba Daniyal, 2008), pp. 10, 11.
4. Faiz Ahmed Faiz, 'Guftagoo—Faiz Ahmed Faiz', *Dunyazad*, no. 35 (Karachi: Scheherzade Publications, 2012), p. 53.
5. Ludmila Vasilieva, *Parvarish-e Lauh-o-Qalam: Faiz Hayat aur Takhleeqat* (Karachi: Oxford University Press, 2006), p. 159.
6. Ibid.
7. Ibid.
8. Ayub Mirza, *Faiz Nama* (Lahore: Classic Publishers, 2006), p. 83.
9. Faiz, 'Guftagoo—Faiz Ahmed Faiz', p. 71.
10. Translation by this author.
11. Mirza Zafarul-Hasan, *Umr-e Guzishta ki Kitab* (Karachi: Idara Yaadgar-e Ghalib, 1978), p. 95.
12. Ibid., p. 94.
13. Faiz, *Poems by Faiz*, translated, with an Introduction and Notes by Victor G. Kiernan (London: George Allen and Unwin Ltd, 1971), p. 25.

12
The Conspiracy-I

Say not the struggle naught availeth
The labor and the wounds are vain.

—Arthur Hugh Clough

Faiz and Alys had been married more than nine years. In October, they were planning to celebrate their tenth wedding anniversary. Their two girls were growing quickly and studying at one of the better English schools in the city. Faiz was working as hard as ever but his home and his two daughters were his respite from work. Outside their home though, things were in turmoil. The new nation of Pakistan had been in existence for four years and it was chaos all around: political disorganization, increasing dependence on the West, financial crisis and no hope of improvement in the lives of millions of toiling workers and peasants. The euphoria of independence had long since worn off and a collective despondency was beginning to set in.

One of Faiz's closest friends and a member of the Communist Party of Pakistan, the Marxist historian Syed Sibt-e Hasan, was scathing in his assessment of the leadership of the new nation: 'The Muslim League leaders felt no sympathy for their people or their nation. They had participated in the independence movement for their own selfish gains. None of them suffered in the least bit by being part of the Pakistan movement, none of them had spent a day in jail, suffered at the hands of the police or lost any of their fortunes. For them, Pakistan was their bounty and their later fights were all about a bigger share of the loot.'[1]

The two newspapers headed by Faiz, *Pakistan Times* and *Imroze* were not the official mouthpieces of the Muslim League. However, Faiz had early on declared his support for Pakistan by naming his very first editorial, 'We are a Muslim League Paper' and expressed the paper's unqualified support for the demand for Pakistan. Both papers had also asserted from the beginning that the 'Pakistan Resolution' of 1940 and Quaid-e Azam Muhammad Ali Jinnah's speeches, essays and ideas should be the basis for all future governance in Pakistan. This implied that the ideals, history and political and cultural elements of all the various ethnic communities in the new state of Pakistan had to be a part and parcel of any future national narrative. Many years later, Faiz said about this dilemma:

> Up till 1947 there was no Pakistani nation. Because there was no country, there was no nation. There were two ideas that existed at the time: First were the Muslims of India who called themselves a nation, but that included the Muslims of both Pakistan and India, and hence it was not a Pakistani nation. Second, people identified with whatever places they lived in, such as Punjabi, Sindhi, Balochi, Pathan etc. Obviously a Pakistani nation had not been created then. Since there was no Pakistan, there could not be a Pakistani nation. When Pakistan was created, we only had the raw materials for a Pakistani nation. A nation evolves over centuries; nations are not born fully developed. So our first task was to establish the details of our nationality, its definition, its destiny, but what happened was that we got tangled up in ministries and presidentships, and in making and breaking governments and this dimension was ignored both by our intellectuals and politicians.[2]

Ordinary people who had supported the demand for Pakistan wanted an independent, democratic nation where the rights of minorities and the poor and downtrodden would be protected. However, soon after the creation of Pakistan and especially after the death of Jinnah in 1948, the Government of Pakistan was taken over by men who looked contemptuously upon these ideals.

It did not take long for bureaucrats, local landowners and capitalists to form a powerful group, cheered on by unscrupulous newspapers and mullahs raising slogans of ethnic and communal hatred, in whose eyes newspapers like *Pakistan Times*, *Imroze* and later, *Lail o Nahar* were 'anti-Pakistan traitors'. Differences between the central government and the provinces were growing and many prominent Muslim League leaders were abandoning the party to join regional or provincial parties. The blood of the innocents slaughtered in the partition had hardly dried before the dash to occupy the lands and properties of those who had fled commenced.

The new neighbouring countries of India and Pakistan had a multitude of common problems to resolve, not the least of which was the problem of Kashmir over which there had already been fighting.

It was under these conditions in 1951 that the first provincial elections on the principle of adult franchise were announced in the Punjab. Several parties fielded their candidates in the election and the Communist Party of Pakistan (CPP) joined the fray. One of its stalwarts and Faiz's lifelong friend and comrade, Syed Sibt-e Hasan, described it thus:

> We knew that in spite of our popularity amongst workers and ordinary people, we would not be able to win more than 2 or 3 seats. But that was not our purpose. We wanted the program and aims of the Party to reach the largest number of people. Restrictions on speeches and writing are usually loosened before an election and it becomes easier to reach more people. As the election heated up, we were delighted to see that thousands of people were coming to our 'jalsas' and listened intently to what we had to say. We were also getting very encouraging news from the rural areas of Multan and Bahawalpur. In Lahore, our candidate Mirza Muhammad Ibrahim was being feted with great enthusiasm by workers. We were very hopeful.[3]

'Mr Faiz, you have to come with us'

On 9 March 1951, polling in the election was supposed to start early. Faiz got home late on 8 March. Things were hectic at the paper because of the approaching election. He went to bed early. Alys, in her book *Over My Shoulder*, wrote about what happened next:

> I woke in the early hours of the morning and saw someone shining a torch on our windows. I realized at once that it was no dream, someone was outside. I slipped out of bed and carefully looked out the window. I saw several uniformed policemen whispering to each other. I came out on to the terrace and glanced down to see several dozen heavily armed policemen surrounding the house. I realized at once that it was a raiding party. I woke Faiz who was still drowsy. I asked him what was going on and he said, it's probably a search party, they keep harassing us journalists and writers, to scare us and keep us

> quiet. I remembered that we had a couple of beer bottles in the house. Faiz did not want to give the police an excuse so he took them from me and emptied them in the bathroom and I threw the bottles in the neighbors deserted front yard. The bottles broke with a bang which seemed very loud in the stillness of the night and the people downstairs seemed to get even more agitated. The banging on our front door got louder. Faiz called out from the terrace 'Who is it?'. Someone said 'Faiz sahib, we want to see you'. He went downstairs and opened the door and two dozen heavily armed policemen barged in and rushed upstairs until our small terrace was crowded with them. Faiz admonished them to be quiet since the children were asleep. Faiz asked them if they had a search warrant to which they replied they did not. 'We have our orders, you must come with us.'[4]

Faiz insisted to the policemen that they either produce a search warrant or go downstairs and allow him to get ready. Reluctantly, they went outside to wait. Faiz dressed in the semi-darkness and reassured Alys that is was probably a precautionary measure in view of the upcoming election and he would return in a couple of hours. She was to write later, 'How was I to know then that it would be more than four years before he would return.'[5]

'A conspiracy against the nation'

Soon after the police had left with Faiz, Alys got news that the prime minister, Liaquat Ali Khan, had just announced on Radio Pakistan that government agencies had uncovered a conspiracy against the Government of Pakistan in which, along with a handful of army officials, a few civilians were also involved. The purpose of this conspiracy, according to the government, was to sow uncertainty and discord within the armed forces and spread chaos in the country. The list of those arrested for this alleged plot included the chief of staff of the Pakistan army, Major General Akbar Khan, Brigadier M.A. Latif then posted in Quetta, Mrs Akbar Khan and the chief editor of *Pakistan Times*, Faiz. This announcement was followed by instructions that people should remain calm.

Alys was taken aback and immediately realized the seriousness of the situation. Within days, the hysteria had reached fever pitch with some people calling for all the alleged perpetrators to be hanged forthwith, without any trials. Faiz was especially singled out by the conservative and religious press since he had long been a thorn in their side for espousing the causes of workers and women.

The next day, the news was flashed in newspapers all over the world with Faiz, as the only journalist and poet and the most well-known accused, being blamed in scurrilous fashion. 'Faiz...the brain behind the conspiracy', screamed a headline in *The Statesman* from Delhi. The *London Times* called him 'the most dangerous Leftist figure in Pakistan'. Subsequent developments would show why Faiz was singled out for special treatment in the mainstream press.

Alys later described the one or two days after Faiz's arrest as the most painful ones of her life. Family and close friends came often but Faiz's elder daughter Salima remembers that other people who used to come to the house day and night gradually stopped coming. It was difficult for people to reconcile the Faiz they knew—soft-spoken, affectionate and peaceable—with the image that was being painted by the newspapers.

The prime minister's speech had already caused a furore. He had accused a 'foreign power' (referring to the Soviet Union) of being behind the conspiracy to depose the government. The purpose, said the prime minister, was to change the existing political system and institute a communist government (under military leadership). The conspirators, it was further alleged, had also enticed a group of army officers to join them. The onus of the blame was thus placed squarely on Pakistan's tiny Communist Party and, by extension, everyone who had 'Left-leaning' sympathies. This—along with the fact that his friend and member of the Communist Party, Syed Sajjad Zaheer, could not be immediately located since he had gone underground—was the reason Faiz was singled out in the press.

A wave of arrests followed, which targeted not just the alleged conspirators but also ordinary workers of *Pakistan Times* and *Imroze*. At the same time, a vigorous anti-Soviet campaign took shape in the press, the thrust of which was that Western capitalists, no matter how bad, could be reasoned with since they believed in

God while the godless Soviet Union and its socialist allies could never be our friends. This manufactured hysteria was part of a worldwide propaganda campaign which attempted to paint the Soviet Union and its neighbouring countries as totalitarian dictatorships even though, until a few years ago, they had been allied with western powers in the struggle against fascism.

It was the beginning of the Cold War and the battle lines were being drawn. In America itself, a similar process was taking place in the form of the 'Red Scare', led by the rabid Senator Joseph McCarthy, who conducted hearings on the imagined infiltration of the US government and armed forces by communists and the hearings of the House Un-American Activities Committee which blacklisted hundreds of artists on suspicion of being 'subversives'. In America, this resulted in thousands of innocent people being arrested, fired from their jobs or even jailed. Faiz was later to write a moving tribute called 'Hum jo tareek rahon main maray gaye' ('We who were killed in desolate alleys'), referring to the two most famous victims of this campaign, the young couple Julius and Ethel Rosenberg, who were executed on charges of being Soviet spies.

The charge of 'atheism' against the Soviet Union was, no doubt, deliberately emphasized since it was bound to provoke a reaction in a country like Pakistan, founded on the basis of religion.

The scare tactics had their desired effect. Fear stalked the country. Many trade unions voluntarily suspended their activities and many Left-wing organizations disbanded themselves for fear of retribution. For a prolonged period, the authorities were unable to present a legal basis for the arrests until it was finally announced that Faiz, General Akbar and their co-conspirators had been arrested under the 1818 Bengal Conspiracy Act. Suspecting, no doubt, that trying to prosecute the arrested under a law that was over a hundred years old would make a laughingstock of the government, the legislative assembly hurriedly passed the Rawalpindi Conspiracy Act specifically to try the conspirators.

In later years, Faiz would recall, 'And then they made a mountain out of a molehill. One reason was that the government was upset with our Army friends and secondly they felt, maybe, that these people are not sufficiently obedient. They wanted to get rid of those people and this provided them a good opportunity. We got stuck in the middle for nothing.'[6]

It is unlikely though, that the renegade army officers were the real targets of the government. The actual aim was to silence all dissenting voices in the country, starting with the fledgling Communist Party and all its affiliated organizations. For the government, people like Sajjad Zaheer, the secretary general of the Communist Party, and Faiz himself were far more dangerous opponents: people who spoke up for the rights of workers, peasants and women and were refusing to toe the official line of the government of the new country. Faiz, especially, as editor-in-chief of two major newspapers, was a dangerous man. His presence when the conspiracy was discussed amongst the group of officers was a bonus for the government.

'Where is he?'

Faiz had been arrested and no one had any idea where he was or why he had been arrested. Despite the best efforts of Alys and his friends to get some news of his whereabouts, there was no sign of Faiz anywhere. The police and intelligence agencies flatly denied that he was in their custody. With each passing day, Alys's apprehensions were mounting. This was compounded by the terrible rumours that soon started flying: that Faiz was being kept in the notorious dungeons of Lahore Fort, that he was being tortured, that he had been blinded by his torturers. Moreover, Alys was afraid that some of these rumours would reach Bebe-ji, Faiz's mother. It was all she could do to control her panic. On the other hand, with each passing day, as the government failed to produce the conspirators or lay any formal charges against them, the mood of the people was turning against the government and in favour of Faiz.[7]

As soon as he had been arrested, the management of Progressive Papers Ltd (PPL), fearing a government crackdown, had dismissed Faiz as editor-in-chief of *Pakistan Times*. Years later, the fact that it had put up no resistance to the unannounced arrest of one of its most illustrious journalists would embolden the military dictatorship of General Ayub Khan to take over PPL completely and muzzle it further. Coincidentally, just a few months earlier,

Alys had been hired as a librarian at *Pakistan Times* and later given the responsibility of writing a weekly column related to the problems of women and children. Because of her hard work and dedication to the job, the management of *Pakistan Times* kept her on after Faiz was arrested and the Rs 400 a month she was earning became the sole sustenance of the young family. At her wits' end how to manage her household on her tiny salary, Alys handed over the entire responsibility for this to her sister-in-law, Faiz's half-sister Iqbal.

Salima and Moneeza were, at the time, studying in the prestigious Queen Mary school. The girls were happy there but there was no question of being able to afford their fees now. They were taken out and admitted to the Kinnaird Mission High School, a venerable institution where fees were lower but the educational standards, still good. In addition, the principal, an Englishwoman, was sympathetic to Alys. Bebe-ji started sending wheat, rice, vegetables and cooking 'ghee' from the village and other family members helped to get daily groceries like bread, milk and sugar at discounted rates.

There was still no sign of Faiz. Several other workers and team members of *Pakistan Times* had also been arrested, including Mazhar Ali Khan, its acting editor in Faiz's absence. Paradoxically, the readership of the newspaper had grown enormously since the arrests, which had emboldened those staff members who had not been arrested, including Alys. It had also increased their workload manifold. Alys, by virtue of her command over English, also had the responsibility of reading and editing the reports sent in from the field. Around this time she also decided to complete her graduation.

After selling their car, Alys had bought a bicycle which she used to ride back and forth to work. She had learned how to ride in London, but this was Lahore, where no one followed any traffic rules. In addition, her daily commute included some of the busiest roads in the city and she knew that a moment's inattention or carelessness on her bicycle could jeopardize the future of her young family.

Lahore is a beautiful city. Wide streets are lined by lush green trees and the entire city is dotted with parks. The only thing that the denizens of Lahore fear is its summer, when the temperature climbs to over 100°F and stays there for months on end. Everything wilts under the sun's fierce gaze. Then the rains come and, after a brief respite, the humidity climbs along with the heat and the city turns into a sauna. It is hard enough for natives of the Punjab to deal with the heat. For an Englishwoman, it must have been excruciating. In one of his letters to Alys from jail later during his imprisonment, Faiz writes:

> When I read of Lahore's temperature in the newspaper, my heart aches. Then I imagine you sitting in an oven-like office, sweat flowing, the children walking home in the summer sun and the long, sweltering evenings crushing the body and spirit like a dead weight. I am aware of all these responsibilities that you are bearing alone, from which there is no immediate escape nor rest; just an endless burden of toil without reward or remuneration. I know all this and I have no words to comfort you except that every journey has an end and as long as one is alive, there is a future.[8]

To protect herself from the sun, Alys wore a wide-brimmed straw hat tied under her chin with a ribbon. The bicycle also had a small basket attached to it to carry books or papers and a bell whose distinctive ring became familiar to morning commuters on Lahore's busy Mall Road. Even the traffic policemen on duty began to recognize her and would sometimes clear the traffic for her to pass and occasionally even salute her. In the evening, she would come home where the girls would be waiting for her. She would take a bath and help them with their homework, then sit down with papers from the office to work some more. For more than four years, while Faiz was incarcerated, the bicycle remained her faithful companion.

Life was gradually settling into a routine. But there was still no sign of Faiz.

'Your father is alive!'

For three months, there was no news of Faiz, where he was or who was holding him. At last, a letter arrived from the district jail at Lyallpur (now Faisalabad). It stated that Faiz had been kept in solitary confinement in Lyallpur jail and he had now received

Sultan Mohammad Khan.

Faiz Ahmed Faiz with elder brother Tufail on the latter's wedding day, 1942.

Faiz's mother Sultan Fatima 'Bebe ji' (far right) with Faiz's younger daughter Moneeza (centre) and his brother Tufail's daughter Yasmeen.

Faiz with Moneeza at her wedding.

Faiz in army uniform at a press conference at the Civil Secretariat, Delhi, 1944.

Faiz standing fourth from right with the editorial staff of *Pakistan Times*, Lahore, 1947.

Faiz, as the editor of *Pakistan Times* and *Imroze*, Lahore, 1948.

Faiz with Pakistani poet Ahmed Nadeem Qasmi, addressing trade union workers at Mochi Gate, Lahore, 1949.

Faiz addressing railway workers, Lahore, 1948.

Faiz with Indian President Dr S. Radhakrishnan and the Ambassador of Pakistan, Raja Ghazanfar Ali Khan, at a mushaira, Delhi, 1955.

Faiz and Alys with older daughter Salima (standing to Alys's left) and Moneeza at their Empress Road residence, 1961.

Faiz going to Moscow from Lahore to receive the Lenin Peace Prize, 1962.
Daughters Moneeza and Salima are standing next to him.

Faiz receiving the Lenin Peace Prize from Prof. Keiblton, Moscow, 1962.

Faiz with Chilean poet Pablo Neruda,
Sochi Beach near Black Sea, Georgia, 1962.

Faiz with his close friend, Russian writer Mariam Salganik, Moscow, 1962. Faiz's fifth collection of poetry *Sar-e Waadi-e Sina* is dedicated to her.

Faiz with Sajjad Zaheer (left) and a Russian friend, Moscow, 1962.

Faiz in Karachi, 1968.

A rare photo of Faiz (extreme right) and his early mentors—Ahmad Shah Bokhari 'Patras' (centre) and Sufi Ghulam Mustafa 'Tabassum' (standing behind Bokhari). Another famous Pakistani playwright, Imtiaz Ali Taj, is on the extreme left.

Faiz with Afro-Asian writers, Afro-Asian Writer's Conference, Tashkent, 1978.

Faiz with Ludmila Vasilieva, Tashkent, 1978.

Faiz with filmmaker Muzaffar Ali, 1978.

Faiz taking a break at a mushaira, Bhopal, 1978.

Faiz with the author, his oldest grandchild, at home in Lahore, 1979.

Inauguration of *Lotus* magazine, Beirut, 1979. L–R: Palestinian poet Mu'in Bseiso, Faiz Ahmed Faiz and PLO leader Yasser Arafat.

Faiz with the Dutt family (date unknown): Nargis sitting to Faiz's left, Sunil Dutt and Sanjay Dutt (sitting in front of Nargis).

Atal Bihari Vajpayee greeting Faiz at a reception given in the poet's honour, Delhi, 1981.

Faiz with Alys, son-in-law Shoaib Hashmi and all four grandchildren (from left): Mira, Yasser, Adeel and Ali.

Faiz with grandsons Ali (the author) and Adeel at home in Lahore, 1983.

Faiz's last mushaira, BBC Television, London, 1984. L–R: Iftikhar Arif, Bilquis Delhvi, Shohrat Bokhari, Dr Gopi Chand Narang, Faiz Ahmed Faiz, Ahmed Faraz and Zehra Nigah.

Faiz's MBE (Member of the Most Excellent Order of the British Empire) awarded for meritorious service during the Second World War.

Chief - Editor

Journal of Afro - Asian Writers Association (English - French - Arabic)

P.O.B. 135/430
BEIRUT - LEBANON
Tel : 800011 - 800211

Date ....

Ref. ....

آج شب کوئی نہیں ہے

آج شب دل کے قریں کوئی نہیں ہے
آنکھ سے دور طلسمات کے در وا ہیں کئی
خواب در خواب محلات کے در وا ہیں کئی
اور مکیں ۔ کوئی نہیں ہے
آج شب دل کے قریں کوئی نہیں ہے
"کوئی نغمہ، کوئی خوشبو، کوئی کافر صورت"
کوئی امید، کوئی آس مسافر صورت
کوئی غم، کوئی کسک، کوئی شک، کوئی یقیں
کوئی نہیں ہے
آج شب دل کے قریں کوئی نہیں ہے
تم اگر ہو، تو مرے پاس ہو یا دور ہو تم
ہر گھڑی سایہ گر خاطر رنجور ہو تم (در مجبور)
اور نہیں ہو تو کہیں، کوئی نہیں، کوئی نہیں ہے
آج شب دل کے قریں کوئی نہیں ہے

Faiz's poem 'Aaj shab' ('This evening') in his handwriting.

IDS 13/24 XF NIL AP 1016 BOMBAY 23 59
MRS FAIZ AHMED FAIZ WIFE OF LATE FAIZ AHMED FAIZ URDU POET LAHORE
PAKISTAN
DEEPLY SHOCKED TO GRIEVED TO LEARN PAKISTAN:
DEEPLY SHOCKED TO GRIVED TO LEARN OF THE SAD AND SUDDEN
DEMISE OF YOUR HUSBAND STOP HE WAS A AGAINST IN URDU
LITERATURE AND A GREAT POET STOP ALL INTELLIGENTIA
WILL MISS HIM STOP MAY HIS SOUL REST IN PEACE(.)
SUNIL DUTT

IDS 82/22 XF 1800 APM 849 BOMBAY 21 VIA ND 28/31
BEGUM FAIZ AHMED FAIZ LAHORE PAK=
FAIZ SAHIB IS GONE STOP IT IS GREATLOSS TO THE LITERURY
WORLD ACCEPT HEARTFELT CONDOLANCES
RAJA KAPOR BOMBAY=

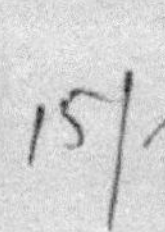

IDS 32/22 XF 1655 APF 6 NEW DELAHI 21 34:-
: MRS FAIZ 102 H MODEL TOWN LAHORE PAK:-
OUR PEARTS GO TO YOU AT THIS
TRAGES MOMENT FAIZ HAS INDEED
~~LET~~ LEFT AN IRRPROABLE VOID MAY
YOU BE ~~GRNTE~~ GRANTED COURAGE TO WITH
STAND THIS CALAMITY:-
INDER GUJRAL

Condolence messages on Faiz's death from Inder Gujral, Sunil Dutt and Raj Kapoor.

permission to see family. He had asked for Alys and the girls to come see him. Salima recounts the moment when she heard the news: 'I came home from school one day and saw Mummy unusually happy. As soon as she saw me, she exclaimed, "Your father is alive!" I screamed with joy, "What? He's alive? Where is he?" I was delirious with happiness.'[9]

Now that they knew he was alive, though, they were afraid of what had become of him. 'My happiness was clouded with fear,' remembers Salima. 'All night, horrible thoughts bothered me. At times, I would picture him in my mind, his fingers broken and his arms and legs cut off. Other times I would see his radiant face with blank holes in place of his shining eyes. It was agonizing. Mummy would suddenly startle, sometimes she would start crying quietly. At last the night passed and we set off for Lyallpur.'[10]

At Lyallpur jail, the superintendent asked Alys how many children she had. Alys pointed at Salima and Moneeza and said, 'those two girls.' 'No boys?' asked the man sympathetically. Alys shook her head. She was used to this particular subcontinental mindset. Boys were considered a family's treasure while girls were, at best, a burden to be borne gracefully. Salima remembered the visit in perfect detail:

> They seated us in a narrow room overlooking the prison courtyard. Those few moments were so hard to bear. Even today, my mind goes numb thinking about it. I looked up and beyond the iron bars I saw a man in a shirt and trouser walking towards us. His gait was leisurely, swaying from side to side. I shook my mother, 'Mummy, he's coming.' She was so quiet, she never came to the window. 'How is he?' she asked. 'He looks okay,' I said and then started a running commentary. He was wearing dark glasses and I suddenly remembered the rumors about him being blinded and I went quiet. A few moments later he entered. With one hand he took off his glasses and smiled at me 'Hello darling,' he said as he embraced mummy. I kept looking into his eyes, they were fine, even brighter than before. I was quiet as I felt the tears well up in my eyes. I did not want him to see me crying but it was useless. We embraced and hugged each other and talked and hugged each other some more.
>
> 'What have you done?' I asked him. 'Nothing,' he said, 'it's

> all rubbish, a lie.' He had never lied to us and I felt that his belief in his truth was absolute. 'There's nothing to worry about,' he said, 'it will be fine.' Later we all came home with new fervor.[11]

Faiz revealed that for the first few days, he had been kept in solitary confinement in Lahore's Central Jail in the middle of the city. However, in the historic Lahore Fort is another place of confinement that strikes terror even the in stoutest hearts. These are the dungeons of the fort which date back to its Mughal past. Sibt-e Hasan describes the place: 'The tourists wandering through the palaces and museums of the Lahore Fort can never imagine that in a forgotten corner of this historic place where there are no sign posts or guards, political prisoners are brought to be tortured with all manner of devilish instruments. In these chambers of anguish and agony, the screams of the prisoners vanish into the walls of the cells without ever reaching those outside.'[12]

Faiz would not talk about what had happened in Lahore when he was 'interrogated' by the police but he was transferred first to Sargodha jail and then on to Lyallpur, where he was kept in solitary confinement for three months. For a man like Faiz, it must have been trying. Prisoners in solitary are completely isolated from the outside world. A single guard on duty is forbidden to talk to the prisoner. A small narrow cell contains a basin in the corner next to a hole in the ground or a basic commode. Every day the prisoner is allowed to stroll by himself in a narrow courtyard for half an hour in the morning and half an hour in the evening. He is not allowed to talk to anyone and, in any case, there is no one around to talk to. For a newsman like Faiz, it must have been disorienting at first. In addition, the prisoner is allowed no papers, books or writing materials. Soon though, the confined person begins to withdraw from the outside world into himself since he has no other choice. For Faiz, his refuge became his poetry. These were the days when he began composing and memorizing some of his most remarkable verses often in the form of 'qitas' or four-line verses, which were easier to memorize. He would write them down on stray bits of newspaper scrap which would show up in his cell or on match boxes or cigarette packets, using a pencil stub that a sympathetic jailer had smuggled in to him.

The muse of poetry had returned with a vengeance and in his

second letter to Alys (dated 14 June 1951), a little over three months after his arrest when he was back in touch with his family, he wrote, 'Since my arrest, I have just finished my sixth poem. That means I have written more in the last three months than in the three years before that.'[13]

Faiz was keeping his spirits up, but he was still unaware of the sword hanging over his neck.

Notes

1. Syed Sibt-e Hasan (Syed Jaffer Ahmed, ed. and comp.), *Mughanni-e Aatish Nafas, Sajjad Zaheer* (Karachi: Maktaba Daniyal, 2008), pp. 46, 47.
2. Faiz Ahmed Faiz, 'Guftagoo—Faiz Ahmed Faiz', *Dunyazad*, no. 35 (Karachi: Scheherzade Publications, 2012), p. 65.
3. Hasan, *Mughanni-e Aatish Nafas, Sajjad Zaheer*, pp. 46,47.
4. Alys Faiz, *Over My Shoulder* (Lahore: The Frontier Post Publications, 1993), pp. 133–4.
5. Ibid.
6. Khaleeq Anjum (ed), *Faiz Ahmed Faiz: Tanqeedi Jaeza* (New Delhi: Anjuman Taraqqi-e Urdu, 1985), p. 308.
7. Alys Faiz, *Over My Shoulder*, p. 135.
8. Faiz Ahmed Faiz, *Saleebain Mere Darichay Main* (Karachi: Maktaba Daniyal, 1976), p. 96.
9. Ayub Mirza, *Hum ke Thehre Ajnabi* (Islamabad: Dost Publications, 1996), p. 162.
10. Ibid., p. 164.
11. Ibid., p. 164.
12. Syed Sibt-e Hasan, *Shehr-e Nigaran* (Karachi: Maktaba Daniyal, 1984), p. 160.
13. Faiz, *Saleebain Mere Darichay Main*, p. 23.

13

The Conspiracy-II

> Life is not an easy matter...You cannot live through it without falling into frustration and cynicism unless you have before you a great idea which raises you above personal misery, above weakness, above all kinds of perfidy and baseness.
>
> —Leon Trotsky

While details of the Rawalpindi Conspiracy Case remained shrouded in mystery for years after the trial ended, it gradually became clear that the actual 'conspiracy' was to ban the fledgling Communist Party of Pakistan (CPP) and muzzle all dissenting voices, especially those that were clamouring for greater political freedom and openness.

These details, as they emerged during the trial and after, left no doubt about the motivations and expected outcome of the charges.

After the end of his service in the British army, Faiz had remained on friendly terms with a number of army officers. This included the seniormost army officer accused in the conspiracy, Major General Akbar Khan, chief of staff of the Pakistan army. He was democratic in his political leanings, although by no stretch of the imagination could he be considered a socialist or communist. There were others in the army with similar political views, who felt that the country was going down the wrong path and change was needed, specifically of a 'Left' or progressive kind. General Akbar Khan was also friends with Syed Sajjad Zaheer, the general secretary of the CPP. The army officers wanted to meet Zaheer to discuss their ideas with him but he had been underground for two years, ever since he had come to Pakistan. He had been under surveillance by the authorities since 1936 as he was the moving force behind the formation of the All-India Progressive Writers' Association. General Akbar requested Faiz's help in meeting Sajjad Zaheer. One day, in March 1951, Faiz and his close friend and mentor Sajjad Zaheer went to General Akbar's house in Rawalpindi. Years later, Faiz had this to say about the meeting: 'One day, we all sat down and discussed what should be done with this country? How could we help better the conditions here? It had been four years since the country was created and there was no constitution, no political structure.'[1]

Those assembled felt that the prime minister was mishandling both the internal and external affairs of the country and that the recent pact with the United States could prove extremely dangerous. It would result in the building of American bases in the country and, in case of war, the Soviet Union could use the atomic bomb against Pakistan. The participants felt that it was necessary to turn Pakistan's foreign policy in a non-aligned direction so that, in the event of a war between the USA and the Soviet Union, Pakistan would be spared. The army officers wanted the political support of the Communist Party to implement the plan to overthrow the government.

After a spirited discussion lasting several hours, Sajjad Zaheer and Faiz convinced the other participants of the meeting not to proceed with this plan. They persuaded them that the conditions of the country made any solution based on force unwise. In addition, the army officers involved had no practical blueprint about what to do if they were to succeed in taking over the government and in any case, the CPP was too small and too weak to assume political leadership of the country. There was no other party that could perform that role and hence the plan was doomed to failure.

Prior to the meeting, another detailed discussion had taken place within the CPP (of which Faiz had not been a part) that had reached the same conclusion. Syed Sibt-e Hasan, a member of the CPP, recalled:

> Some Army officers under the leadership of General Akbar Khan wanted to change the government. They were unhappy over the government's stance about Kashmir and they felt that ordinary people were sick of the self-serving policies of the Muslim League. They felt that people would welcome a change of government. A meeting of the party's Central Committee was held and a vigorous discussion took place over 2-3 days. We knew that social revolution was not the task of a handful of Army officers. It needed to be led by workers, peasants and

> enlightened members of the middle class under the guidance of a revolutionary party. After we got details from the Army officers, our suspicions were confirmed. They had no clue about how to reform Pakistan's politics or its economic conditions; no ideas about how to empower ordinary people, how to compose the new government and, most importantly, what help they wanted from the CPP. It did not take us long to reach the decision to ask the Army officers to refrain from such childish maneuvers.[2]

In his memoirs, General Akbar Khan later confirmed that the meeting between members of the army who had proposed the plan and the representatives of the CPP had ended with a general agreement to do nothing. He thought that was the end of the matter and had not even bothered to remove his notes of the meeting from his writing table. These were later presented as evidence against the accused. Even before the so-called conspiracy took place, General Akbar had been on the radar of his superiors as someone who was too independent-minded and had not been subservient enough even to the British. One of the police officers who arrested the accused wrote years later:

> Many senior British officers like (Commander in Chief of the Pakistan Armed Forces after partition) General Gracey preferred Pakistani officers who were subservient and servile. The officers involved in the conspiracy were not their hand puppets. They were all brave officers with strength of character but Ayub Khan (who succeeded General Gracey as Commander in Chief after he was promoted out of turn) was the son of a non-commissioned officer; groveling before the British was in his blood. General Gracey wanted him installed as the Commander of the Army not just to weaken Pakistan but also to hand over the actual command of the Army to a General loyal to the British. He succeeded in his scheming.[3]

This same General Ayub Khan was later to launch the first successful army coup against a civilian government in Pakistan.

Free in prison

For approximately three months after his arrest, Faiz and his co-conspirators were kept in solitary confinement in Sargodha and then Lyallpur jail. They were then shifted to Hyderabad Central

Jail, where a special tribunal had been constituted to try them. It was in Hyderabad jail that they were finally informed of the charges against them. All of them were both amused and infuriated to see the list of charges, which contained many outright lies as well as repetitions. Some of the accused were inclined to dismiss the charge sheet as a joke but Sajjad Zaheer, General Akbar and Faiz argued that the charges should be taken seriously since some of them carried sentences of life in prison or even the death penalty. They were aware the government, desperate to bolster its sagging popularity and maintain its iron grip of terror over the nation, could resort to anything. In addition, whatever the outcome of the trial, the proceedings would be part of the historical record and the charges had to be refuted vigorously.

Faiz's letters to Alys from prison, published many years later under the title *Saleebain Mere Darichay Main*, provide a glimpse of his various states of mind during his confinement. One remarkable thing is his unshakeable belief in his own innocence. He had written in an early letter from jail: 'Ever since I got here [jail], I feel no fear or apprehension whatsoever in my heart. There was never much to begin with because I have not done anything which might be considered morally wrong. Not just that, I am not guilty of anything which might be considered legally or traditionally wrong either.'[4]

Faiz was kept in Hyderabad jail for twenty-six months (4 June 1951 till July 1953). The legal proceedings continued for eighteen months, until 1 November 1952. On 5 January 1953, the verdict was announced and Faiz was given a sentence of four years in prison. The other co-conspirators received similar sentences.

In typical fashion, he wrote to Alys:

> By now you must have received the bad news. Don't worry yourself. We can spend the next few years the same way we have spent the last few. Think about it, what does this new predicament mean? At most two or two and a half more years of parting. If you look around you, it would be hard in India and Pakistan to find any virtuous man who had not spent more than this time in prison during the British era. And none of them were the worse for wear. Unfortunately, there is no easy path to goodness and redemption, what I have been asked of in this cause is not at all out of the ordinary.[5]

Faiz's time in jail was, poetically, one of the most fruitful periods in his life. Years later, he recalled how his poetic muse returned:

> The first requirement of poetry writing is availability of time. However, it's not just about time. The thing is that in the jail cell one begins to experience the same state one experiences in adolescence. New perspectives become visible in everything, new colors, more awareness. This was especially so when I was in solitary confinement for four months, when I had no paper, pen, letter or newspapers...nothing to do apart from observation of nature. Many things were revealed at that time. I have written in one of my letters for instance: do you know how many colors there are on the neck of a wild pigeon? Or that if you observe a Peepal tree from dawn till dusk, how the colors of its leaves and branches change with the movement of the sun? When seasons change, what effects it creates. How the first breeze of cool air of rainfall arrives after summer. These sensations of man become much more acute and sharp in prison because there is no other way of their satisfaction. Resultantly the mind, consciousness and emotions develop more perspicacity, and the astonishment regarding many things that one loses in everyday life; that state of astonishment experiences a revival.[6]

In jail, Major Ishaque Mohammad was Faiz's self-appointed 'guardian' and had learned when Faiz was in the process of writing a new poem. In his essay 'Roo-dad-e qafas' (Jail diary) about his jail experiences with Faiz, published as a preface to Faiz's third verse collection, *Zindan Nama* (Prison Notebook), he writes: 'I...was familiar with his [Faiz's] moods. When he would be composing verses, he would go quiet and would start humming to himself. After a while, he would look around and I could tell that he wanted an audience. We would confer amongst ourselves and then would go up to him and start pestering him. If he had finished composing something, he would recite a verse or two, otherwise, he would tell us affectionately to get lost. We knew that meant he was working on something and we would spread the word.'[7]

Faiz also got a chance to catch up on his much-neglected reading during his incarceration. His letters to Alys from prison contain astonishingly astute two-to three-sentence 'reviews' of the books he was reading. He had been a teacher of English in college and had mastery over Urdu, Arabic and Persian as well, and he had loved reading since he was a child. He specifically requested that the 'diwan' of the Arabic poet, Abu Tamam, be sent to him in prison. He requested Alys to send him Reynold Nicholson's *A Literary History of the Arabs*, Ernest Turner's *A History of Courting*, Arnold Toynbee's *A Study of History*, Sarvepalli Radhakrishnan's *Indian Philosophy* and others, indicating his abiding interest in human culture and civilization and its evolution. He had always been fond of literature and his reading list also included books such Alphonse Daudet's *Sapho*, Sean O'Casey's play *The Star Turns Red*, the poems of T.S. Eliot, the short stories and novels of Chekhov and Maupassant, James Aldridge's novel *The Diplomat*, Upton Sinclair's *The Jungle*, the stories of Gogol and the works of Shakespeare. He also asked to be sent the books of Havelock Ellis and Nietszche.[8]

Writing about Chekhov, the famed Russian physician and author, he had this to say in one of his letters to Alys: 'What love, what affection drips from Chekhov's writings. His dramas are so fresh and novel that we can't call them tragedies...the basic point of his dramas is the jewel of hope and sympathy which pervades every scene.'[9]

Elsewhere he writes: 'I have first started Turner's "A History of Courting". It's a spicy item and I'm reading it slowly so it doesn't end too soon. I have also started reading philosophy and if the mind is prepared and ready for it, philosophy is similarly enjoyable.'[10]

Another time, he says: 'I'm reading a poem by Eliot. Time, which is both a killer and a nurturer, it's a beautiful poem although the results that Eliot draws from it are quite senseless.'[11]

About Nietszche's *Thus Spake Zarathustra*, he writes: 'I have not read this book before although I have read some of Nietszche's important works. If he had been alive, he would have fought the Nazis because they completely distorted his ideas and deformed the real contours of his writing. He, too, was an ignoramus but a very sensitive and poetic one.'[12]

Death comes visiting

One sweltering day in July 1952, Faiz was particularly happy. His beloved older brother Tufail was coming to see him. They had been very close since childhood. When their father had died unexpectedly, Faiz had wanted to quit his studies to go to work and support his mother and the rest of their family but Tufail had strictly forbidden it, insisting that he complete his studies. Tufail had, instead, assumed the entire burden of supporting the large family. During the Conspiracy Case, it was Tufail who had helped Alys find a lawyer willing to take on the case.

This time, Tufail was bringing good news. The dispute with extended family members over their father's ancestral lands had finally been resolved in their favour. Tufail felt that if they managed the lands judiciously, the entire family, including Alys and her two young daughters, could be financially comfortable.

Their meeting was not to be. In the early morning hours of 17 July 1952, Tufail suffered a fatal heart attack and died on the spot. Faiz wrote about his feelings in his next letter to Alys: 'This morning, instead of my brother, Death came to greet me. Everyone was very kind. They took me to see my life's most prized possession which was now dust. And then they took it with them.'[13]

Even at the moment of saying eternal goodbye to his older brother, Faiz did not lose hope. It took him just a short time to regain his composure and begin his letter to Alys:

> In the arrogance of my grief, I kept my head high and never lowered my gaze before anyone; how difficult this was, how agonizing, only my heart knows.
>
> But now I am alone with my grief inside my jail cell and I do not have to hold my head high any longer. There is no shame here in surrendering to the tyranny of my pain. But please do not worry. This wound is sudden and unwarranted but I am strong enough to bear it and not bow my head. I only wish I was outside and could offer the strength of my arms to those weaker than I whose sorrow is more burdensome than my grief.[14]

Faiz was haunted by the thought that it was he who was responsible for Tufail's death; that if Tufail had not been coming to see him, he would still be alive: 'I keep trying to not think of his wife and children or my mother. I have no strength to write to them. And what would I write? I snatched away my mother's first born. Yes, it was I who deprived everyone of his presence.'[15]

The very next day, there emerged from his imagination, a haunting elegy for his brother titled 'Noha' (Elegy):

I reproach you, brother, going away
You took away the book of my past
In it were so many cherished images
My childhood and my youth
In its place, going away, you left me
This blood-colored rose of your sorrow
For the last time, listen, agree
Never have I returned empty-handed from you
Come take away this radiant flower
And return to me the book of my past.[16]

A month after Tufail's death, Faiz received news of the death of Rashid Jahan in Moscow. She had been ailing for a long time and the news was not unexpected but it was still shattering: 'I read the news of Rashida's death in Moscow. If I had been outside, I might have wept bitter tears but there are none left to shed. Instead of weeping, there is a deadening of the heart. With her departure, our subcontinent has lost a great treasure of virtue and humanism.'[17]

In October of the same year, Alys's father, Goeffrey Osmond George, fell seriously ill. Faiz advised Alys to rush to London but she was reluctant to leave him while the trial was still ongoing. Faiz knew that his father-in-law was probably very worried about both his daughters facing such difficult circumstances so far away (Christabel's husband, Dr M.D. Taseer, had died suddenly and unexpectedly of a heart attack in 1950). Alys was also worried about the cost of such a trip. She never made the trip and her father died soon after. Faiz wrote to Alys: 'I will not mention your fresh grief, nor try and console you. There are no adequate words for the frightening finality of death, only love and the pain of sorrow can provide some recompense and no words are needed for either.'[18]

'Traitor to his nation'

While Faiz was fighting his inner demons in prison, Alys and the girls had to deal with those outside. Knowing that its legal case was weak, the government and its agents had started a malicious campaign of character assassination and slander against Faiz and the other accused. The real purpose of this was to divert the attention of the masses away from their very real problems and to diffuse the growing resentment against the government. Faiz's personal popularity and his status as a journalist were a significant problem for the government and he was thus singled out for the most vicious slanders: that he was a Russian agent, that his wife was a British spy, that he was an atheist, etc. No one dared to say anything to Alys because of her fiery temper but her young daughters were fair game. Salima recounts:

> One day my class fellow Nazli invited me to a birthday party at her house. I told Mummy, who encouraged me to go. It was the first friendly invitation in many days. Mummy dressed me up and when I got there, I was taken to the drawing room where there was no birthday stuff, just six men sitting around a table who started interrogating me. I swore to myself to refuse to answer any of their questions. 'Are you Faiz's daughter?' 'Yes,' I said, with my head held high. 'Is he in jail?' 'Yes.' 'Do you hear from him?' 'Yes.' Actually, they wanted to find out if he had any links to the outside. We had no news of Abbu [Father] but I was not about to admit defeat to those bastards. After interrogating me for two or three hours, they let me go. I came home and for the first time embraced mummy and wept inconsolably. She reassured me as she wept too and abused them no end.[19]

There were others though, who came to see the family often, offering words of encouragement and hope and helping keep their spirits up. Salima especially remembers how it was ordinary people, those not constrained by a fear of losing their jobs and their positions in society, who were the kindest of all—the milkman, the bakery man, the man who sold them vegetables: 'They would often say: "Have you met him? How is he? Don't worry, Allah will unite all of you soon". Those few words of encouragement from these poor people were like music to my ears. But there were plenty of others who enjoyed mentally torturing us.'[20]

Dast-e Saba

In November 1952, while Faiz was still in Hyderabad jail, his second collection of poems *Dast-e Saba* (The East Wind's Hand) was published. Its cover was designed by renowned Pakistani painter Abdur Rahman Chughtai who also served as chief guest at the book's launch in Lahore. It was the first ever launch of an Urdu book and was graced by many noted literary luminaries and intellectuals of the time, including Faiz's teacher Sufi Tabassum, Dr Sajjad Baqir Rizvi, Ahmad Nadeem Qasmi (who read a brief paper to the audience), and dozens of ordinary people. Alys read out hundreds of messages of congratulations and good wishes from both within and outside Pakistan. The large gathering helped dispel some of the gloom surrounding Left-wing activities and gave courage to many who had been cowed into submission. The spontaneous outpouring of good wishes was also a fitting response to the vilification campaign being carried out by the government.

Inside prison too, the publication of *Dast-e Saba* was an occasion for great rejoicing. The prisoners actually obtained permission from the jail authorities to hold a little 'party' to commemorate the occasion. As usual, it was left to Syed Sajjad Zaheer, Faiz's dear friend and mentor, to pronounce the final verdict on the new book: 'When the historian of tomorrow writes about the important events of 1952, there will probably be no mention of the Rawalpindi Conspiracy Case. The publication of "Dast-e Saba" though will be remembered as an important historical event.'[21]

The mysterious 'Kulsoom'

Faiz dedicated his second collection of poems to 'Kulsoom', the name given by Bebe-ji to Alys when she and Faiz had married. When the book first came out, his friends and acquaintances, including his fellow prisoners, not aware of this fact, were mystified. They did not dare ask Faiz who this 'Kulsoom' was, and he enjoyed their discomfiture. In a few hours, though, all was revealed. In truth, Alys had not been happy with the dedication either, but Faiz had convinced her: 'As far as the dedication goes, if you want to call yourself Alys, that is your choice since the book is yours. I wrote "Kulsoom" because, first of all, it's an Eastern name. Secondly, people will probably ask you about it and that might be some source of amusement for you. In any case, you can do as you wish.'[22]

In a further popular rebuke to the government, the first edition of *Dast-e Saba* sold out in weeks and a second edition was brought out. When Faiz heard, he wrote, 'You have written that you people are preparing a second edition, what does this mean? If the book is selling well, write to me, I will be happy.'[23] In less than three months, a third edition was needed and Faiz wrote: 'Very happy that the second edition was popular but I am amazed as to who you are selling these books to. Ten or twenty years ago, it was different. I know I had some permanent customers amongst college girls but who are these new buyers and what do my ramblings mean to them, I don't know. All I know is that ordinary people do not have the money to waste on books. If they are still buying our books, that's wonderful.'[24]

And in a further mischievous reference to 'Kulsoom', he wrote: 'I enjoyed what you wrote about "Kulsoom", great fun. A little doubt is good for fame and it's also good that I don't have even a passing acquaintance with anyone named Kulsoom. Otherwise some lady would have decided that the book was dedicated to her and imagined that we were expressing our hidden love and it would have been no surprise if she had a heart attack because of this revelation.'[25]

In one of his earlier letters, Faiz also gave a glimpse of the secret of his genius, writing about his poem 'Zindan ki ek shaam' (A prison evening): 'I am particularly happy with this poem...I don't mind telling you that no one else today can write like this and no one will be able to, for a long time to come. This is not because I am arrogant about my ability. My talent is very limited and there are many people who have more ability than I. The secret is hard work, toil and sweat, especially in writing.'[26]

Alys's letters to Faiz were also later published under the title *Dear Heart: To Faiz in Prison*.

Free at last

On 5 January 1953, the verdict in the Conspiracy Case was announced. By this time, the case had become an international cause. Faiz Ahmed Faiz, the poet who had been imprisoned for his democratic, humanistic beliefs, was a name on everyone's lips. Faizs' old friend, the British historian Victor Kiernan, who had first translated of one of Faiz's poems in 1943, had published an English translations of all of his poems until then. This had helped popularize his poetry in the English-speaking world. To no one's surprise, the accused were all pronounced guilty and received varying jail sentences. Faiz was sentenced to a further two-and-a-half years in prison but, before he could complete his sentence, Pakistan's political landscape changed again. On 24 October 1954, the then governor general of Pakistan, Ghulam Muhammad, dissolved the legislative assembly for his own political purposes. This assembly had formulated the special Rawalpindi Conspiracy Act, which had enabled the special tribunal to try the accused. Lawyers for Faiz and the other accused immediately started arguing the entire case afresh, based on this new political development. On 12 April 1955, the federal court of Pakistan declared the special tribunal null and void. Faiz and his 'co-conspirators' were honourably released on 20 April 1955 and, a few months later, the entire episode came to a close when the new legislative assembly voided their remaining sentences.

Salima remembers Faiz's return: 'The news of Abbu's [father's] release had reached us a week before and people had started asking when he would come. One day, I got home in the evening and saw some familiar faces from a distance. I realized that Abbu was home. When I got in, there he was. He stepped forward and embraced me. I was delirious with joy. He reassured me and said "Look, here I am, I'm back. And I won't go anywhere again."'[27] Moneeza, only nine at the time, remembers: 'It was as if we had all gone mad from the intensity of our emotions. Abbu was very excited too. I said to him "Promise us you won't go to jail again." He said "Well, I didn't go because I wanted to, they took me, so I went". When I pestered him, he said "Alright, I won't go again," and I was happy.'[28]

Prison poetry

During the four years of Faiz's incarceration, two volumes of his poetry were published and they remain his best-loved and most-recited poetry. The first, *Dast-e Saba* was published to great acclaim. The second, *Zindan Nama* (Prison Notebook) was not dedicated to anyone and it has been presumed that Faiz himself considered it a continuation of *Dast-e Saba*. Both volumes contain a variety of nazms as well as ghazals, and the subjects Faiz developed and refined in his poetry during his incarceration remained his focus for the rest of his life.

Two sentiments pervade his poetry of the period: the sorrow of incarceration and his fierce love for his country and its people. Faiz himself termed these sentiments both a testament to the struggle for a brighter future and a sense of the everlasting bond between his own destiny and that of his nation.

Faiz would send every new poem to Alys, who would get it published in a newspaper or literary magazine from where it would soon find its way around the country. Faiz's poems from his first three months in solitary confinement include some of his best-known ghazals and nazms and include his signature qit'a, the four-line stanza that became an anthem for prison poetry:

> If ink and pen are snatched from me, shall I
> Who have dipped my fingers in my heart's blood complain—
> Or if they seal my tongue, when I have made,
> A mouth of every round link of my chain?[29]

In jail, Faiz would find the time and freedom to hone and polish his poetic craft to perfection, and he would later describe this process: 'Being in jail is a very basic experience, like being in love. It automatically opens up new avenues of thought and feeling…all sensations are sharpened, like the beginning of youth and the wonder of things like the first break of dawn, the bluish hue of evening and the gentleness of the breeze.'[30] In the time that jail afforded him, he would experiment with new styles and new ideas and come up with his unique voice. In his understated way, he would describe some of these poems as 'not bad' even by his own exacting standards. He wrote to Alys about two of these poems, 'Irani tulaba ke naam' (To the Iranian students) and 'Come back Africa', 'This week, I have started a poem on the martyred students of Iran and Iraq. For the first time since coming to jail, I feel satisfied with one of my creations…it is totally different from the traditional style and the old masters (of poetry) would undoubtedly disapprove but who cares?'[31]

Faiz's preferred forms of poetry remained the nazm and the ghazal (he composed about an equal number in prison: thirty-two ghazals and thirty-one nazms), and he managed to mould both these forms into his own unique style in the 'poetic laboratory' that was prison. This was undoubtedly a greater achievement in the case of ghazals, since this form is traditionally bound much more tightly by poetic, cultural and literary conventions. Faiz himself referred to the difficulty of introducing new topics, especially the politics of protest, into the ghazal genre:

> It is impossible to go beyond a limit in ghazal. Ghazal has inbuilt limitations of such nature that you can only go to an extent and not beyond it. It happens that as you get more skilled in the language of ghazal, the variety decreases, because the art becomes easier for you and it becomes difficult to incorporate something new. The reason is the same, its inbuilt limitations, because ghazal has a limitation in idiom, as well as in form and structure...During my imprisonment, I explored how much room we can create in it for other topics. The pioneer of stretching the limits of ghazal was Ghalib. The second pioneer was Iqbal, who showed that you can talk about any subject in ghazal, provided you keep the language that of ghazal. It is not permissible to change the language for ghazal. You can bring other subjects in it, but you cannot change the language.[32]

Faiz's prison poetry forced people to think about some basic things: What is good? What is evil? Is evil imprisoned inside prison walls or does it roam free in society? It also persuaded people to think beyond the limits of their selves and their homes, about the sorrows and injustices of the larger world where people who may be just like the reader live, love and hope.

And for Faiz himself, his time in prison brought him face to face with a stark reality: the selfishness of idealism. In one of his letters to Alys, he wrote: 'For the first time, I realized that to hold something so close that one's near and dear ones suffer along with oneself, even though it means little to them, is wrong. If you look at it this way, idealism or abiding by certain principles is also a form of self-centeredness. Because in the fervor of your convictions, you forget what others hold dear.'[33]

It would not be the last time that Faiz would face this regret.

Notes

1. Khaleeq Anjum (ed.), *Faiz Ahmed Faiz: Tanqeedi Jaeza* (New Delhi: Anjuman Taraqqi-e Urdu, 1985), p. 308.

2. Syed Sibt-e Hasan (Syed Jaffer Ahmed, ed. and comp.), *Mughanni-e Aatish Nafas, Sajjad Zaheer* (Karachi: Maktaba-e Daniyal, 2008), pp. 46–9.
3. S. Muhammad, 'The Truth behind the Rawalpindi Conspiracy Case', *Daily Dawn* (Karachi), 16 November 1984.
4. Faiz Ahmed Faiz, *Saleebain Mere Darichay Main* (Karachi: Maktaba Daniyal, 2011), p. 22.
5. Ibid., p. 132.
6. Faiz Ahmed Faiz, 'Guftagoo—Faiz Ahmed Faiz', *Dunyazad*, no. 35 (Karachi: Scheherzade Publications, 2012), p. 57.
7. Faiz Ahmed Faiz, *Nuskha hai Wafa* (Lahore: Maktaba Karvaan, 1985), pp. 207–8.
8. Mazher Jameel, *Zikr-e Faiz* (Karachi: Culture Department, Government of Sindh, 2013), p. 393.
9. Faiz, *Saleebain Mere Darichay Main*, p. 22.
10. Ibid., p. 189.
11. Ibid., p. 199.
12. Ibid., p. 95.
13. Ibid., p. 101.
14. Ibid.,pp. 102–2.
15. Ibid., p. 102.
16. Published in Faiz, *Nuskha hai Wafa*, pp. 153–4. The translation here is by this author.
17. Faiz, *Saleebain Mere Darichay Main*, p. 104.
18. Ibid., p. 129.
19. Ayub Mirza, *Hum ke Thehre Ajnabi* (Islamabad: Dost Publications, 2004), pp. 159, 60.
20. Ibid., p. 166.
21. Sajjad Zaheer, 'Sar-e aaghaaz' in *Zindan Nama* (Karachi: Maktaba Daniyal). p. 1971.
22. Faiz, *Saleebain Mere Darichay Main*, p. 111.
23. Ibid., p. 135.
24. Ibid., p. 147.
25. Ibid., pp. 147–8.
26. Ibid., pp. 110–11.
27. Mirza, *Hum ke Thehre Ajnabi*, p. 167.
28. Moneeza Hashmi, personal recollection.
29. Translation by V.G. Kiernan.
30. Faiz, *Nuskha Hai Wafa*, p. 307.
31. Faiz, *Saleebain Mere Darichay Main*, p. 99.
32. Faiz,'Guftagoo—Faiz Ahmed Faiz', p. 56.
33. Faiz, *Saleebain Mere Darichay Main*, p. 21.

14

Slings and Arrows

> Whether 'tis Nobler in the mind to suffer
> The Slings and Arrows of outrageous Fortune,
> Or to take Arms against a Sea of troubles,
> And by opposing end them?
>
> —William Shakespeare

Faiz's beloved homeland had undergone a series of tumultuous changes while he was in prison. Several governments had rapidly changed hands and things were going from bad to worse. Pakistan had become party to several military blocs and pacts and America, the new imperialist superpower, was making its presence felt in the country. The rapidly rising expenditure on armaments was crushing the economy.

In 1955, Faiz was released from jail and came back to Lahore to find a city sagging under the weight of gloom. There was famine in several parts of the country, industry was stagnant and people, more impoverished than ever, were either despondent or dismissive. For Faiz, who had seen with his own eyes the sacrifices made for independence, it was a painful sight. He rejoined *Pakistan Times* and its sister newspapers, *Imroze* and *Lail-o-Nahar* as chief editor. His fame had risen to new heights during his incarceration and his return to the world of journalism was a shot in the arm for his peers.

But this was not the *Pakistan Times* that Faiz had proudly represented before and right after Independence and Partition. Journalism itself had become a profession where salaries and perks were the main focus of employees and their cliques. Various industrial and trading houses had placed their own paid agents inside newspaper offices to sing their praises in exchange for suitable fees. The free, fearless, independent journalism, which Faiz and his fellow journalists had practised, had largely vanished, to be replaced by narrow self-interest. In addition, Pakistan's rulers had become increasingly intolerant of even the slightest criticism.

For Faiz, it was intolerable. He started working to restore some of the ethical, democratic journalism he and his co-workers had founded, but soon realized that even within *Pakistan Times*, there were many who wanted none of it. Years later, he would describe the degeneration of Pakistani journalism:

> At that time [before 1947] people used to start a newspaper to promote a particular ideology, to spread a particular political doctrine to people. Journalism had not yet become a business. Afterwards people discovered that it can be used to make money, so it became a business. Secondly, when Ayub Khan seized Pakistan Times [in 1958], people were afraid that it could happen to them as well. Up until then people thought that as long as they did not break any laws in what they wrote no one would touch them. After the military governments, this sense of security was lost. People began to write under pressure. So one reason is that it became a business, the second reason is that people became afraid, and third reason is that the sense of a pride in your profession was lost. When you write a good ghazal, people praise it and you feel satisfaction in producing quality work. Till then there was a competition between newspapers about who would report a particular piece of news first or who has written the best editorial. Afterwards newspapers became a business and people who saw it as a craft got discouraged and left.[1]

Despite this, Faiz continued writing in *Pakistan Times* against the injustices he saw around him and criticizing the government's domestic and foreign policy. At the same time, the paper continued to appreciate every step the government took in improving relations with the socialist bloc. This was usually in the shape of cultural or scientific exchanges.

His old friends in the Progressive Writers' Association wanted him to become more active in the organization. Faiz was deeply grateful for their support while he had been in prison, including their generous reception of *Dast-e Saba,* but he was wary of getting too involved with the day-to-day organizational matters of the association. No doubt remembering the acrimonious splits among members that had occurred in the early days of the organization, he pleaded lack of time owing to his duties at the newspaper and remained on the sidelines. He frequently participated, though, in discussions on broadening the scope of the organization to include progressive writers and artists from other countries.

At the offices of *Pakistan Times*, things were gradually going from bad to worse. The guiding light and founder of the paper, Mian Iftikharuddin, and his group had been sidelined, as had Faiz's old colleagues and friends. One such close friend and colleague, Marxist historian Syed Sibt-e Hasan, wrote later: 'Some people at Progressive Papers had started malicious whispering campaigns against Faiz. These were people who hated that he was the Chief Editor and who were unwilling to listen to or accept anything he said. They would complain that Mian Ifitkharuddin had imposed Faiz on them, sometimes they would make fun of his poetic temperament, other times they would grumble about his personal friendships with politicians and bureaucrats. It was a very painful time for Faiz.'[2]

Zindan Nama

A short time after his release, Faiz's new collection of poems *Zindan Nama* (Prison Notebook) was brought out. Although *Dast-e Saba,* had been released while he was in jail, more than half of that volume contained poems which had been written before he had been incarcerated, whereas *Zindan Nama* consisted of poetry written entirely behind bars. It is thus remarkable not just as a poetic description of Faiz's own condition, but as a chronicle of that era. Prison literature, including prison poetry, often consists of a writer or poet's lamentations against the world, injustice and oppression, usually from a personal standpoint. It is like a record of the screams of prisoners echoing around the prison walls. Faiz's prison poetry, though, according to one commentator, is typified by a specific element, a defiance of authority that is, so far, unique in this part of the world. Sibt-e Hasan writes: 'Our literature contains a large treasure of prison writings. Strangely enough, the inventor of this is Ghalib. Except that Ghalib's imprisonment was of a purely personal nature.[3] Those who embraced prison in the service of their country include Maulana Muhammad Ali Jauhar, Maulana Hasrat Mohani, Maulana Abul Kalam Azad and Maulana Zafar Ali Khan. And the leader of this caravan which lit up dark prison nights is Faiz.'[4]

Poems such as 'Aa jao Africa' (Come, Africa) and 'Hum jo tareek rahon main maray gaye' (We, the martyrs of unlit paths) speak not just to Faiz's personal sorrows or to those of his people but to all the world. His defiance and determination to fight and surmount the odds shine through and this is the key to the universal appeal of his poetry.

His friend and companion in prison, Major Ishaq Mohammad, wrote a detailed preface to *Zindan Nama* which he named 'Roodaad-e qafas' ('Prison memoir'). He and Faiz were together in prison for almost four years. Major Ishaq's essay, therefore, is an intimate look at the day-to-day prison life of Faiz and his co-accused; how they lived, what they thought, what they talked about and what they felt. At one point, remembering their time in Hyderabad Central Jail, he writes:

> The days of the trial inside Hyderabad jail were strange. For three months, all kinds of government toadies had been demanding in newspapers, advertisements and public gatherings that all of us should be shot. Some newspapers had even come out with special 'Traitor' editions. In this atmosphere of harassment, every free man in the country had begun to fear that he would be next. Fear and paranoia reigned supreme and our families, relatives and friends had already decided that we were done for. But inside jail, it was like we were on a picnic. Everyone would be laughing, we were hopeful and resolute and would sing qawwalis and mimic other people; one reason for this was that we were convinced that we would be released. Another might have been that when faced with a catastrophic danger, one either panics and flees or one decides to face one's fear and fight it out.[5]

In the Preface to his fourth edition of poetry, *Dast-e Tah-e Sang* (Hand under the Rock), published after his release, Faiz wrote: 'Basically, both these volumes [*Dast-e Saba* and *Zindan Nama*] are a continuation of the same strand of feelings and sensations which started with [his famous poem]"Mujh se pehli si muhabbat meri mehboob na maang" (Do not ask of me, my Love, that love of old).'

In addition to political poems such as 'Aa jao Africa' and 'Hum jo tareek rahon main', *Zindan Nama* also contains intensely personal work like the searing 'Mulaqat' (Meeting) and the incandescent 'Daricha' (Windowsill) in which Faiz melds his favourite symbols of 'saba' (east wind), 'abr-e bahar' (spring clouds) and 'mah-e taabnaak' (brilliant moon) with religious and poetic imagery to create a haunting vignette of pain and redemption. There are also the intensely sad 'Aye roshnion ke shehr' ('O city of lights'), the defiant 'Bunyad kuch to ho' (No matter the pretext) and the light-hearted 'Fikr-e sood-o ziyaan tau chootay gi' (Free of trivial worries).

Zindan Nama would prove to be his most popular and enduring work.

In jail, Faiz had also started compiling a list of the critical essays on prose and poetry he had written over the years. This was finally published in 1962 under the title *Meezan* (Collection). It contained a total of thirty-one essays divided into four parts: Literature and the ideology of literature, Problems, The Ancients (or Ancestors) (with essays on the poets Ghalib and Hali, novelist Ratan Nath Sarshar, short-story writer Prem Chand, etc.) and Contemporaries (with writings on Iqbal, 'Josh', 'Patras' Bokhari and many others). Faiz himself was not too enthusiastic about these essays, dismissing them as being only of 'historical importance', although he did write in the preface: 'I have never had the time or the energy to debate literary matters in detail. I have had the opportunity, though, of talking about these matters on radio or in different gatherings. These essays are a result of these talks. This is why they are addressed not to litterateurs but to ordinary people who want to learn something about literature.'[6]

First Asian Writers' Conference, Delhi

The conspiracy case had not even been fully dismissed yet when, in 1956, Faiz's old compatriot from the All-India Progressive Writers' Association, famed Indian writer Mulk Raj Anand wrote to Faiz inviting him to a literary conference for Asian writers in Delhi. One day, soon after Faiz's release, the Pakistani High Commissioner in India, Raja Ghazanfar Ali Khan came to visit. He had been a leading member of the All-India Muslim League and a trusted lieutenant of Muhammad Ali Jinnah's, serving in the interim Government of India in1946 and later as a minister in Pakistan. Faiz later remembered the circumstances:

> [He came over] and as soon as he came in, he roared with laughter 'You came [out of prison] at the perfect moment. Great timing. Next month we are arranging a mushaira in Delhi on Iqbal day, you need to come. I said, Raja sahib, I haven't even been properly exonerated yet, I'm still out on bail, who's going to let me go to Delhi. What if I flee? Don't you worry about it, that's my responsibility. Raja sahib insisted so I said yes but I was certain that in spite of his dedicated services to the government, he wouldn't be able to do anything. A few days later though, we got permission to go to Delhi.[7]

The Pakistani delegation set off from Lahore and crossed over at the Wagah border into Amritsar. Faiz was particularly attached to the city. This was where he had begun his teaching career, where he had met his lifelong friends and mentors, Sahibzada Mahmooduzzafar, Dr Rashid Jahan and later Syed Sajjad Zaheer, and where the initial activities of the Progressive Writers' Association had started. This was the city where he had first become acquainted with the family of Dr M.D. Taseer and where he had met and fallen in love with Alys. Faiz always referred to his time in Amritsar as the happiest in his life.

He took his companions all around the city—the narrow streets and lanes, Jallianwala Bagh, Darbar Sahib and to the building of the former Mohammadan Anglo-Oriental College, to point out where he had lived and taught. The delegation then proceeded to Delhi where it received a royal welcome and it was obvious that Faiz was the centre of attention. His close friend, Zehra Nigah, who was in Delhi at the time, remembered his visit later: 'How proud Faiz sahib was of the love and devotion he received from all quarters. Many years after partition when Faiz sahib visited Hindustan for the first time, I was also there. I saw people standing in long queues to see and greet him, [they were] kissing his hands and feet, showering their affections on him. Kings would be envious of such a welcome.'[8]

The Asian Writers' Conference was the first of its kind, its stated objective being to formulate a stance on the neo-colonial system of oppression which had been fashioned after the Second World War and the nominal 'independence' of former colonies. In just half a century, the world had been through two horrific World

Wars in which tens of millions had perished along with materials and resources worth billions. The world had also witnessed the senseless destruction of Hiroshima and Nagasaki. It was felt necessary for Asian writers to examine the problems of their history, politics and culture in the framework of their own languages. After some heated discussions, the conference adjourned without issuing a formal statement, agreeing to meet again in Tashkent in the Soviet Union.

Faiz also had the opportunity of reciting his poetry to an adoring audience at a mushaira organized in honour of Allama Muhammad Iqbal on Iqbal Day. The President of India, Dr Sarvepalli Radhakrishnan, presided, and Faiz was the main attraction. He recited a number of his poems, which had become just as popular in India, while he was incarcerated, as they were in Pakistan. The day after the mushaira, Raja Ghazanfar Ali Khan came to see Faiz: 'The next afternoon, Raja sahib came to my room and said he had not invited Pandit Nehru [then Prime Minister of India] for reasons of protocol. He said [Nehru] had called him to complain and he was coming this evening just to listen to the Pakistani poets.'[9]

Red Star

The delegation had just returned from Delhi when an invitation was received for Pakistani journalists to visit the People's Republic of China. They were to accompany then prime minister, Hussain Shaheed Suhrawardy, on his official tour. Faiz was appointed the head of the delegation. He must have been eager to visit China, which had successfully undergone a workers' and peasants' revolution in 1949. Friendly relations between China and Pakistan was something Faiz, too, would have considered desirable, as a counterpoint to Pakistan's increasing dependence on the United States and the Western bloc. The prime minister's visit had been cancelled once before and the same thing happened again. When the delegation reached China via Hong Kong, it learned that the prime minister would not be coming. Instead of the Chinese government, the delegation was warmly greeted by the Chinese Journalists' Union. Faiz's poems, 'Peking' and 'Sinkiang' were written in memory of this first visit to China.

By this time, Faiz was weary. According to Sibt-e Hasan, 'The two years, 1957 and 1958, were very hard on Faiz. Supposedly he was the chief editor of Progressive Papers Limited but his position was merely ornamental. He was assigned no work and none of his suggestions were paid heed to. This period of enforced limbo was very hard on him and it affected his poetry as well.[10]

In April 1958, Faiz resigned as chief editor of Progressive Papers and his sojourn in journalism came to an end.

Tashkent

The first Afro-Asian Writers' Conference[11] in Delhi in 1956 had resolved to meet again in Tashkent in the Soviet republic of Uzbekistan. The meeting was planned for October 1958. Faiz was a member of the organizing committee and requested the Pakistani government to send a large delegation of senior writers, poets and journalists. The government, though, wary of offending their American 'friends' at the height of the Cold War, reluctantly agreed to grant travel visas only to Faiz and poet Hafeez Jullundhri. For Faiz, Pakistan's participation in this conference was essential since it was a continuation of the Asian Writers Movement that had arrogated to itself the task of analysing and resolving the linguistic, cultural and literary problems of all newly liberated Asian and African nations. The movement was thus decidedly anti-colonial, and one of the first tasks confronting it was to work urgently on translating literature from different languages of the region into other languages, thus making it widely accessible. There were writers representing India and Pakistan, the Soviet Union, North Korea, Vietnam, Algeria, Indonesia, Iraq, Congo and many others. Most of these countries, including India and Pakistan, had fought long and hard to gain their independence. Many had fought decades-long wars against their colonizers and most had been born after the holocausts of the First and Second World Wars. A fervent desire for peace and fraternity had thus been a central element of their struggles. In addition, at the height of the Cold War, when the old imperialist nations of Europe and the Americas were beginning to tighten their noose around the Socialist bloc, especially China and the Soviet Union, there was a perpetual danger to world peace, which was unacceptable to the newly independent nations of Asia and Africa. A single spark could cause a conflagration, which could turn their dreams of freedom to ashes.

As soon as the conference started though, there was a squabble. The Indian delegation had raised objections to the use of the words 'imperialism' and 'colonialism' in the resolutions proposed at the conference. It was the same disagreement that had plagued the All-India Progressive Writers' Association. The Indian delegates objected to 'politicizing' the conference by the use of these words, while the others insisted that in newly liberated, underdeveloped countries, no facet of life was free of politics. In the end, it was left to Faiz to give a speech in which he reminded the Indian delegates of the struggles and sacrifices they had made for their own independence just a few years back and to ask what would be left of Indian literature if everything related to India's freedom struggle were expurgated. This made sense to everyone, and draft resolutions were prepared, discussed and finally approved.

After the conference, Faiz received invitations to visit other Soviet cities. Later, he specifically singled out the beauty of the historic cities of Samarkand and Bokhara in his writings.

The thousand-year Rudaki celebration

The thousand-year celebrations for Tajikistan's celebrated poet Abu Abdollah Jafar ibn Mohammad Rudaki (858–941), popularly known as 'Adam ul-Shoara' (Adam of Poets or the First Poet), were also held around the same time as the Tashkent conference. Rudaki (sometimes written as Rudagi) is regarded as the first great literary genius of modern Persian and one of the founders of Persian classical literature. Faiz proceeded to Dushanbe in the Soviet Republic of Tajikistan to attend the festival. He realized that in Dushanbe he no longer needed an interpreter since the local language referred to as 'Tajik' or 'Tajiki' is a dialect of Persian, which he could understand and speak. Faiz described his visit:

> The Rudaki celebrations were very exuberant. There was an exhibition of books and letters about Rudaki in the city's main library and I was delighted to see that (Indian scholar) Maulana Shibli Nomani's 'Shair-ul-Ajam' ('History of Persian Poetry') had pride of place. In the evening, we saw a play on Rudaki's

> life written by our dear friend Mir Ali Mir Shakir. Some scenes are still etched on my heart, especially the one where Rudaki's eyes are put out on the order of the King and he cries out 'Oh Lord, they are putting out my eyes, open wide the eye of my heart![12]

During the day, the delegates met students and ordinary citizens, and Faiz commented on how people in Dushanbe knew more of Allama Muhammad Iqbal's Persian poetry by heart than people in Pakistan or India. At the city's main hospital and medical college, the principal described to them how, before the Soviet revolution, the area they had been touring was empty fields and forests where the local people would come to hunt jackals. There was no school around for miles. The local mullah in the mosque was the only source of information or education and there was no doctor or hospital anywhere.

From Dushanbe, the delegates were to proceed to Moscow but, due to bad weather, they made an unscheduled stop at Baku, the capital of the Soviet republic of Azerbaijan. Their hosts had already called the local writers' union and they were received at the airport by the president of the Azerbaijani Writers' Union, who, Faiz and his companions later discovered, was also the president of Azerbaijan. It was the first time Faiz realized that in this new Soviet society, artists, poets, actors and musicians did not have to remain confined within their narrow artistic sphere but could participate in politics as well. Politics was not the exclusive fief of a certain class of people.

Later, Faiz and his companions stayed a few days in Moscow and he wrote glowingly about the city: Its beautiful historic buildings, the wide tree-lined boulevards, the intersections with monuments and statues at every corner and, unusually, the total lack of any advertising billboards which are a ubiquitous eyesore in every big city.

Syed Sajjad Zaheer organized a small poetry recital in his room where Faiz read 'Hum jo tareek rahon main maray gaye', his moving ode to Julius and Ethel Rosenberg, the young couple executed in America on trumped-up charges of being Communist spies. When someone finished translating the poem in English, a man at the back suddenly got up weeping, covered his eyes with his handkerchief and abruptly left the room. Faiz later found out that this was Albert Kahn, the well-known progressive American journalist and writer who had been a personal friend of the Rosenbergs and was a trustee for their two young children.

The romantic revolutionary

Faiz met many people during this, his first, trip to the Soviet Union but the meeting he treasured the most was with renowned Turkish poet, Nazim Hikmet. They met at a mushaira and immediately hit it off. They remained friends till Hikmet's death in 1963. Hikmet was a poet, playwright, novelist and memoirist whose poetry has been translated into more than fifty languages. He was acclaimed for the 'lyrical flow of his statements' and has often been described as a 'romantic revolutionary'. He was repeatedly arrested for his political beliefs and spent much of his adult life in prison or in exile. Faiz described their first proper meeting:

> He was a very handsome man, slim and well built with golden hair and brown eyes, very fair with sharp features. He was probably eight or ten years older than me but looked very young. He belonged to a family of royals [but] spent his entire life fighting for the rights of ordinary people...We started talking about poetry, its language and form, a conversation which continued over many years. He would say, 'There is no such thing as totally free verse. Joining words together in rhythm is itself a kind of discipline, and this is what raises poetry above prose and since poetry evolved from the womb of music, therefore its first condition is a specific rhythm, tone and melody. But people often think that this can only be done in the ways outlined by our ancestors in the past. This is wrong. Actually, every language has a certain covert and scattered rhythm. If you pay attention to it, you can extract many kinds of vocal images from it. What we should be doing is to use the natural rhythm's [*sic*] of our own language to create our poetry. But we usually don't do that. Take your language Urdu, or mine, Turkish. They each have their own cadence but in our poetry, we try and mimic the patterns of Arabic. Why? Those patterns were designed by the Arabs for their own language, for their own songs and melodies and the real origin of their rhythm is the specific gait of the camel. Why should we imitate it?'[13]

Hikmet had spent a long time in Turkish jails and, after being released, had finally gone to Moscow. The Turkish government sentenced him to death in absentia but he was given a royal welcome in Moscow. He was given the rank of a minister, advised the government on various cultural projects and lived out the rest of his life peacefully in the Soviet Union.

Boots on the ground

Faiz was still at the Tashkent conference when Pakistani politics turned another somersault. General Ayub Khan, who had been promoted out of turn to chief of army staff at the urging of Pakistan's last British commander-in-chief, General Sir Douglas Gracey, overthrew the civilian government to install the first of Pakistan's many military dictatorships. Ayub's civilian political benefactors had supported his elevation to a four-star general because he was thought to be appropriately subservient and unambitious. It was not the last time that Pakistani politicians would make such a mistake. Once again, the country was gripped by fear and uncertainty. Widespread arrests followed immediately after, including of political activists and everyone of a 'Leftist' bent, from peasant and student leaders to trade-union workers, journalists, writers and poets. Faiz was shocked and dismayed but resolved to return to Pakistan. Soviet writer Alexander Surkhov, in the preface to his Russian translation of Faiz's poetry, wrote of Faiz's decision to return, despite the dangers:

> We were in Moscow reading poems at a writer's gathering…I asked [Faiz] what his plans were for the near future? He looked at me with his deep, dark eyes which betrayed a hint of sadness and said with a slight smile 'first I will go to London to meet some friends, then, of course, Karachi, Lahore, back to my homeland'. 'but you know that over there…'. The same smile played over his lips 'Obviously, I must go back'. 'But imprisonment is certain…'. 'Maybe, and if one has to go to jail for a great cause, one should absolutely do so'. 'But what if…it's something worse than jail'. [Faiz] looked out the window at the statue of Tolstoy in the garden and glanced up at the frozen sky. He was still smiling. He paused in his particular style and then said softly 'If it's something worse than jail, that would be

horrible. But a struggle is, after all, a struggle, you know that...'. This was his calm, confident answer.[14]

Faiz, the film writer

Faiz was due to go to London for the screening of a film he had written *Jago hua savera* (Awaken, it's dawn). Alys had already arrived in London with the girls, her first trip home since 1938. Faiz had never been involved with the film industry, although as early as 1947, a film made in Bombay called *Romeo Juliet* had used one of his poems as a song. Subsequently, several of Faiz's poems were used in feature films, including the Dilip Kumar-starrer *Mazdoor*. After his release from prison, Faiz had become extremely popular, partly as a result of his constant demonization by the mainstream press. In Pakistan, he was welcomed back from prison a hero. It was during this time that he met A.J. Kardar, son of the famed film-maker A.R. Kardar, who was originally from Lahore and had been one of the pioneers of the film industry there. He eventually ended up in Bombay where he introduced many legendary artists to the Hindi film industry, including Naushad, Majrooh Sultanpuri and Suraiya.

A.J. Kardar persuaded Faiz to write a film script which Faiz based on one of his favourite novels, *The Boatman of the Padma* (a translation of Manik Bandhopadhyay's classic, *Padma Nadir Manjhi*), about the lives of Bengali fishermen. He also participated in the direction of the film. Earlier, there had been an attempt to make a film based on the Faiz poem 'Hum jo tareek rahon main maray gaye' about the life of the American couple Julius and Ethel Rosenberg but it had come to naught. *Jago hua savera* was filmed almost entirely in East Pakistan and Faiz wrote most of the songs for the movie. The film did not do well at the box office, probably because of its unusual subject matter and a total disinterest on the part of the Pakistani establishment to promote it, but was feted at several international film festivals. Faiz's poems though, continued to be used in feature films. There were several other attempts to make films in which Faiz was involved, none of which came to fruition. Faiz would have a ready answer for people who would ask him when there would be good films made in Pakistan. He would say, only half in jest, that it would happen when instead of shooting films, the film-makers would be shot! The film-makers, Faiz maintained, refused to accept that a film could be realistic and entertaining at the same time. Another film that Faiz made much later, in the early 1970s, when he was cultural advisor to the government of Prime Minister Zulfiqar Ali Bhutto was also made with A.J. Kardar. However, that film never saw the light of day due to contractual disputes between the film-maker and the crew.

Faiz's only English poem was also a screenplay for a documentary about two artefacts recovered from the ruins of Mohenjodaro. 'The Unicorn and the Dancing Girl' describes the march of human civilization through the ages and was made into a documentary film under the aegis of UNESCO in 1963.

Faiz knew that films are a very powerful medium in which multiple creative endeavours can be combined to communicate a very effective message. He had written in one of his essays that it was strange that all other creative activities were considered 'art' while film had been designated an 'industry', thus relegating it to the commercial sphere only. While Faiz was not wholly opposed to the commercial aspects of art, it was his view that the real purpose of films, like all art, is to reflect human life—its joys and sorrows, its agonies and ecstasies, its purpose and ends. He was also painfully aware, though, that like all art forms, films were beholden to financiers and profiteers and subject to their whims. In spite of this, he maintained an active interest in films and his poetry continues to grace films today.

Back in prison

Faiz flew from London to Karachi where his friends advised him to not go on to Lahore. The military government had rounded up and imprisoned anyone with even the remotest socialist or communist sympathies. The martial law junta had no clear policy about what to do next and was trying to enforce the writ of the state through brute force. Faiz, though, was having none of it. It was Salima's birthday in a few days and he was determined to get to Lahore. A friend of his, now a minister in the Ayub government, assured him that he would not be harassed. In Lahore, Alys and the girls were waiting for him eagerly. He was given a royal welcome and Salima's birthday was celebrated in grand fashion.

After a day or two, though, the inevitable police party showed up. Faiz later described his second arrest:

> It used to be that if there was some change of government or upheaval, opponents of the government would be locked up as a precaution. But Ayub Khan went a step further and arrested everyone whose names appeared in their CID files going back to 1921. Many of them hadn't done a thing…when I was arrested I said I hadn't done anything, why had I been arrested? I was sent to Moscow with an official delegation. They said, yes, we know you haven't done anything, it's just a precaution. If we feel you pose no danger to the government, we'll let you go. Or you can write down that you won't do anything to oppose the government. I said what's to write? I haven't participated in politics for a long time. They said, well then you write that you support the government. I said I would not write anything of the sort. Every few days, some high official would come and ask the same thing and I would refuse. After a few months, they said, fine, you can go home.[15]

During his incarceration, Alys was questioned by the police several times as well about Faiz's 'secret links' with the Soviets. It later transpired that when Faiz had gone to the Soviet Embassy with Hafeez Jullundhri to get his visa for the Tashkent conference, they had left the embassy together. Faiz, ever absent-minded, had left his bag inside and went back to get it. Some overzealous intelligence officer took a picture of Faiz emerging from the embassy alone and this was assumed as 'proof' of something clandestine. The police also wanted to know about the money that Alys had used to buy a car in London. It was bought from the money she had inherited after her father's death but the Pakistan government assumed that it was payment from the Soviet government for something sinister.

While Faiz was in jail, his old friend, Mian Iftikharuddin, died suddenly. It was a great blow. Mian Iftikhar and Faiz had been friends for close to forty years. He had fought for progressive causes all his life starting with the All-India Progressive Writers' Association. He was also a stalwart of the independence struggle and had been the driving spirit behind the founding of Progressive Papers Limited. Faiz had borrowed Rs 300 from him to buy Alys a wedding ring. Faiz wrote a haunting elegy for his old friend called 'Na ganwaao navak-e neem kash' (Do not waste the half-drawn arrow) which is included in his collection *Dast-e Teh-e Sang*.

An offer to return

Faiz was released from jail in April 1959. Outside jail, the police officers on duty surrounded him and insisted that they would not let him leave unless he wrote down his new poem 'Aaj bazaar main pa-bajaulan chalo' (Walk today in the bazaar, feet enchained) for them. Faiz had written it during his first imprisonment when he had been brought to Lahore from Montgomery jail for dental problems. While he was being taken to Lahore's dental hospital in a tonga, people on the street recognized him, and gathering around the tonga, started chanting slogans.

At first, Faiz refused but the police officers pleaded with him, invoking their love for him, and at last he relented and wrote it down for them.[16]

Alys was still working for *Pakistan Times* when one day, a familiar car drove up to the house and there was a knock at the door. A highly placed police official had come to visit. Faiz received him politely. The man told him that he had come not as a police officer but as a friend and well-wisher to convey a message. The government wanted him back as chief editor of *Pakistan Times* and *Imroze*. He would be given every facility, whatever he wanted. Faiz asked if the man was an emissary of the government and he said yes.

Faiz's answer stunned the man: 'Nothing doing. Principles are not for sale. Tell the government to hand the newspapers back to Progressive Papers Limited and let us run them the right way. Then we'll see.'[17]

And that ended Faiz's long association with *Pakistan Times*.

Notes

1. Faiz Ahmed Faiz, 'Guftagoo-Faiz Ahmed Faiz', *Dunyazad*, no. 35 (Karachi: Scheherzade Publications, 2012), p. 71.
2. Syed Sibt-e Hasan, *Sukhan dar Sukhan* (Karachi: Maktaba Daniyal, 2009), p. 40.

3. Ghalib was imprisoned for six months on charges of gambling and failing to pay his debts.
4. Syed Sibt-e Hasan, 'Paara paara daaman-e sidq-o wafa', in *Mataa-e Lauh-o-Qalam* (Karachi: Maktaba Daniyal, 1973), p. 302.
5. Faiz Ahmed Faiz, *Nuskha hai Wafa* (Lahore: Maktaba-e Karvaan, 1985), pp. 203–4.
6. Faiz Ahmed Faiz, *Meezan* (Karachi: Urdu Academy, Sindh, 1987), p. 7.
7. Faiz Ahmed Faiz, *Mataa-e Lauh-o-Qalam* (Karachi: Maktaba-e Daniyal, 2011), p. 97.
8. Ashfaq Hussain, *Faiz ke Maghrabi Hawalay* (Lahore: Jung Publishers, 1996), p. 242.
9. Faiz, *Mataa-e Lauh-o-Qalam*, pp. 97–8.
10. Hasan, *Sukhan dar Sukhan*, p. 42.
11. The 'Afro-Asian Writer's Association' was founded after the 1956 Asian Writer's Conference. It organized semi-regular conferences of writers in various places also later published the magazine *Lotus* of which Faiz remained the editor while in Beirut.
12. Faiz Ahmed Faiz, *Mah-o-Saal-e Aashnaai* (Karachi: Maktaba Daniyal, 2008), p. 34.
13. Ibid., pp. 81–2.
14. Faiz, *Mataa-e Lauh-o-Qalam* , pp. 286–387.
15. Ibid., pp. 34–5.
16. Hasan, *Sukhan dar Sukhan*, p. 54.
17. Ayub Mirza, *Faiz Nama*, (Lahore: Classic Publishers, 2006), p. 258.

15

The Lenin Peace Prize

Man is made by his belief. As he believes, so he is.

—Bhagavad Gita

Faiz was still debating his future when he was offered the position of director of the Lahore Arts Council, formed immediately after partition by noted artists and litterateurs of the city, including Faiz himself, M.D. Taseer, noted singer-actress Noor Jehan, the famed painter Abdur Rahman Chughtai and playwright Imtiaz Ali Taj. It was located in an abandoned property on Lahore's Mall Road, which 'resembled a stable. There was a layer of dust an inch thick on the portraits in the National Arts Gallery and stray dogs wandered around the courtyard.'[1]

Faiz was neither a painter, nor a musician, nor a singer or actor. But he was passionate about the arts and culture and, despite his laid-back veneer, he had tremendous organizational energy and capability.

His friend, Syed Sibt-e Hasan later wrote:

> Perhaps once a year [at the Arts Council], an artist would display their works; even that would be seen by very few people since no one ever heard about it. When Faiz sahib took charge of this dying institution, it came back to life. He [Faiz] was not a musician or painter but he had an irresistible personality. He would treat young artists so affectionately that people would be drawn to him. They would flock to [the Arts Council]. There would be a drama rehearsal going on in one room, a tabla playing in another, a painting or photo exhibition in a third and a puppet show going on in yet another. And in the courtyard young painters would be standing with their easels, painting. Faiz sahib had a small tea house built for the artists on the premises and people would sit there past midnight discussing everything under the sun. Occasionally, Faiz would come out of his office and sit with everyone and things would liven up even more. Very soon, [the Arts Council] became one of the most active institutions in the city. Faiz was so happy those days. He

> had the freedom to propagate the Fine Arts the way he wanted to and all the artists in the city were collaborating whole heartedly in this endeavor.[2]

Faiz had a small temporary structure built on the premises where art classes were held, and persuaded an Italian architect to design a new building free of charge. Faiz then started raising money for a permanent structure. His dream was to open an arts council in every city across the country so that every corner of the nation could enjoy art and culture.

Of course, it was inevitable that Faiz's activities would come to the notice of the government. He was, in any case, under constant surveillance for his 'dangerous' and 'subversive' ideas. At first, the government ignored what he was doing. Then, when it became obvious that what Faiz was doing was beginning to be lauded far and wide, the people in power decided that the arts council could be used for government purposes. Until then, foreign dignitaries and guests who expressed a desire to savour Pakistani culture in the form of paintings or music or dance performances, had nowhere to go. Once, the Shah of Iran, on a visit to Lahore, was made to sit in the gallery of the Punjab Assembly to hear a qawwali while the performers sat on the street outside.

The Lahore Arts Council could now serve this purpose admirably. But those in power were envious and afraid of the hold Faiz had on young artists and terrified that some of them might become 'infected' with his socialist ideas.

A high official in Ayub Khan's government wrote later:

> When Faiz sahib was in charge of the Arts Council, the Chief Justice of the Supreme Court of Pakistan said to me that it would really help the Arts Council if President Ayub came to visit. The President happily agreed but the Punjab Governor, the Nawab of Kalabagh refused to come. I went to see him personally. He had a high police official sitting with him. Nawab sahib told me categorically to not take the President there. He abused Faiz sahib for a few minutes and then pointed at the police officer 'I have kept this pet Alsatian to deal with Faiz'.[3]

Faiz worked at the arts council for three years, from 1959 till 1962. As its fame and creative output grew, so did the opposition from government and religious quarters. They knew, of course, what Faiz was trying to do: raise awareness among ordinary people about social and political matters through the arts. And this, as far as Pakistan's rulers were concerned, was dangerous and subversive.

'The pain was such...'

In the three years that he worked at the Lahore Arts Council, Faiz turned a moribund institution into one of the most vibrant artistic institutions in the Pakistan. There were arts councils in other cities such as Rawalpindi, Peshawar and Karachi, but while Faiz was in charge of the Lahore branch, none of them could match it in terms of the profusion of artistic and cultural activities being conducted there. While the Lahore Arts Council and its plays, art exhibitions, puppet shows and musical performances were lauded all over Pakistan, some people, especially those opposed to any cultural or artistic activity, including Pakistan's increasingly strident religious lobby, were increasingly opposed to it. Faiz had to fight on many fronts to keep the activities of the council going. In addition, he had now achieved international recognition and received invitations to travel all over the world for literary and poetry seminars and meetings.

Faiz had been a smoker since he was a college student and had developed respiratory problems because of his chain-smoking. His smoking habit had become particularly ingrained after his imprisonment and, in spite of attacks of breathlessness that left him completely drained, he could not quit. In February 1962, he almost fainted from a spell of extreme breathlessness and was taken to hospital where the doctors had to work hard to restore his breathing. He was later told that he had had a heart attack. His physical activity was severely curtailed by his doctors and he was put on a special diet and confined to his home after he got back from hospital. It was at this time that he decided to resign from his duties at the arts council. He was tired of the constant opposition and felt he had done enough.

A serious illness, a brush with death or a significant loss can, paradoxically, help to clarify one's priorities and weed out the trivialities that occupies so much of our day-to-day lives. It makes it easier to focus on what one finds truly meaningful. In 1967, Faiz wrote his poem, 'Heart Attack' about his experience:

From the ecstasies of pain that night the feral heart
Sought entanglement in the soul's every vein;
An exit from every hair tip,
And far away, in your courtyard, it was as if
Every leaf, washed in my forlorn blood
Looked angry at the beauty of the moon.[4]

The prize

After Faiz returned home from hospital, he was confined to his room and his physical activity was restricted. There would be a stream of visitors coming in all day. One day, the phone rang. Faiz answered and listened quietly for a few minutes. When he hung up, his expression was one of puzzlement and disbelief. After a pause, he told his assembled visitors it was a friend calling to inform him that he had been awarded the International Lenin Peace Prize.

Previously called the Stalin Peace Prize, the prize was the Soviet Union's equivalent of the Nobel but unlike the Nobel, it was given to several people annually who, in the eyes of the selection panel, had 'strengthened peace between peoples'. In Left circles, it was considered a great honour and previous recipients had included the American civil rights activist W.E.B. DuBois and actor Paul Robeson, Chilean poet Pablo Neruda, noted German playwright Bertolt Brecht and Cuba's Fidel Castro. Faiz would share the prize that year with Pablo Picasso and four other people. At the news, a silence descended upon the room. Everyone realized the significance of the award and that it was being awarded in recognition not just of Faiz's poetic efforts, but also his literary activities, his efforts on behalf of trade-union workers and peasants, his fearless journalism, his struggle against fascism, his role in the international peace movement and many other social and political activities. It was an honour not just for Faiz but for the entire country. Soon, there was an outpouring of congratulatory phone calls, telegrams, letters and visitors, and even though his doctors had forbidden Faiz from seeing too many people, no one paid any heed, least of all Faiz himself. After consulting Alys and a few close friends, Faiz sent a missive to the Soviet government thanking it and accepting the award. He agreed to go to Moscow to receive the award in person, provided Pakistan's military government allowed him to do so. He also sent a telegram to the President of Pakistan requesting permission to leave for Moscow. Even though he was not under detention or any official restriction, in fact, the CID was camped permanently outside his house and his activities were kept under strict surveillance.

To Moscow

Fortunately for Faiz, some intelligent people in Ayub Khan's government had begun advocating a more balanced approach towards the Soviet Union and its allies, in imitation of India's 'non-aligned' foreign policy, no doubt realizing that the large size and population of the Soviet Union meant ample opportunities for trade and commerce. Permission for Faiz to travel to Moscow was quickly granted but his doctors had strictly forbidden air travel, so he had to travel by sea. It was decided that the family would accompany Faiz by train to Karachi, where he and Salima would board an Italian ship to Naples. There they would take a train to Rome, Hungary, Czechoslovakia, Poland and then on to Moscow. After receiving his prize, Faiz planned to travel on to London, where Alys and Moneeza would meet them.

In spite of the fact that they had presidential permission to travel, the Karachi CID subjected Faiz and Salima to a lot of checking and stoppages before they were able to finally leave aboard their ship. The ship took them to Naples from where they boarded a train that was to take them to Rome and onwards. Salima remembers the journey as being quite memorable:

> When we reached Rome, a friend of Abba's had booked us into the Grand Hotel, this very fancy place. I pointed out the tariff to Abba. It was outrageously high and he said we can't afford this. So the next day we shifted to a more modest hotel. We boarded the train two days later and Abba being Abba, had no idea that the train journey was going to last three days. He had just looked at the arrival time, which was 9 a.m. and he assumed it was the next day after we boarded. And, of course, it was my first time out of Pakistan so I was clueless. The train set off and we discovered that there was no restaurant car so there was no food to eat and the train didn't stop anywhere. By night-time we

were hungry and tired but the train kept on going. Finally, the next morning the train stopped somewhere, maybe Vienna, and we rushed off, ravenously hungry and finally found some sandwiches. When we finally got to Moscow, there was a reception committee to receive us. It was the first time that Abba and I had travelled alone together. It was also the first time I learned to wash his socks when I realized he didn't know how to do it![5]

'The night is fractured and they shiver, blue those stars, in the distance'

Before Faiz arrived in Moscow, he and Salima were taken to Sochi in the Soviet Republic of Georgia on the Black Sea. Faiz was admitted to a sanatorium for a complete medical check-up. As it happened, Chile's renowned poet Pablo Neruda was also in Sochi at the time and it gave Faiz a chance to meet and get to know him and his wife. Faiz knew Neruda's work well, although they had never met. Besides being renowned poets in their own languages, they shared a common ideology. Neruda believed, like Faiz, that a popular movement can only succeed if it manages to merge with the flow of history. Revolution is not just about changing the present. It also involves examining the past, discarding what is redundant while retaining what remains vital, and forming clear and healthy ideas about the future. Like Faiz, Neruda had a deep understanding not just of his own nation's history, but also of the history of his entire region.

Years later, in response to a question, Faiz would say:

> 'I cannot claim a friendship [with Neruda]; he is a great man, but definitely I have been in his company. It happened that when I went to Soviet Union in 1962 [to receive the Lenin Prize] by coincidence I got to stay at a sanatorium where he was staying as well. For a month we stayed in the same place and this is how we met. However, I only got to study his poetry afterwards. That is, I had come across a few poems randomly, but had not properly read any collection. After meeting him I studied him to the extent to which I could find the translations of his work, but translations of his poetry were not readily available in those days.[6]

The foundation of love

The award ceremony was held in the Kremlin Grand Palace Hall and was attended by writers and artists from all over the Soviet Union and the world. In his brief but memorable speech,[7] Faiz referred to the greatness of the Lenin Peace Prize since it was associated with the name of Lenin, 'the most venerable flag-bearer of human struggle today', and peace, 'which is the first condition of human life in all its beauty'. Faiz went on to say with his characteristic humility that he could 'find nothing in my life's work which is worthy of this honor' except the 'ideals and principles which I and my comrades have held dear, the fervent desire for peace and freedom, which in itself is so compelling as to elevate all those who work for it'. And then, in his singularly poetic manner, he called peace and freedom 'so very beautiful and radiant...everyone can imagine that peace is amber waves of grain and eucalyptus trees, it is the veil of a newly-wed bride and the gleeful hands of children, the pen of the poet and the brush of the painter and that freedom is the guarantor and tyranny the murderer of all those things that differentiate humans from animals: intelligence and awareness, justice and truth, bravery and chivalry, goodness and compassion.' He referred to 'the two forces that have been locked in struggle since the dawn of humankind: creation and destruction, progress and decline, light and darkness, love of freedom and hatred for it'. He pointed out how 'before today, humans had so little control over the bounties of nature that every group could not hope to satisfy their basic needs and so there was at least some justification for snatching and looting, but not anymore. Human ingenuity, science and industry have progressed to the point where today, everyone can be fed, clothed and satisfied, provided these boundless treasures of nature and production are not used just to satisfy the lusts of a few people but for all of humankind'.

Towards the end, he pleaded to those assembled 'today, when we can look down upon our world from the stars, these irrational selfish attempts to grasp a few bits of the Earth, to establish our dominion over a few people seem beyond reason'. 'Are there not enough people among us,' he asked, 'who can convince the others to sink these guns, bombs, rockets and cannons into the sea and instead of trying to subjugate one another, set out together to conquer the heavens, where there is no shortage of space and no one need fight another, where there are countless skies and uncounted worlds'.

Faiz ended his speech with a verse from one of his favourite poets, the great Hafez of Shiraz:

> Every foundation is faulty I saw
> Except the foundation of Love, faultless.

The land of Pushkin

Faiz's poetry had already become very popular in the Soviet Union. The first Russian translations of his poems had appeared in 1954, during his first incarceration. After he was awarded the Lenin Peace Prize and got wide coverage in the Soviet press, several volumes of his poetry were published repeatedly—each impression running into hundreds of thousands selling within days. It helped that many of the translations had been done by popular, contemporary Soviet-era poets. In just a few years, he had become known throughout the Soviet Union. Everywhere he went, he was showered with affection and he, in turn, returned the love by visiting the Soviet Union as often as he could for the rest of his life. One of his Soviet friends once wrote that it was not humanly possible to count every visit Faiz made to the Soviet Union.

Onwards, to London

Immediately after Faiz had received the Peace Prize, Salima and he went on to London as planned. Alys and Moneeza had already arrived. They were to stay on in London a while. The girls were growing up and Pakistan was still in the grip of a military dictatorship. All political activities, especially any involving poets, writers, journalists, trade unionists or any grouping that the government deemed 'dangerous', were strictly prohibited. Faiz and his family were under constant surveillance and he was watched wherever he went. There was no question of being involved even in a cultural or artistic activity. Under the guise of a 'strong centre', the Pakistan government had suppressed all regional, provincial and ethnic political parties.

Faiz and Alys had decided to stay in London for a few years. England was a natural choice. There were people of South Asian origin all over, and London was a flourishing centre of Urdu cultural and literary activity. Faiz bought a small house in Finchley, north London. Salima started college and Moneeza was in high school. Faiz had lots of plans, which he described in letters to friends. To one friend, he wrote that some publishers wanted to publish a collection of Pakistani literature, both poetry and short stories, and he was making the selection. To another, he described his desire to compile a modern history of Urdu literature. Sometimes he would want to do translations, at other times he would find himself wanting to work on something else. All of this came to naught, though.

One reason was that he was now an internationally renowned literary personality and would be invited all over the world: to conferences, universities, colleges and gatherings of one sort or another. Another may have been the city of London itself. As his friend and translator, Victor Kiernan wrote: 'It's unfortunate that [Faiz] with his family, instead of settling in one of many peaceful and romantic places, for example my ancestral city Manchester or the Lake district where at one time many poets flourished[8] or Edinburgh, chose to settle in London, that gigantic agglomeration of bricks, smog, noise and people.'[9]

It was not as if Faiz stayed in London long enough to concentrate on a weighty project anyway. During their relatively brief stay in London, he travelled frequently all over Western and Eastern Europe, Cuba, Algeria, Syria and many other places. While in London, he would participate frequently in radio programmes for the BBC's Urdu service.

But despite all the activity, he was not happy. When the girls would go off to school and Alys to work (she worked at a school for special children, called at that time ESN school), he would get restless. Ever since his first imprisonment, especially the three months he had been held in solitary confinement, he dreaded being alone. The London weather did not help; cloudy, cold and often wet, it was not conducive to the health of someone who already suffered from breathing difficulties. The fast-paced, impersonal life of the West and the feelings of alienation it inevitably brought on also weighed upon him. In a rare half-complaining mood, he once told the renowned English scholar of Urdu (and avowed communist), Ralph Russell: 'But there is such a feeling of alienation here that it's hard to persuade oneself to do anything. And the worst thing is that life feels so artificial. If you want to see someone, first get an appointment. Even to see friends you have to call ahead and set a time. What kind of life is this?'[10] Although he laughed off his comments in the same conversation, it was clear that his heart was not in London.

Faiz in English

There are any number of Faiz translations available in English today. Some are better than others but the very first translation was done by the British Marxist historian Victor Kiernan (1913–2009). He had studied at Cambridge University and came to India in 1939. He had been friends with Alys before he came to India, since they both shared the same political views. He and Faiz also later became friends. Kiernan had an interest in Iqbal's poetry and was one of the first to translate it into English. It was during that project that he and Faiz got to know one another. He would later try his hand at Faiz's poetry as well, and his translations, according to most commentators, remain some of most authoritative to this day. This, too, was no doubt because he and Faiz shared the same social and political outlook. The first volume of thirty-nine of Faiz's poems translated by Kiernan was published in Lahore in 1962. In 1971, it was republished under the aegis of the United Nations Educational, Scientific and Cultural Organization (UNESCO). Until then, a few isolated translations of Faiz's work had appeared in Russian and Czech literary journals, but this work introduced Faiz to an international audience for the first time. The volume's popularity was such that it is still in print today.

Hand under the Rock

Faiz's fourth slim volume of poetry, *Dast-e teh-e Sang* (Hand under the Rock), was published in July 1965. Its preface is the acceptance speech Faiz made at the Lenin Peace Prize ceremony. It also includes one of several 'autobiographical' essays by Faiz. By now, he was a world-famous poet. People would stop him on the street to greet him, talk to him and just be in his presence. For an extremely private person like Faiz, it must have been quite an adjustment. He enjoyed the affection that people showered upon him, but sometimes the burden was hard to bear. He said more than once that he felt guilty for not having done enough to justify all the love and praise he had been given from a young age.

Faiz described his state of mind while the poems of *Dast-teh-e Sang* were composed. The very first poem in the collection expresses it well. When Faiz wrote in the first verse 'Yun hai ke har ek hamdam-e daireena khafa hai' (It is as if lifelong friends are angry [with me]), it reflected quite accurately what he faced upon his release from prison in 1955. The religious right and its allies in the mainstream press now had more ammunition against him. Henceforth, a prominent Urdu newspaper, whose founder had once been a compatriot of Faiz's during the independence struggle, would refer to Faiz until his death as the 'convicted Faiz Ahmed Faiz' or 'the formerly imprisoned Faiz Ahmed Faiz'. In addition, partly as a result of his incarceration, his poetry had become enormously popular both in Pakistan and internationally. His stature had grown and so had people's jealousies. Faiz experienced this first hand when he came back to work for *Pakistan Times*. He wrote: 'The period after Zindan Nama was one of some mental turmoil. I had to give up my profession [journalism] and had to go to jail again, then martial law came.'[11]

Dast-e Teh-e Sang also includes two moving elegies for Faiz's friend and comrade Hasan Nasir (1928–1960), titled 'Mulaqat meri' (My encounter) and 'Khatam hui baarish-e sang' (The hail of stones has ended).The scion of an aristocratic family of Hyderabad, Nasir, who was the grandson of Nawab Mohsin-ul-Mulk, chose a life of activism and struggle. He migrated to Pakistan in 1947 and eventually became secretary-general of the Communist Party of Pakistan (later banned in 1951 after the Rawalpindi Conspiracy case). He was arrested in the early years of the Ayub military dictatorship in 1960 and brutally tortured to death in the dungeons of Lahore Fort.

Cuba

During his stay in London, Faiz was invited to many countries. One such invitation was from the president of the newly liberated island nation of Cuba, Fidel Castro, who invited Faiz to visit the country to participate in its national day celebrations. Around the same time, a big Pakistani newspaper had persuaded Faiz to record his impressions of different countries in the form of a travelogue, which the newspaper would serialize. *Safarnama Cuba* (Cuba Travelogue) was published in 1963 in three parts (it was later also published as a slim book). In his typically incisive style, Faiz wrote about his impressions of Cuba and its people and about the history of its liberation struggle, starting with the arrival of Columbus in the Americas. He gave an account of the exploits of Castro and his band of revolutionaries, including Argentinean doctor Ernesto 'Che' Guevara. Towards the end, Faiz described the efforts of the young revolutionary government to build a new nation. Big corporations which had, with the collusion of the previous government, been sucking the Cuban economy dry had been kicked off the island and society was being reorganized along socialist lines.

Back in Pakistan

The Ayub dictatorship was still strong but had decided to loosen some of the restrictions on civil liberties and even allow limited political activity. Faiz, who was very restless in London, decided to return to Pakistan, prompting one exasperated commentator to remark: 'When Faiz ought to stay in Pakistan he comes out, and when he ought to stay out, he goes back.'[12]

Faiz returned to the port city of Karachi where he had decided to settle. A bustling metropolis, Karachi was founded as a sleepy fishing village several hundred years ago. The British, realizing its strategic and economic value, developed it as a port, with the result that by the turn of the last century, Karachi was already the largest wheat- exporting port in the East. It grew exponentially after partition and with the influx of economic migrants of various ethnicities and religions came more cosmopolitan, liberal values. To this day, despite its governance issues, Karachi is more 'westernized' than any other city in Pakistan.

Faiz had always loved the Karachi. The weather was temperate, with sea breezes blowing in the morning and at night. In the 1960s, Karachi was a vibrant, open city which Faiz felt would be conducive to the cultural and literary activities that he loved. There were a variety of hotels, nightclubs, coffeehouses, cinemas, libraries, playgrounds and, of course, the ocean, all of which made Karachi a magnet for both tourists and settlers. In addition, Faiz's old friends, Colonel (Retd) Majeed Malik and his wife Amina lived in Karachi. Faiz had first got to know Colonel Majeed Malik in the 1930s. It was at his encouragement that he had joined the army during the Second World War. Colonel Malik had distinguished himself as a journalist working for the Reuters News Agency before the War. His wife Amina was an educationist. She had visited Faiz regularly in jail in Hyderabad. In addition to these two close friends, Faiz already had a vast circle of admirers in Karachi who knew him through his work as a journalist, his trade-union activities and, more recently, as a recipient of the Lenin Peace Prize. The newspaper which had published his Cuba travelogue had already published the news of his return and had extracted a promise from him for a regular contribution of a poem or an article.

Abdullah Haroon College, Lyari

As soon as Faiz arrived in Karachi, his friend, Dr Shaukat Haroon, the daughter of Sir Abdullah Haroon, businessman, philanthropist and politician whom the Quaid-e Azam, Muhammad Ali Jinnah, had once called 'one of the pillars of the [All-India] Muslim League', delivered a message from her mother, Lady Nusrat Haroon. They wanted Faiz's advice about the Abdullah Haroon School, set up many years before partition by the family to care for and educate orphaned children. No one in the family had the time or energy to oversee it. The school had by then progressed to class 10, but it catered primarily to poor children and the standard of education had deteriorated. Faiz was immediately interested since it was a project close to his heart. He asked for a few weeks to examine the school's affairs before making a commitment and then plunged into the task with his characteristic enthusiasm. He examined the school records closely and also went around the local area of Lyari, one of the most densely populated and poorest areas of Karachi. There were no schools, hospitals or government offices for miles and local families could not afford to send their children to far-off schools.

After a couple of weeks, Faiz advised Lady Haroon that the school be immediately upgraded to a two-year college and in a couple of years to a full-fledged college offering a bachelor's degree. He also recommended the immediate hiring of quality faculty, building of more classrooms and offices and the establishment of a vocational school for technical skills. He agreed to oversee all of this, provided he was given a free hand with no outside interference.

Faiz's suggestions were readily accepted and he was offered the post of principal of the college. He was also appointed vice-president of the Abdullah Haroon Memorial Trust. Lady Haroon came to see Faiz and told him nervously that for the moment, the trust had decided on a salary of Rs 3,000 a month for him but that, as soon as things improved, it would be increased.

True to form, Faiz objected, saying he could not accept such a large salary, and offered to work for Rs 1,200 a month. Later, Dr Shaukat Haroon explained to him that they could not offer the principal less than Rs 1,800 a month, since some of the teachers made that much and the principal could not be paid less than a teacher.

Faiz immediately got down to work. Within a couple of years, the standard of education at the college had improved dramatically. Faiz persuaded some renowned teachers to join him at the college. More than his work at the college, though, were the efforts he made to interest the local people in education. He introduced a variety of extracurricular activities at the college. Whenever any person of note came to Karachi—poet, writer, intellectual, politician—he or she would invariably be invited to the college. Debating and literary societies were set up, a library was built, playing fields were renovated and games and matches with other colleges were organized.

Faiz's other great service to the area was the setting up of the Abdullah Haroon Vocational Institute, where unemployed youths were given technical training in various fields. Faiz was always willing to lend a hand to intelligent young people who had few resources. He also initiated welfare projects within the college, including a small dispensary where the local people could get basic medical care.

Faiz and his family would stay in Karachi for eight years, until 1972 and, like with most places he lived in, he would leave his mark on the city.

Notes

1. Hameed Akhtar, 'Faiz: Shakhsiat ki chand jhalkian', *Afkar*, Faiz number (Karachi: Maktaba Afkar, 1965), p. 200.
2. Syed Sibt-e Hasan, *Sukhan dar Sukhan* (Karachi: Maktaba Daniyal, 2009), pp. 58–9.
3. Qudrat Ullah Shahab, 'B'yaad-e Faiz', in *Adab-e Latif* (Lahore: Maktaba Jadeed Press, 1988), p. 50.
4. Translation by this author.
5. Salima Hashmi, personal recollection.
6. Faiz Ahmed Faiz, 'Guftagoo—Faiz Ahmed Faiz', *Dunyazad*, no. 35 (Karachi: Scheherzade Publications, 2012), p. 51.
7. The full English text (although not a very good translation from the original Urdu) is available at http://pdf.aj-pak.org/downloads/the_lenin_prize_oration.pdf
8. The Lake District at one time or another was home to Wordsworth, Tennyson, Coleridge, Keats, Shelley and many others.
9. V.G. Kiernan, 'Faiz' (tr Sehr Ansari), in *Nuskha hai Wafa* (Lahore: Maktaba Karvaan, 1985), p. 380.
10. Ibadat Barelvi, 'Chand yaadein, chand ta'asurat', *Afkar*, Faiz number (Karachi: Maktaba Afkar, 1965), p. 188.
11. Faiz Ahmed Faiz, 'Faiz az Faiz', in *Nuskha hai Wafa*, p. 310.
12. Ralph Russell, *The Pursuit of Urdu Literature: A Select History* (London: Zed Books, 1992), p. 240. Available at http://www.columbia.edu/itc/mealac/pritchett/00urdu/3mod/faiz_russell_1992.pdf

16
Karachi

Yahan se shehr ko dekho tau halqa dar halqa
Khinchi hai jail ki maanind har aik simt faseel.

Look at the city from here, concentric
Like a prison all horizons are rampart bound.

—Faiz Ahmed Faiz

In later life, Faiz would retain a great affection for Karachi, the city where he lived with his family for eight years. The reasons for this were many, including some deeply personal ones: the weddings of both Salima and Moneeza would take place in Karachi and Faiz's two older grandsons would both be born in the city. In addition, he had a wide circle of admirers in Karachi and was given a royal welcome when he arrived in the city. The Abdullah Haroons, one of Karachi's most respected families, were also close friends of Faiz. In short, he had every reason to feel welcome and happy in Karachi. He also had the opportunity to do work that was close to his heart in a social and political environment that was (by Pakistani standards) relatively free and open. And he loved both the city's temperate weather as well as its tolerant ethos. Karachi had not yet begun to experience the violent convulsions of sporadic violence which would later engulf it. Many of the city's most prominent writers, poets and intellectuals counted him as a friend and admired his work. He was also popular amongst Sindhi-language progressive writers. Faiz had been writing regular columns since his stay in Cuba and a prominent newspaper in Karachi had offered to publish these along with his poetry.

Karachi Arts Council

The promotion of art and culture had been of abiding interest for Faiz. This was a period of rapid growth in Karachi. Many new housing societies were being built, including the Pakistan Employees Cooperative Housing Society (PECHS), where Faiz and his family lived, and the Defence Housing Authority, which were meant for the affluent; Nazimabad, North Nazimabad and Federal B Area, for the middle class; and Liaquatabad and Shah Faisal Colony for workers and labourers.

Faiz was staunchly opposed to this haphazard 'development' of the city and he was not shy about expressing his opinion in lectures, seminars and conferences. While urban development was necessary, given the city's rapidly expanding population, he felt that it needed to take into account the city's rich cultural heritage and to complement it. Rather than razing everything to the ground, development should incorporate the best parts of the past into the present. In addition, he thought that Karachi's shoreline was a great asset which should be appropriately utilized in building up the city. As usual, though, crass commercial interests were riding roughshod over any voice of reason.

As he had done in Lahore, Faiz decided to help rehabilitate the Karachi Arts Council, located at the time in a small building behind the Sindh Assembly, surrounded by an overgrown, unkempt lawn. The council had come into being after partition through the efforts of some concerned citizens, including some highly placed officials. The president of the arts council was always the local commissioner while the vice-president was selected by council members. In 1964, Faiz was appointed the vice-president and immediately set about raising money for a new building, which he soon accomplished. He also invited artists from all over the country to exhibit their works there. Very soon, the new arts council had blossomed into a dynamic organization. It hosted the centenary celebrations of Mirza Asadullah Khan Ghalib. Faiz also made a special effort to showcase Karachi's indigenous people, like the Sheedis and the fishermen community, by holding special events celebrating their dances, folk festivals, and the like. He commissioned documentaries on Ghalib and Iqbal, on Mangho Pir and Lyari and on the Sufi shrines in and around Karachi.

Idara-e Yaadgar-e Ghalib

The establishment of the Idara-e Yaadgar-e Ghalib (Institute of Ghalib Studies) was one of the Faiz's proudest accomplishments in Karachi. The institute was the brainchild of Faiz and one of his close friends, Mirza Zafarul Hasan. They knew each other through a mutual acquaintance—Faiz's old friend, Progressive poet Makhdoom Moheyuddin. About Mirza Zafarul Hasan and Faiz, one commentator wrote: 'Mirza sahib's love [for Faiz] is such that he cannot hear a word against Faiz and if Faiz is being praised somewhere, he preens as if the praise is for him.'[1] Mirza Zafarul Hasan was associated with radio broadcasting and was familiar with organizing literary activities. He had once organized a mock trial of Mirza Hadi Ruswa's acclaimed novel, *Umrao Jaan Ada*, where Faiz was appointed chief justice. He also organized a debate on Ghalib in which Ghalib's admirers and detractors squared off in a public forum. Both of these events remained talked about in Karachi for a long time. Faiz was convinced of Mirza Zafarul Hasan's passion for literature and the arts.

Ghalib's centenary fell in 1969 and events were being held to commemorate him all over the world. Faiz wanted Karachi to be the first city in Pakistan to celebrate Ghalib's centennial. He and Mirza Zafarul Hasan helped set up the Idara-e Yaadgar-e Ghalib and were selected as its first president and first honorary trustee respectively. Most of the notable litterateurs of the city were members and its patrons included some of Karachi's biggest benefactors, including Roshan Ali Bhimjee, the head of Eastern Federal Union (EFU) Insurance, Pakistan's largest insurance company, Mahmoud Haroon, veteran Pakistani politician and chairman of Pakistan's oldest English-language newspaper and Hakim Said, founder of Hamdard Laboratories, Pakistan's oldest and most trusted manufacturer of traditional medicines.

While they had plenty of support from Karachi's affluent, Ghalib lovers decided to raise money on their own through printing and selling special calendars and writing implements. Idara-e Yaadgar-e Ghalib celebrated Ghalib's centenary in style, with seminars, lectures, mushairas and musical evenings aplenty. The noted Pakistani painter Sadequain was commissioned to create special calligraphic murals of Ghalib's poetry. It was also decided to set up a permanent Ghalib library, which would be a resource for Ghalib lovers. It exists to this day.

Faiz and Alys were enjoying their relatively peaceful time in Karachi. Over the country at large, though, and over Karachi as well, the shadow of the military dictatorship still loomed large. Compared to Lahore, Karachi had a relatively liberal political atmosphere and Faiz successfully managed to keep himself apart from politics during his stay. He was well aware, though, of the ongoing struggle in both halves of the country. From 1962, Pakistan's military dictator Ayub Khan had started efforts to legitimize his rule by introducing his own version of 'democracy'. His attempts to muzzle opposition to his rule would be reflected in Faiz's next collection of poetry. But before its publication, Pakistan and India would be at each other's throats.

'Arise from dust, my son': The 1965 war

Faiz's entire life was dedicated to promoting peace and friendship between people and between nations. This did not mean that he was in favour of peace at all costs. When the difficult choice of what to do during the Second World War came up, he calmly examined the situation from both sides and enlisted in the British army in defence of his homeland. And at the end of the War, just as coolly, he gave up a well-paid position in the army to return to teaching when he felt that staying on would mean betraying his principles.

As Pakistan's most illustrious intellectual, he was faced with a similar choice when the 1965 war between India and Pakistan broke out in September. On principle, Faiz was staunchly opposed to war which he knew served little purpose other than to fill the coffers of the war-mongers. It was always the ordinary people on both sides who paid in lives and blood. As someone who had personally participated in India's freedom struggle, he was especially opposed to any enmity between the two neighbours. He knew that ordinary citizens had nothing to gain from India and Pakistan going to war with each other. In addition, for Faiz and others of his generation who had witnessed the carnage of partition with their own eyes, it was very painful to see the war drums being beaten on both sides of the border to encourage more slaughter. It demeaned the blood of the innocents killed in partition and it made the chances of peaceful coexistence that much more difficult. And, of course, it strengthened the hands of neo-imperial powers that retained a keen interest in the riches of the subcontinent.

In the run up to the 1965 war, Faiz was one of the few people who insisted on dialogue instead of hostilities but, of course, such voices were ignored. Once the war had commenced, Faiz was invited by the Government of Pakistan to Islamabad to advise the government on how to proceed. He had already declined to participate in the jingoistic mania pervading the country by refusing to write any patriotic songs or anthems. He later recalled: '[The government] wanted to consult me. I agreed. They wanted to pay me. I said it's my national duty, I don't want any money. They insisted and offered me large sums but I refused. I told them to arrange accommodation and food, that's all'.[2] Talking about his advice to the government, he said, 'I told them that it will not be possible in light of the economic condition of both countries to prolong this war beyond a couple of weeks. But the government refused to listen to us and kept pumping up the war hysteria. I told them to not raise it so high that it would be difficult to bring it back down.'[3]

He was right, since he had based his advice on an analysis of the ground realities. In less than three weeks, both governments accepted mediation from the USSR and USA and a truce was signed in the Soviet city of Tashkent. As Faiz had predicted, the military adventure achieved nothing except wasting precious economic resources and human lives and further poisoning the relationship between the two countries.

Years later, when asked his opinion about the war, Faiz had this to say: 'The first thing is that I didn't initiate the 1965 war, Ayub Khan did that. Nor am I responsible for the 1970 war, Yahya Khan did that. It is true that in the time of war it is obligatory to defend one's country, and something has to be done. However, I had a fundamental disagreement with these wars. There were incompetent and myopic people on both sides who created conditions for the wars. The truth is that I was against (both) wars.'[4]

Refusing to write patriotic songs or anthems to promote the war, Faiz expressed his sentiments in poetry in his heart-rending poem 'Sipahi ka marsiya' (Soldier's elegy) with its iconic opening verse 'Arise from the dust, arise my son'. It is a moving tribute to the fallen on both sides. Faiz's soldier is a Pakistani warrior as well as an Indian hero who fights to defend his motherland and finally succumbs to the insanity of a war not of his own making. For Faiz, 'any soldier killed in a war to defend his land and his nation, is a martyr. And "Sipahi ka marsiya" is for every soldier who has died defending to uphold the banner of the freedom of his land and his nation.'[5]

Also in 1965, the Karachi magazine *Afkar* published its Faiz number. This was long before the time when such commemorative editions began to be published about any and all poets and authors. The editor, Sehba Lakhnavi, included everything about Faiz's poetry and life that he could get his hands on. The issue was well researched and widely acclaimed and became a valuable resource for everyone who wanted to learn more about Faiz. It remains a resource for students, researchers and authors even today.

Father-in-law

Salima and Moneeza were both eventually married in Karachi. Faiz and Alys were devoted to their daughters and Faiz's biggest regret was that because of his imprisonment and periods of exile, he had missed some precious years of their growing up. His letters from jail are filled with these regrets, such as this one (dated 28 August 1951):

> I received your letter dated the 23rd along with pictures of the children. How beautiful are they. And how they have grown. Along with many other regrets, the biggest is that I cannot see them growing up in front of me. Although I have no worries about their upbringing under your supervision. The little part that I can play in their upbringing is to teach them to be happy and to spoil them to their hearts' content so they cannot become selfish, greedy and stingy (and I know this will not happen) and to make them aware what is honorable and what is not.[6]

When, as is still the custom in the Indian subcontinent, someone would offer their 'sympathies' that Faiz and Alys had no male children, they would be told off in no uncertain terms. Faiz was proud of his daughters and would often remark that they were educated, intelligent, ambitious and hardworking. They managed their own households, worked and, importantly for him, earned their bread without 'selling my name; when I see them, my head rises as high as Everest with pride'.[7] At the same time, he also felt, 'Because of my fame, I have become a handicap for my daughters and their husbands. This is one of my heartaches.'[8]

Alys and Faiz were an enlightened and progressive couple. At the same time, in their domestic life, traditional values prevailed. Alys had made sure that both the girls learned conventional Eastern religious and moral values from Faiz's mother, Bebe-ji. So it came as a shock to Alys when Shoaib Hashmi, their older son-in-law-to-be, who was studying in London at the time the Faizes were living there, came to her and asked for permission to marry 'Cheemie' (Salima). Alys knew that they were friends, of course, but she was still taken aback and asked him to meet Faiz. Faiz described the incident years later: 'One day, he [Shoaib] came to see me and said, "you are like my father, if you give your permission, we would like to marry." I glared at him in mock-fury and said, "Boy, you are stepping over your limits. What manner is this of asking for a girl's hand? Do you have a mother, an elder? Go tell them to ask us for her hand, we'll think about it."'[9]

When asked about his insistence on the conventional way, Faiz said, 'Listen, I liked Shoaib and so did Cheemie but there is a way of doing everything in an established social system other than just the boy and girl liking each other. The parents should agree as well. In society, waywardness causes disharmony. Some basic principles cannot be ignored and for a young couple, what better than to have their elders' blessing as well as love for each other. This is what marriage means in socialism.'[10]

When asked about the wedding of his younger daughter Moneeza, Faiz said: 'By that time, they were smarter. The whole rehearsal took just a few minutes, it was quite easy.'[11]

Both Moneeza and Salima's elder sons were born in Karachi under the supervision of one of Faiz's oldest and dearest friends, Dr Shaukat Haroon, whom the girls affectionately called 'Shaukee khala' (Aunt Shaukee).

'The moon of your countenance'

Dr Shaukat Haroon was the daughter of Sir Abdullah Haroon, one of the leading lights of the All India Muslim League as well as a close personal friend of Quaid-e Azam Muhammad Ali Jinnah.

Dr Shaukat Haroon had graduated from Lady Hardinge Medical College in Delhi in 1942. She had later married an eminent lawyer from whom she had two children. In 1949, her husband was killed in an air accident but instead of relying on her father or her husband's inheritance, she went to England to study further and came back to Karachi to work and raise her children on her own.

Faiz met Shaukat, or 'Shaukee' as she was affectionately known in the family, in 1953 in the Karachi jail hospital, where he was transferred from Hyderabad jail when he fell ill during his imprisonment. She was friends with Begum Amina Majeed Malik, who sent her a message to take special care of Faiz since he was so forlorn in those days. They became friends and stayed so for the rest of their lives. She was devoted to Faiz and he, in turn, cared deeply for her. When he first met her at the hospital where he was under treatment, Faiz was so taken with her that he wrote two ghazals in her honour. It is surmised that his famous poem from *Zindan Nama* titled 'Ae habeeb-e amber dast' (O friend with amber perfumed hands) is also about Dr Shaukat Haroon.

Moneeza's husband, Humair Hashmi, remembers Shaukat: 'She was a tall, fair lady with a no-nonsense air. Moneeza would often visit Karachi when she was studying in college. She became "Shaukee khala" to Moneeza and was her surrogate mother, mentor and confidante. Whenever Faiz saw them together, a sense of joy and fulfilment could be felt in his demeanour. [Shaukat] normally wore saris, had a neatly cut and elegantly styled hairdo and smoked expensive cigarettes, always in long, beautifully carved cigarette-holders. She always smelled wonderful and lavishly gifted perfumes and saris to her acquired "niece".'[12]

Dr Shaukat Haroon died unexpectedly of a sudden heart attack at the age of forty-nine. She had just seen Faiz off at Karachi airport where he had boarded a plane to Lahore to attend a mushaira in his honour. He was sitting with friends in Lahore when he got a phone call and went up to receive it. When he came back, it was as if he was sleepwalking and mumbling in disbelief.

He was devastated and became extremely quiet for several days. This same quiet had engulfed him after his mother's death and, again, after his beloved comrade Sajjad Zaheer's death. A few days later, three elegies emerged from his imagination, all included in his collected works under *Marseeyay* (Elegies). They are titled 'Door jaa kar qareeb ho jitnay' ('The nearer you are from afar'), 'Chand niklay kisi jaanib teri zebaai ka' ('Let the moon of your countenance rise somewhere') and 'Kab tak dil kee khair manain' ('How long must we guard our heart'). The last two were sung beautifully by Pakistan's renowned singer, Farida Khanum, also an ardent admirer of Faiz's.

Moneeza remembers: 'It was 1968, summer I think. I remember because I was pregnant and she was my gynaecologist, she was supposed to deliver the baby. We were all shattered when we heard and Abba most of all. He was inconsolable for days.'[13]

In the Skies over the Valley of Sinai

The might of Pakistan's military dictator Ayub Khan had already started declining after the brief war of 1965. Ordinary people, crushed under the twin burdens of military dictatorship and spiralling inflation, were restless and angry and they were being egged on by, among others, Ayub's brilliant and mercurial former foreign minister, Zulfiqar Ali Bhutto. However, the one military dictatorship fell only to be succeeded by another, when General Yahya Khan imposed a second martial law right after Ayub Khan suddenly resigned. Once again, the country was under the shadow of tyranny, prompting Faiz to write his melancholy 'Aaj ke din na poocho mere dosto/door kitnay hain khushiyaan mananay ke din' (Today, do not ask friends/how distant are the days of merriment).

In 1970, while still in Karachi, Faiz was offered editorship of the weekly *Lail-o-Nahar* (Night and Day), which was being published again after a long break. It remained in publication for a year and a half. Faiz had returned to journalism after a long break and Pakistan's political and social landscape had changed considerably. Faiz worked hard as usual, in particular on the thirty-nine editorials he wrote for the paper. It was a tumultuous time in Pakistan's history and most of his editorials were about the election campaign of 1970, its importance after more than a decade of military dictatorship and most particularly, the growing resentment and hostility between the eastern and western parts of the country. His editorial in the last week of 1970 pointedly referred to the dangers of ethnic and communal politics being stoked both by the Pakistan People's Party headed by Zulfiqar Ali Bhutto as well as East Pakistan's Awami League headed by Sheikh Mujibur Rahman:

> The Awami League and the People's Party should remember that in spite of elections, there is still a martial law government in the country...it is therefore necessary and prudent that the Awami League should consider the sentiments of the people of West Pakistan and the People's Party should lend a sympathetic ear to the grievances of the people of East Pakistan and a middle ground should be found. Politicians in West Pakistan should realize that no force in the world can turn East Pakistan's majority into a minority...[the Awami League's] logic seems to be that since you considered us a colony and looted us for so long, we will now do the same to you. This is a very dangerous trend...this will result in strengthening the separatist mindset in both halves of the country and the result will be a division of the country into two...How wise and patriotic is it to waste time and energy over insignificant matters while ignoring the very foundation on which the progress and security of the entire country depends.[14]

In 1971, two Faiz books were published. Faiz's letters to Alys from prison were published by none other than Mirza Zafarul Hasan under the title *Saleebain Mere Darichay Main* (Crucifixes in My Window). Alys had first raised the idea of publishing these letters while Faiz was still in prison in 1953. No doubt, part of the reason was financial, since she was under tremendous financial stress trying to raise her two young daughters by herself. At that time, Faiz had written to her: 'It would be better to not ask me about publishing [the letters]. I'm afraid they will appear ridiculous in print...How I wish ASB[15] was still around to decide about such matters. At any rate, if you decide to publish them, they should be in Urdu. Unless I take great care, my English writing appears too ornamental and awry.'[16]

Despite Faiz's characteristic misgivings, these letters form the perfect complement to his prison poetry, considered by many to be the apex of his poetic achievements. They provide the backdrop to the creation of some of the best-loved poems, both in the context of what was going on around him and, even more importantly, what was going on in his mind as he composed the poems.

The other important publication to appear in 1971 was Faiz's fifth collection of poetry, *Sar-e Wadi-e Sina* (In the Skies over the Valley of Sinai). Faiz had originally titled the collection *Lahoo ka Suragh* (The Mark of Blood) after the moving poem he had written in 1965 to mark the death of a young protestor against Ayub Khan's regime. Faiz's younger son-in-law Humair Hashmi recalls: 'His new book of poetry had just come out and he mentioned that he had decided to name it "Lahoo ka Suragh". I told him it sounded ridiculous, like an Urdu detective novel! He was quite amused by my reaction and asked me what I thought it should be called. I told him why not a Persian name like "Dast-e Teh-e Sang", his last collection? And I suggested "Sar-e Wadi-e Sina" which was also the title of one of the poems in the collection and he agreed.'[17]

Sar-e Wadi-e Sina contained several poems about Palestine inspired by the 1967 Arab-Israeli war. It was dedicated to his friend, the Soviet writer Maryam ('Mira') Salganik. The other major theme in the collection was the holocaust that was about to engulf Pakistan and, like the last one in 1947, this one, too, would tear the country apart.

Notes

1. Mazher Jameel, *Zikr-e Faiz* (Karachi: Culture Department, Government of Sindh, 2013), p. 616.
2. Ayub Mirza, *Hum ke Thehre Ajnabi* (Islamabad: Dost Publications, 1996), p. 236.
3. Ibid pp. 237–8.
4. Faiz Ahmed Faiz, 'Guftagoo—Faiz Ahmed Faiz', *Dunyazad*, no. 35 (Karachi: Scheherzade Publications, 2012), p. 66.
5. Agha Nasir, *Hum Jeetay Jee Masroof Rahay* (Lahore: Sang-e-Meel Publications, 2011), p. 166.
6. Faiz Ahmed Faiz, *Saleebain Mere Darichay Main* (Karachi: Maktaba Daniyal, 2011), pp. 32–3.
7. Mazher Jameel, *Zikr-e Faiz* (Karachi: Culture Department, Government of Sindh, 2013), p. 629.

8. Ibid.
9. Ibid.
10. Ibid.
11. Ibid.
12. Humair Hashmi, personal recollection.
13. Moneeza Hashmi, personal recollection.
14. Faiz Ahmed Faiz, Editorial, *Lail-o-Nahar* (Karachi), 28 December–3 January 1971.
15. Ahmad Shah Bokhari 'Patras', Faiz's old friend and teacher.
16. Faiz, *Saleebain Mere Darichay Main,* pp. 9–10.
17. Humair Hashmi, personal recollection.

17
Bloodstains

Kab nazar main aayegi be-daagh sabzay ki bahaar
Khoon k dhabbay dhulain ge kitni barsaton keba'ad.

When will the gaze find Spring's verdant carpet, unmarked
How many rains will wash away the bloodstains.

—Faiz Ahmed Faiz

During the Ayub Khan military government, the country's education ministry formed a standing committee on culture. Faiz was appointed its chairman. Culture and its various forms had always been of special interest to Faiz and he accepted the responsibility eagerly. The committee was tasked with conducting a comprehensive cultural survey of both the western and eastern wings of Pakistan and submitting a report to the government to formulate an official cultural policy.

For Faiz, the question of a Pakistani culture was a central one.

When did Pakistan's history as a nation begin? Did it, as claimed in some quarters, begin with the arrival of the boy conqueror Muhammad bin Qasim in Sindh? Or did it begin with the rise and fall of the Mughal empire in India? What about Mohenjo-daro and the ancient Indus Valley civilization and other remnants of the civilizations that existed in the area that is present-day Pakistan? Where did they fit in? Were they not a part of Pakistan's culture and history?

According to Faiz, 'culture' is actually the sum total of a community's way of life: how it lives, what it eats, what it wears, how it celebrates, how it mourns. In addition to this overt aspect of culture, the hidden or covert side consists of customs, traditions, superstitions and beliefs; how the community's (or nation's) members relate to each other, their beliefs, hopes, dreams, or what might be called the collective value system of a society, which reflects and reinforces their external appearances. A central aspect of this way of life is the language that ordinary people use to communicate with each other.

Talking of Pakistani culture, Faiz said: 'When Pakistan came into being, its geographic boundaries were determined. The same cannot be said of its historical borders. Where should this new Pakistani nation begin its history? From the ancient civilizations of Mohenjo-daro and Harappa? From the arrival of Muhammad Bin Qasim in Sindh, the Mughal era, from Sir Syed Ahmad Khan, the War of 1857 or the Pakistan Resolution? This is a crucial point but there is no need for confusion. The central elements of any civilization are its people. Therefore all those things in which a people feel pride are their civilization.'[1]

Faiz drew attention to the multicoloured and unusually vibrant canvas that was Pakistani culture with its multiplicities of language, arts, music and traditions. And to those who were afraid that paying attention to Pakistan's remote past would somehow dilute or contaminate its present, Faiz pointed out that moribund aspects of past culture are automatically excluded from the present. Only those things survive which have relevance to the present, a prime example being the various languages spoken in Pakistan, which thrived because there were still people to speak them.

In his characteristically lucid manner, Faiz talked about the two streams of Pakistani culture: 'The first stream is the folk heritage of Punjabi, Sindhi, Balochi and Pashtoon people and the second is our classical traditions including Urdu, Persian and Arabic. Unfortunately, our people are familiar with either one or the other (leading to much confusion). Another problem is that after partition, English medium schools proliferated like weeds and so we had a whole generation of people who knew nothing about either our folk heritage or our classical traditions.'[2]

Dreams are wiser than men

General elections were held for the first time in the history of Pakistan, on 7 December 1970 under the military government of General Yahya Khan, who had deposed Ayub Khan in a bloodless coup after a series of popular demonstrations. The polls in East Pakistan, originally scheduled for October, were delayed by disastrous floods and rescheduled for December and January 1971.

East Pakistan, although much smaller in size, had a bigger population than the western wing of the country; there were a total of 56,941,500 registered voters in the country, out of which 31 million were from East Pakistan, while less than 26 million were from West Pakistan. Resentment against the perceived economic (and military) domination of the Eastern wing by the West was at its peak. It had been building for decades and, in fact, had started right after partition, when the Quaid-e Azam had announced the elevation of Urdu as the national language, relegating Bengali—the language spoken by a majority of the country's population—to regional status. In the run-up to the 1970 elections, the Awami League, led by Sheikh Mujibur Rehman, and the National Awami Party of the 'Red Maulana' Bhashani, had skilfully exploited the resentment of the East Pakistani people into a national movement for greater autonomy from West Pakistan.

The results of the election saw the Awami League win 160 seats in the 300-seat National Assembly, giving it a clear majority. Zulfiqar Ali Bhutto's recently formed Pakistan People's Party won the majority of the seats in West Pakistan with eighty-one seats, mainly in the Punjab and Bhutto's native Sindh. His party slogan of 'Roti, kapra aur makaan' ('Bread, clothes and shelter') had resonated strongly with Pakistan's poor and middle classes. He was the first politician in Pakistan's history to speak directly about the concerns of the ordinary man. The voter turnout was 63.1 per cent, the highest in the history of the country.

The Awami League did not win a single seat in West Pakistan and Bhutto's Pakistan People's Party likewise had no presence in East Pakistan. While Sheikh Mujibur Rehman and his Awami League were entitled to form a central government in Pakistan, the fact that they had no seats in West Pakistan gave Bhutto and the West Pakistani leadership, including the army, the excuse that they had 'no mandate'. Despite pleas from saner voices, including Faiz's, on both sides, who foresaw the bloodbath that was imminent, Bhutto coined the slogan 'Idhar hum, udhar tum' ('We over here, you over there'), fanning the flames of hatred. Under the circumstances, a compromise proved elusive and in March 1971, the Pakistan army began its infamous Operation Searchlight to crush all nationalist opposition and 'pacify' the population of East Pakistan. Shortly thereafter, Sheikh Mujibur Rehman declared Bangladesh's independence from Pakistan. The war which would claim the lives of some 3 million Bengalis would go on for nine more months and would end in the unconditional surrender of all West Pakistani forces in Bangladesh. With it would end the Quaid-e Azam's dream less than twenty-five years after it came into existence. Bangladesh's independence would also shake the basic ideology of Pakistan to its foundations.

As for Faiz, a friend described his state in those harrowing days. Faiz had invited him to a hotel in Rawalpindi where he was staying: 'The room was silent. The lights were off. A soft voice called out "Who is it?" I said, "Faiz sahib, where are you?""Bhai, come over here". He was lying flat on the bed, hiding his head under the sheet. The East Pakistan surrender was complete. I said, "Faiz sahib, have some hope." He replied, "Bhai, there is a constructive aspect in every destructive act but to destroy your own home like this...the agony is unbearable. This should never have happened. That we would live to see Pakistan defiled like this, it's unthinkable."'[3]

Faiz had many friends in East Pakistan. He had been there several times and was on friendly terms with journalists, trade-union activists, writers and poets. Many of these friends were massacred in the bloodshed, since writers, poets, teachers, journalists and political activists were specifically targeted by the Pakistan army and its proxy militias. Faiz had foreseen the bloodbath and had written his chilling poem 'Hazr karo mere tan se' (Fear my being) in March 1971 specifically about East Pakistan. Several more poems about the heart-rending slaughter in East Pakistan followed in 1971. There were millions, in both East and West Pakistan who, like Faiz, were appalled at the fraternal genocide taking place in front of their eyes. Others, though, like members of Al Shams and Al Badr, the Pakistan army proxy militias, were not impressed with Faiz's compassion. They would have preferred that Faiz write paeans to their exploits against the Mukti Bahini, (the Bengali 'Liberation Army'). The chorus of voices against Faiz rose high enough for some of his friends in interior Sindh to take him into 'protective custody' and he remained their guest for about six weeks.

Pakistan National Council of the Arts

After the fall of Dhaka in December 1971, Zulfiqar Ali Bhutto took charge of Pakistan at the head of his Pakistan People's Party. Pakistan, now reduced to just its western wing, was in a shambles. The gloom and despondency pervading the country was palpable and the successful independence struggle of East Pakistan, now Bangladesh, had emboldened separatist sentiments in all the minority provinces of the country. There was a real danger that what remained of the country would come apart at the seams.

Faiz was heartbroken at the wanton bloodshed. Having been in the thick of the struggle for independence from the British less than twenty-five years earlier, it was extremely painful for him to see the country torn in half. For people like Faiz, the wounds of partition had just begun to heal and this new one was unbearable. Faiz did not want to live in Pakistan any longer and applied through a friend, a senior member of Bhutto's cabinet, for permission to leave the country. Instead, he was summoned to Islamabad for a personal meeting with Bhutto, who made an impassioned plea to him to stay on in Pakistan. Bhutto was an extremely intelligent man and a shrewd politician. He knew that Pakistan was teetering on the brink and the news of someone like Faiz leaving the country at this juncture would be disastrous to the country's image. Bhutto reminded Faiz of the 90,000 prisoners of war still in Indian jails, the economic challenges facing the traumatized nation and the fact that for the first time in Pakistan's history, a democratically elected government was at the nation's helm. How would it look, he asked, if someone like Faiz, who had spent a lifetime preaching hope, faith and self-reliance, left the country at this point? There would be no restriction on Faiz travelling in and out of the country but he had to stay in Pakistan. His country and his government needed him. Bhutto knew of Faiz's passion for culture and the arts and offered him the post of advisor to the government on cultural affairs.[4]

Faiz knew Bhutto was right and agreed to his request. This was, in fact, part of the work he had already started under the Ayub Khan government. A senior official in Ayub Khan's government had called a committee in the summer of 1968 under the aegis of the ministry of education, in which arts councils, arts institutions and representatives from all over Pakistan had taken part. The conference had convened a Standing Committee on Art and Culture and Faiz had been selected its chairman. Faiz and his committee members eventually travelled the length and breadth of (both East and West) Pakistan and held discussions with over 300 poets, writers, artists and cultural experts. Their comprehensive report for promotion of art and culture was submitted to the government six months later, by which time the Ayub government was counting its last days, and the report was consequently shelved.

After his new appointment as cultural advisor, Faiz's first act was to establish a new national institution by the name of Pakistan National Council of the Arts (PNCA) with himself as chairman. Islamabad, Pakistan's new capital, was undergoing a period of expansion. A piece of land was allocated for the new arts council and Faiz busied himself with formulating plans for its development. He threw himself into the task with his characteristic energy, using the same report they had submitted to the earlier government as the blueprint. His first priority was developing an outline for a national theatre. A new drama theatre was built in the garrison city of Rawalpindi, adjoining Islamabad. The most work went into developing the 'folklore and cultural research wing' of the PNCA. With dedicated researchers and artists from all over Pakistan, Faiz's team combed the length and breadth of the country to find examples of ancient cultural artefacts for preservation and display. This included samples of recordings of local dialects and languages, as well as folk songs and tales from all over the country. Many of these folk songs and anthems were recorded by the most popular artists of the day to be presented to the public and preserved for posterity in an extensive audio archive. All of this was accomplished under the auspices of another newly created institution, the Lok Virsa [Folk Heritage] Museum, which remains the largest such collection in Pakistan. An important aspect of the work was to obtain, catalogue and store precious artefacts from Pakistan's past to make sure that they were not stolen and smuggled abroad to be sold to international art collectors, something that had been going on for years. This idea had come to Faiz when he had first met Pablo Neruda in 1962 in the Soviet Union: 'Other than his own country, he [Neruda] loved the ancient civilizations of Latin

America, which had been annihilated by foreign invaders. His life's most precious possession was the collection of ancient artifacts he had accumulated at his home.'[5]

A National Art Gallery under the aegis of the PNCA was another accomplishment. For the first time in the country's history, works of art from all over the country were solicited for display in the capital. A performing arts department was also created, with folk artists from all over Pakistan especially invited to perform not just nationally, but internationally as well. Faiz also began the work of setting up Pakistan's first academy of letters for the country's writers and poets, an institution that is still running strong.

International University of Taxila

The International University of Taxila was one of Faiz's ideas while he was still at the PNCA. The idea was first proposed at an international UNESCO conference held in the Indonesian city of Yogyakarta. Faiz was a part of the Pakistani delegation, which, along with presenting an overview of cultural activities in Pakistan at the conference, also proposed the creation of an international university at Taxila, close to Islamabad. The ancient city of Taxila, later designated a UNESCO World Heritage site, had once been one of the foremost centres of higher learning in this part of the world, with students from far and wide coming to study under the tutelage of renowned teachers and scholars. Faiz briefed the conference about the vast Buddhist ruins which still existed at the site and proposed that an international university be constructed there for the study of Buddhism and the Pali language. This would help Pakistan unearth and conserve more ancient artefacts, as well as significantly promote international tourism. It would also help curb the illegal theft and smuggling of many of these priceless relics abroad.

Moreover, it would help strengthen and grow Pakistan's ties with neighbouring countries such as Nepal, Sri Lanka, Burma, Thailand, China and Japan, where Buddhism was widely practised.

Faiz's suggestion was enthusiastically received and unanimously accepted. Faiz submitted a report to the Pakistani government in 1974, detailing the proposal as well as UNESCO's wholehearted support for it. Despite Faiz's hard work, though, the idea never materialized.

'Slings and arrows' and Punjabi poetry

The Bhutto government had proclaimed socialism as its official policy and had initially gathered most Leftist and progressive Pakistanis into its fold. After he came to power, though, and especially after he sent the army into Baluchistan to quell the restive population in the aftermath of the 1971 war, many Leftist and nationalist leaders, especially those who belonged to provinces other than the Punjab (the majority province) and Sindh (Bhutto's home province) parted ways with the Pakistan People's Party. Faiz did not. He had never been in favour of fanning the flames of further conflict, preferring always to search for a compromise solution. Faiz's stance, as in the past, was seen by some as a betrayal of socialist principles and, as before, he was accused of being a coward, a collaborator with the government, more concerned about his job than his principles.

Faiz, who never responded to personal attacks, had already answered these accusations numerous times in the past. He had never been afraid to express exactly what he was feeling in his poetry and his poems like 'Mere dard ko jo zabaan milay' (If my pain could find a voice) and 'Paon se lahoo ko dho daalo' (Wash the blood from your feet) from this time continued this tradition. If he did not 'toe the party line', so to speak, it was because he never had, even when he had been accused by his Progressive friends in 1947 of having 'sold out' to the Muslim League after *Subh-e azadi* first came out.

A common grouse against Faiz had always been that although he was a Punjabi, he never wrote much Punjabi poetry. In fact, he did write a few Punjabi poems but was never satisfied with them and admitted: 'One reason that I have never written [poetry] in Punjabi is the unattainably high standard that has been set by our classical Punjabi [Sufi] poets like Bulleh Shah, Waris Shah, Baba Farid and Shah Hussain. And it's not enough to just be familiar with the language…you also have to know its mood. I never paid much attention to Punjabi during my education.'[6]

A collection of Faiz's Punjabi poems, titled *Raat di Raat* (All

Night), was published in 1975 from Lahore[7], but this actually contained just a few original Punjabi poems, the rest being translations from Urdu done by the book's compilers. In the foreword, Faiz warmly praised the compilers for their efforts, but later in life remained steadfast in his view that he did not have enough command over the Punjabi language to write Punjabi poetry: 'I do not have as firm a grasp of the classical Punjabi poetry tradition as I do over the Urdu tradition. And now the configuration of my brain and mind has become such that it's suitable only for Urdu poetry.'[8]

Nevertheless, Faiz's poetic brilliance shines through even in Punjabi poems like 'Rabba sacchiya' (True master). Faiz's good friend and renowned Punjabi poet Ustad Daman, upon reading another of Faiz's Punjabi poems, commented though: 'What a wonderful Punjabi poem Faiz has said in Urdu.'

'Parting is such sweet sorrow'

In December 1973, Faiz was invited to the Soviet republic of Kazakhstan for the fifth conference of Afro-Asian writers, the organization that he had helped found. A large writers delegation from India was also invited, including Faiz's dear friend and former comrade, Syed Sajjad Zaheer. The conference was to be a joyful reunion of old friends, some of whom were meeting for the first time after partition. Many of the writers had been members of the All-India Progressive Writers' Association and knew each other well. Unfortunately, Faiz's joy at meeting Sajjad Zaheer would be short-lived, since he had a heart attack during the conference and passed away. The conference thus became a memorial service for Sajjad Zaheer. The Indian delegation chartered a special flight to take his remains back to Delhi for burial. Faiz accompanied it and, on the way, composed his heart-rending tribute to his old friend 'Na ab ham saath sair-e gul karenge' (No longer will we stroll the garden together). It was a huge loss for Faiz, the end of one of the journeys of his youth which had started in 1935 in Amritsar.

Upon his return from Delhi, Faiz learned that the Pakistan parliament had given its final approval for the official establishment of the PNCA. It had been placed under the chairmanship of the minister of education and Faiz appointed its director general. Sensing that he was being sidelined again for political purposes and already weary of Islamabad's 'court intrigues', Faiz went to Prime Minister Bhutto and requested permission to relocate to Lahore, citing as a reason the fact that Lahore was where both his daughters and his grandchildren lived. He was appointed 'special advisor' to the PNCA and permission was granted for him to return to Lahore. In Lahore, he founded a new institution for the study and compilation of classical music with the help of his friend, music maestro Khwaja Khurshid Anwar, and in the same building, created a small art gallery where painters and artists from all over the country were invited to display their works.

Sigh of relief

Faiz lived in Islamabad as the head of the PNCA for approximately four years, from 1972 to 1976. It was the first time in Pakistan's history that he was being feted and honoured by a Pakistani government. In addition, his salary was reasonable, Islamabad was a quiet, green city at the foot of the Margalla mountains, he was doing something he loved and felt he was making a difference. Alys had also found a position with UNICEF (the United Nations Children's Fund) and was assisting Faiz in his cultural projects. They had started building a house in Lahore and more grandchildren were on the way. Moneeza's younger son, Adeel, was born in 1973 and Salima's daughter, Mira, came along in 1974. Around the same time, one of the Urdu newspapers started a whisper campaign against Faiz, citing as its chief grievance the fact that the People's Party government had handed over culture to a 'communist'. By this time, Faiz had discovered the headaches of being close to power. His old friend Sibt-e Hasan later wrote: 'Whenever Faiz would come to Karachi, we could tell he was unhappy. It was not his nature to complain but he was tired of government officials who would smile and say one thing to his face and then try and create hurdles in what he was doing. He would spend half his time sitting in government offices. On top of that, he felt constricted by his official position and could not speak up or write poetry properly...he knew his poetry was being suffocated.'[9] According to Sibt-e Hasan, Faiz's four years in

Islamabad were 'poetically barren'. Faiz often felt that he had been much freer in prison, where he could think or write whatever he wished.

Moving to Lahore, therefore, was a blessing and relief for Faiz. He created a Music Research Cell in collaboration with his friend, Khwaja Khurshid Anwar, and got busy recording and archiving Pakistan's classical and folk music. This was also the first time that he had had a chance to spend an extended period of time with his family and the sense of regret that he had often felt while Salima and Moneeza were growing up was now mitigated, since he was amongst his grandchildren. He would often remark humorously that he had nothing to do; that he was just getting a pension. He was now also a world- renowned literary personality and received invitations to mushairas and literary gathering from all over Pakistan, invitations he rarely refused. He would make a special effort to show up at students' gatherings and workers' or trade-union rallies or meetings.

To Bangladesh

In 1974, Faiz, as chairman of the PNCA, accompanied an official delegation to Bangladesh along with Prime Minister Bhutto. He was looking forward eagerly to the trip; to seeing his old friends and old haunts, having conversations and making amends for all that had happened just a few years before. As it happened, the trip was a painful reminder of how quickly the two nations had drifted apart. Talking about it later, Faiz said: 'Nothing happened, we came back the same way we had gone...when we came back [to Dhaka after touring other cities], it was if there was a curfew, the roads were deserted, no one in sight. [Bangladeshi leader] Mujeeb embraced me warmly and said, "Faiz bhai, write something." I told him I have written plenty but he insisted, "Faiz bhai, write something about us too." I told him I would. And on the plane, on the way back, a poem came to me.'[10]

The poem was his iconic 'Hum ke thehre ajnabi' ('We, who became strangers'), which became popular worldwide. It accurately expressed the sentiments of Faiz and many people in Pakistan about the upheaval that had torn the nation asunder just a few years earlier.

Two more books

Earlier, in December 1973, Faiz's old friend and admirer Mirza Zafarul Hasan had persuaded him to allow the publication of another book of his collected prose works, *Mataa-e Lauh-o Qalam* (*Riches of Pen and Paper*).

It consisted of four parts: the first contained interviews, speeches and essays by Faiz; the second consisted of letters, opinions and forewords by him; the third part was scripts of radio plays as well as radio and TV speeches; and the last consisted of some essays written about Faiz. As usual, Faiz had been reluctantly persuaded to allow this material to be published and he wrote in the preface that perhaps 'one or two things might be worth a look'. The book comprises a valuable resource for researchers, though, and contains Faiz's usual penetrating insights into a variety of subjects, some presented in an unusual format like that of a play.

In 1975, Faiz had compiled a travelogue of the Soviet Union at the insistence of friends. He called it *Mah-o Saal-e Aashnai* (Months and Years of Intimacy). The book consists of both his impressions of the land of the October Revolution, recorded with a journalist's eye, and a reflection of the socialist dream as seen through the eyes of a believer. The journalistic impressions become particularly acute when Faiz describes the lands and civilization of the Central Asian republics with their Muslim heritage, which Faiz shared.

A special treat for Faiz-lovers is a poem that Faiz wrote specifically at the request of Soviet writers to celebrate the anniversary of the October Revolution of 1917, which had led to the birth of the USSR. That poem, titled 'Murgh-e bismil ki maanind shab tilmilayi' (Evening writhed like a wounded bird) is not included in any of the Faiz published collections but is available in *Mah-o Saal-e Aashnai*. In addition, the book contains Faiz's translations of several noted Soviet and international poets, including Nazim Hikmet and Rasul Gamzatov.

Faiz was happier in Lahore amongst his friends and family than he had been anywhere in the world. Pakistan's next convulsion though, was just around the corner as was the next twist in Faiz's life.

Notes

1. Mazher Jameel, *Zikr-e Faiz* (Karachi: Culture Department, Government of Sindh, 2013), p. 641.
2. I.A. Rehman, 'Faiz, mehroom tabqaat ki awaz', in Sheema Majeed (comp.), *Baaten Faiz Say* (Lahore: Rohtas Books, 1990), pp. 42–3.
3. Ayub Mirza, *Faiz Nama* (Lahore: Classic Publishers, 2003), p. 302.
4. Ahmad Saleem, *Faiz: Yaadein, Baatein* (Lahore: Sang-e-Meel Publications, 2011), pp. 33–5.
5. Faiz Ahmed Faiz, *Mah-o Saal-e Aashnai* (Karachi: Maktaba Daniyal, 1980), p. 59.
6. Rehman, 'Faiz, mehroom tabqaat ki awaz', p. 43.
7. Faiz Ahmed Faiz, *Raat di Raat* (Lahore: People's Publishing House, 1975).
8. Nusrat Chaudhry, *Faiz ki Sha'eri: Ek Mutale'a* (Lahore: Nigarshat, 1987), p. 95.
9. Syed Sibt-e Hasan, *Sukhan dar Sukhan* (Karachi: Maktaba-e Daniyal, 2009), p. 99.
10. Mirza, *Faiz Nama*, p. 315.

18

Wanderer-I

> Nor does anyone know what it is that he will earn on the morrow: Nor does anyone know in what land he is to die.
>
> —Quran 31:34

By 1976, Faiz was back in Lahore. He was glad to be away from the suffocating 'court intrigues' of Islamabad and amidst his family and old friends. He was still formally associated with the Pakistan National Council of the Arts (PNCA) but, as he jokingly remarked to a friend, 'I'm on a pension'. In addition to giving him a chance to spend time with his children and grandchildren, something he had always longed to do, this was also a time when he travelled all over Pakistan to attend literary gatherings, mushairas and all kinds of meetings. He was especially keen to speak at students' gatherings and workers' meetings and there was no shortage of invitations since he was now a world-renowned poet and literary figure.

On Pakistan's political horizon though, the storm clouds were already gathering. Zulfiqar Ali Bhutto had ridden to power on the back of a popular movement against the Ayub military government. In the process, Quaid-e Azam's Pakistan had been dismembered and the 'two-nation' theory which formed the bedrock of Pakistan's founding lay in tatters. The bloody 1971 war and its aftermath had emboldened the separatist elements in all the minority provinces of Pakistan to agitate against the 'hegemony' of the Punjab, and there was a real danger that the remainder of Pakistan would succumb to civil war and anarchy. It was under these circumstances that a chastened Pakistan army invited Bhutto and his Pakistan People's Party (PPP) to form the government. Even though the PPP had majority electoral support in just two of the country's four remaining provinces (Bhutto's native Sindh and the Punjab), he was a shrewd and intelligent man and his motto of 'Islamic socialism' was carefully calculated to appeal to everyone. Once in government, though, he quickly abandoned his popular mantle, preferring to rely on the time-tested method of dispensing political patronage as a means of garnering votes. The time was ripe for an overhaul of Pakistan's antiquated social and political system but Bhutto, himself a patrician feudal lord from Sindh, was not the man for the job.

Soon after he took office, he dismissed the elected Government of Baluchistan, Pakistan's largest province, and sent in the army to pacify the restive population. This was followed in rapid succession by a number of reactionary measures, which blatantly violated his campaign promises of democracy and freedom: muzzling trade unions, cracking down on all political activity opposed to his government, declaring members of the Ahmadiyya community non-Muslims. Predictably, Bhutto's popular support quickly melted away. His heavy-handed and haphazard 'nationalization' of key industries also earned him the undying enmity of Pakistan's 'captains of industry', while his half-hearted attempts at 'land reform' led nowhere. As Pakistan's economy and industry stagnated in the worldwide recession of the early 1970s, Bhutto came to rely more and more on the repressive apparatus of the state to keep dissent against his regime in check.

By 1976, when Faiz returned to Lahore, political agitation against the PPP government was beginning to gather steam. Faiz had already sensed the mood in the country and had wisely distanced himself from association with the government. As the anti-PPP movement escalated, though, Faiz was vilified as a government supporter. Years later, his detractors complained that he had not actively spoken out against the repression of the Bhutto government in its last years. While there may have been a grain of truth in this, Faiz likely felt that the worst civilian government, answerable to the ballot box and the people, was still better than the best military dictatorship, answerable to none. In addition, Faiz had realized early on that the PPP government would not be able to deliver on its extravagant campaign promises but had decided to persist in Islamabad until parliament passed the Pakistan National Council of the Arts Act, which would make the PNCA a permanent entity in Pakistan's cultural landscape.

In the meantime, he continued to do whatever he could to help those struggling for a more just and socially progressive Pakistan.

Faiz had personally helped leaders of the North-West Frontier Province's Marxist–Leninist Mazdoor Kissan Party (MKP), including his friend Afzal Bangash, to hide at his elder daughter's house in Lahore when they had to go underground during the peasant uprising in Hashtnagar. Faiz's elder daughter Salima remembers:

> They both came here [Afzal Bangash and Sher Ali Bacha] to this house after Abba called from Islamabad to tell us they were coming. They were supposed to meet Mustafa Khar [PPP governor of the Punjab] in connection with the peasant uprising in Malakand. All the servants were sworn to secrecy and no one was allowed to go in the room except my mother-in-law who served them food. None of these things are on record. We kept them in hiding here for about ten days and then they left. Bangash sahib had warned us ahead of time that it was dangerous for all of us for them to be here because Khar was a ruthless governor but Abba insisted that they come so they did.[1]

Allama Iqbal's Payaam-e Mashriq

The centenary of Muhammad Iqbal, revered as Pakistan's national poet, fell in 1977. Iqbal was the man who first espoused the idea of a separate homeland for India's Muslims, carved out of its Muslim-majority provinces. Faiz knew Iqbal since they shared a common birthplace and had been briefly acquainted in Faiz's youth. When the Iqbal Academy, the official agency tasked with promoting Iqbal's work, approached Faiz to write something in connection with Iqbal's centenary, he agreed to translate Iqbal's Persian collection, *Payaam-e Mashriq* (Message of the East), into Urdu. Even though what was eventually published was only a brief selection from the collection, it was still a rare treat for poetry lovers in the subcontinent: a versified Urdu translation of one of the greatest poets of the subcontinent by another world-renowned Urdu poet. Faiz wrote in the preface with his characteristic humility that he had 'accepted the task [of translation] with some reluctance', since it 'gave me a chance to study the beautiful collection again and secondly, a translation, whether good or bad, would give those lovers of Iqbal unfamiliar with Persian to be able to appreciate the meaning of the original at least to some extent.'[2]

Operation Fair Play

As the anti-Bhutto movement gained steam, Bhutto announced fresh elections in early 1977. The results were overwhelmingly in favour of the ruling PPP but accusations of widespread rigging and ballot stuffing began immediately. As the situation spiralled out of control, with daily street demonstrations and clashes, the army stepped in once again and on 5 July 1977, Pakistan's third, and most brutal, military dictatorship took over.

Faiz was in Lahore at the time, looking after the Music Research Cell he had put together. Salima remembers:

> It was something he liked doing, he was very happy with it. I had gone to London for a holiday and I arrived there on 5 July. I got off the flight and the airline people told me what had happened. And, of course, my first thought was 'What about Abba?' I asked them who had been arrested and they said so far it's only PPP officials, the cabinet and so on. I came back after two weeks and by that time, they had started shadowing Abba, our phones were being tapped and there was a police jeep permanently parked outside our house. He was very annoyed. He knew he would not be allowed to do anything any longer, so he decided to leave and he wrote to Zia [General Zia-ul-Haq, the leader of the coup] that he was asking permission, as always, from the head of state to go abroad and Zia wrote back saying, 'You're welcome to leave, you won't be stopped.' And while he was still debating, the military government started showing its true colours. Journalists began to be arrested and publicly flogged; there was widespread, brutal repression against the Left; activists, trade-union and student leaders, writers, they all began to be rounded up and it was obvious that they [the army] had the full support of the West. At first it had seemed that their target was just the PPP government but pretty soon it became obvious that there was a much broader objective: complete annihilation of the Left, including all trade unions, student unions, really, any organized Left groups in the country, including all minority groups. He [Zia] had the full support of the Jamaat-e Islami, so it was their vision of governance and public behaviour that was being enforced. Abba didn't leave immediately, he didn't want to, so he stayed on for a while to see if it would be possible for him to stay and do whatever it was he could do. But it soon became obvious that if he didn't leave soon, he might not be allowed to leave at all, letter or no letter.[3]

Once he had decided to leave, Faiz didn't waste any time. He flew to Islamabad, then Karachi and on to Delhi, where he had been invited by the Indian government to participate in Allama Iqbal's centenary celebrations. He had planned to stay briefly in India and then fly on to London and Moscow. His reception in India was so rousing, though, that he stayed longer than planned. The initial plan was just to have Faiz attend some ceremonies in three major cities in connection with Iqbal's centenary, but when word got out that Faiz was in India, invitations poured in from all over the country. His fans, friends and well-wishers in Gwalior, Bhopal, Chandigarh, Punjab, Haryana, Bombay, Hyderabad, Lucknow and dozens of other cities refused to heed his plea that he would return in a few months and spend more time with them. He ended up spending several weeks in India, far longer than he had anticipated.

In the meantime, newspapers in Pakistan, ever eager to take a dig at Faiz, started publishing rumours that he planned to take up the post of vice-chancellor of Aligarh Muslim University. Replying to a friend, Faiz stated unhesitatingly that if he desired a vice-chancellorship, there were plenty of universities in Pakistan where he could take up such a post. Faiz was no doubt aware that in spite of his great affection for India and its people, the symbolic significance of someone like him taking up permanent residence in India would be used by 'short-sighted people' to foment more trouble between the two countries.

The chief minister of Indian Kashmir called up Faiz personally to invite Alys and him to Srinagar to celebrate their wedding anniversary there. Faiz wryly replied, 'But how can we come to Srinagar? We don't recognize your government there!'[4]

Calcutta University was very keen to have Faiz teach Urdu there. Later, when Alys and he were in Beirut and both were pining for their home and children, this was the only offer he seriously considered, and that too, 'only because it would have meant that he could be closer to us, at least it was in the subcontinent. But he also said, "I can't do it because it will make things very difficult for all of you [Salima and Moneeza's families]."'[5]

For five years, from 1978 to 1983, Faiz and Alys travelled all over the world: London, Moscow, Berlin, Cairo, Beirut, Delhi, Tokyo, Korea. This self-imposed 'exile' took its toll. The only place they did settle in for a while, was, of all places, Beirut—the once-exquisite, now war-torn capital of Lebanon.

Lotus *and Beirut*

The idea of a journal for the Afro-Asian Writers Association (AAWA) had been floated by Faiz as early as 1962, while he was in London. He strongly believed that the colonized and formerly colonized nations of Asia, Africa and Latin America had a strong, independent literary tradition, which reflected their ideals of freedom and struggle. These works did not (and could not) find adequate expression in the West. A literary journal would provide a common platform for writers from these areas to express their ideas and would also be a way for writers from different continents to develop solidarity. At last, in 1968, a literary journal named *Lotus* began to be published from Cairo, the headquarters of AAWA. Its editor-in-chief was Egyptian writer and journalist, Yusuf al-Sibai who would later become Egypt's minister for culture. In 1978, al-Sibai was assassinated by a Cypriot nationalist unhappy with Egyptian president Anwar Sadat's attempts at making peace with Israel (which would also lead to Sadat's assassination by officers of his own army a few years later).

The post of editor-in-chief of *Lotus* fell vacant after Al-Sibai's death, although the journal continued publication. In 1979, at the sixth conference of Afro-Asian writers in Luanda, Angola, Faiz was appointed editor-in-chief and Alys was assigned to help him. An important consideration in Faiz's selection, besides his numerous international honours and accolades (including the 1976 Lotus Prize for literature given by AAWA), was undoubtedly his strong command over Arabic and English, as well as his working knowledge of French.

It provided Faiz with another opportunity to pursue his lifelong passion: showcasing the best anti-colonial and anti-imperialist writings from the Afro-Asian region to introduce a global audience to the freedom struggles of oppressed nations.

The Palestinian people's struggle for freedom had always held a special place for AAWA. Palestine had always occupied a prominent place in AAWA conferences and there had been several resolutions condemning Israeli aggression and expressing solidarity with the Palestinian struggle. The Palestine Liberation Organization (PLO) and its chairman, Yasser Arafat, admired AAWA for its principled stance and so, when the question of a central headquarters for *Lotus* was raised, Arafat and the PLO offered Beirut as a home. Faiz, who had recently left Pakistan, accepted and was received warmly in Beirut by Palestine's celebrated poet, Mu'in Bseiso. About his first impressions of Beirut, Faiz later wrote:

> I had first seen the beautiful land of Lebanon and Beirut about fifteen years before when this city was full of tourists and the rich...this time, when we passed through it, it was a ruin. A hotel, a couple of restaurants and a few buildings were all that was left. There were piles of rubble everywhere with the burnt out shells of cars and trucks scattered around. This was the coastal area destroyed by the Israelis and the Christian Fascist militias. But inside the city where the Palestinians were in control, it was very different. One or two buildings were damaged but it was business as usual, shops were loaded with fruits and things to eat, people appeared happy and the roads were filled with cars and traffic.[6]

Faiz was taken to meet Yasser Arafat the same day he arrived in Beirut. Arafat welcomed him warmly and Faiz got to work to set up the headquarters of *Lotus*. The Arabic edition was already being published from there under the guidance of Mu'in Bseiso. Alys joined Faiz a few days later in December. Alys recorded her first impressions of Beirut in *Over My Shoulder*:

> Our apartment was on the sixth floor of a residential block in a middle class area. Two more apartments nearby were reserved for Lotus staffers. Before I could complain to Faiz that he had not come to the airport to receive me, he explained that there had been firing in the neighborhood just this morning and for safety reasons, he had been confined to the apartment. Faiz showed me our home. It was a two room apartment with balconies on both sides with the sea on one side. Because of the conditions in the city, Faiz's movements were restricted to an area with a one mile radius.[7]

Because of his close friendship with 'Abu Ammar' (Yasser Arafat), Faiz was provided extra security and was carefully monitored even during his evening walks. Both Faiz and Alys missed the children and grandchildren terribly. It was obvious to both of them that the situation could not continue indefinitely. Beirut was under siege and for Faiz and Alys, it was amazing that the Palestinians went about their day-to-day lives despite the daily bombings and fighting. For Faiz, it was testament to their resilience and a stark demonstration of their belief in the truth of their cause. He was familiar with the history of the area known as historic Palestine, a fertile land that had been occupied by conquerors for centuries.

From the ancient pharaohs of Egypt to the Ottoman empire, this area had always been under the rule of foreign invaders. From the fourteenth to the nineteenth century, the Ottomans had ruled there and when the Ottoman Empire declined and fell, Western powers moved in to take its place. The discovery of oil in the Middle East worsened the prospects of independence and, following the Second World War, with the formation of the State of Israel, the area was in a permanent state of war. It was perhaps also not a coincidence that the central city of the Palestinians, Jerusalem, is also the birthplace of three of the world's most widely practised religions: Judaism, Christianity and Islam. It has thus remained contested between these three faiths for hundreds of years.

Faiz had started raising his voice for the Palestinian cause long before he arrived in Beirut. In 1967, during the Arab-Israeli war, Faiz had written his stirring poem, 'Sar-e wadi-e Sina' (In the Skies over the Valley of Sinai) about which his dear friend, Marxist historian Sibt-e Hasan had this to say: 'His [Faiz's] poetry is usually restrained but the poem he wrote for this war, "Sar-e Waadi-e Seena" has echoes of the battleground in it; as if some fervent Arab poet is reciting a battle hymn urging on his fellow fighters.'[8]

The scenes of death and destruction that Faiz and Alys were to witness during their time in Beirut would affect them both deeply, as would the courage and suffering of the Palestinian people. Faiz did not write much about his time in Beirut in later years. Alys, however, recorded some memories of their stay: 'A Lebanese woman used to come to clean our apartment. An anti-Muslim group had killed her husband, her son had disappeared and she had a daughter who was an invalid. But every day, she would cross the "green line" [the line of demarcation separating the predominantly Muslim areas of west Beirut from the Christian east] for work. We would observe her courage and be amazed.'[9] The Pakistani ambassador's house was located close to Faiz and Alys's apartment and they would end up spending quite a bit of time together. Faiz and Alys also had a few close shaves with death: 'Kidnappings were common. There used to be firing in broad daylight on roads and in alleyways. One day, Faiz and I decided to go to the Alhamra shopping centre to a cinema. All of a sudden, the firing started all around us and a jeep rushed by us, firing as it went. It happened so suddenly that we were shocked. We ran and took refuge behind a wall in a street. A short time later, everything was back to normal as if nothing had happened. After that, we went to the cinema, ate dinner and strolled back home.'[10]

It was also not unusual for artillery and air bombing to start without warning. Yasser Arafat and his top lieutenants never slept in the same house for more than one night for fear that it would be targeted by Israeli bombings. Alys wrote in her memoir:

> [One] night, the office of the Iraqi airline which was underneath our apartment was attacked. The explosion was so loud that it shattered all the windows in our apartment and turned the curtains into rags. The couch on which I used to rest often was buried under a pile of rubble. If anyone had been in that room, it would have been a miracle if they had survived. Every bulb in the house had shattered. Some people came in to check on us and then left. Faiz said to me, come to the bedroom. He lay down on the bed, turned over and was soon snoring.[11]

Unlike Faiz, Alys was under no restriction and could go sightseeing, but things in Beirut were going from bad to worse: 'Sometimes, while eating, we would end up bumping into a wall and realize that our building had shook because a piece of a rocket had struck it. It was often not even possible to tell who was fighting who, who was firing, who was dying.'[12] Inevitably, ordinary civic services were affected. Garbage would pile up in the streets for months and would decay and stink. Often, elevators in buildings would not work, making it hard for children and the elderly to reach their homes in the upper floors. The garbage piles would keep rising higher and higher. If anyone passed by the piles at night, she would see thousands of tiny eyes reflected inside the garbage from the light of the street lamps. These were the street rats that would forage in the garbage at night. During the daytime, flies would descend like a 'black blanket' on the rotting food and refuse. In spite of this, life continued.

'An ocean of blood'

Around this time, Salima and her children came to Beirut to visit. Salima remembers:

> I remember I got this very sad letter from him [Faiz] in which he said I missed your childhood and now I'm missing theirs [the grandchildren's]. So we decided to go. I remember we got to Beirut airport and it was complete mayhem. Mama had said Abba would be at the airport but there was no sign of him so we got really panicky. Suddenly, we saw him and it was fantastic. Then, of course, to get from the airport to the Muslim side was quite a journey. We would be stopped first at one check point, then another by these different militias; there were bombed-out buildings and burnt shells of tanks and trucks on the roads, it was quite a sight. Finally we got to the apartment and it was this tiny little two-room flat. So the kids camped in Mama and Abba's room and I was in the other room.[13]

Soon after this, Faiz became ill. He had suffered from breathing problems for a while, compounded by his chain-smoking habit. He had also developed heart problems early in the 1960s. The doctors in Beirut could not fix the problem and his condition did not improve. Finally, some Soviet writer friends of his arranged for him to go to Moscow for treatment. Once word came that Faiz was better, Salima went on to London while the children stayed with Alys in Beirut for a while. Alys remembered later: 'We had found a beautiful swimming pool nearby. Everything was fine except for the echoes of occasional shooting. Once we were in the pool and the shooting started so we ran underground in our swimming clothes. We came back after 10 or 15 minutes and the hustle and bustle returned. The children loved to look at the sea from the verandah. They would ask me questions like "Why is the sea brown today?" or "Why are the waves so high today?" When the firing would start, they would startle but soon they got used to it.'[14]

The scenes of death and destruction that Faiz and Alys would witness in Beirut would stay with them for the rest of their lives: 'We lived our whole lives in those two years…There was Moussa, our bodyguard and driver with his five lovely children and his exquisite wife, his tall handsome father lived in a camp near Sidon. The old man so wanted to be buried in his homeland…but there was a bombing by the Israelis on the camp and when one of the refugees went there to bury his parents, there was nothing left to bury, not a brick was left standing.'[15]

About the incongruity of Faiz, by now an old man himself, living in such a place, Salima says:

> You know, Beirut was a natural nesting place for exiles of every kind, from all over the Middle East; Kuwait, Iraq, Syria. And it was the only place he was offered a job, even though his salary was tiny; but his heart was very much with the Palestinians and Beirut offered him a place to be close to an actual political struggle. It was hard for him to be there; he was putting his life in danger but he felt that this was the place he needed to be. And then of course he met all these wonderful people there, intellectuals like Mahmoud Darwish,[16] Mu'in Bseiso, Adonis,[17] and so many other brilliant writers and poets from all over the Arab world; journalists on the run from different parts of the Arab world and many others. Beirut in those days was a base where all the dissidents from all over the Arab world had gathered so he felt at home in some ways.[18]

The significance of so many independent-minded writers and poets being in Beirut was not lost on Israel. These were the days when the plans for an Israeli invasion of Lebanon to 'flush out' the PLO were being drawn up and it was obvious to the Israelis that the longer they waited, the more the plight of the Palestinians would be broadcast to the world through the voices of people like Faiz and his compatriots.

For Faiz, after a long time, he was back in the thick of a political struggle. It may have felt like being back in the heady days after partition when the dream of making a just, socially progressive new nation from the ashes of the old seemed within reach. After his harsh treatment in the Rawalpindi Conspiracy Case, Faiz had distanced himself from politics and decided to focus on culture and the arts but it was always obvious that active engagement on the political front was needed to bring about any meaningful change. For a long time now, though, he had been reluctant to risk imprisonment or worse. As he said once, as one gets older, 'the soul is willing but the body is not'. Beirut offered him the chance, through a combination of circumstance and will, to engage once again in the life-and-death struggle between 'creation and destruction, progress and decay, light and darkness, justice and oppression'.[19]

Did he ever wish to be somewhere else where he could read and write in peace? Where dodging bombs and bullets was not part of one's daily routine? London may have seemed like a natural choice. The list of rebels and free thinkers who had made the city home was long. Karl Marx himself had composed *Das Kapital* in London; another rebel of his time, Sigmund Freud, when he finally left his beloved Vienna to escape the Nazis, had come to London and eventually died there and, of course, London was where Syed Sajjad Zaheer and his compatriots had laid the foundation of the All-India Progressive Writers' Association. Alys would, in all probability, have been happy to be back home. Salima remembers:

> He used to go to London; he had lots of friends there but firstly, what would he live on? They had no money and this [the editorship of *Lotus*] offered a small salary. And he liked the idea of a magazine for Afro-Asian writers, he had worked to set up the Afro-Asian Writers' Association and he had been one of its leading lights for many years; there was an Arab edition [of *Lotus*] that Mu'in used to bring out, a French edition that used to come out from Tunis and the English edition that Abba brought out. And if the Israelis had not invaded and laid waste to Beirut, *Lotus* had a lot of potential.[20]

Faiz could have chosen to immigrate to the West, perhaps to become an academic. Even with his 'communist' credentials, he could have obtained a university position in Europe, Canada or even the Soviet Union. Even the United States might have been willing to take a chance if he had promised to 'behave'. Says Salima:

> He never had much money at all except for a short time with the PNCA, when he had a decent salary. Beirut was very tough to survive on that tiny editor's salary. Luckily Mama [Alys] was used to living frugally. The only thing he was tempted by was when he was offered a position of Urdu Chair at Calcutta University, that was the only time he thought about it and only because it would have been closer to us, his family, and to Pakistan. But he didn't want to live anywhere in the West. Even when we lived there briefly in 1962 (after Faiz received the Lenin Peace Prize), he hardly stayed in London. He had his 'yaars' [friends], other people in exile like Alex La Guma[21] but he couldn't live in the West. He was never happy there. Beirut was still the third world. He would have loved to go and live in Calcutta but that wasn't possible, especially during the Zia dictatorship. He knew it would make life even more difficult for us in Pakistan.[22]

Life in Beirut went on amidst the bombing and the gunfire but time was running out. Soon, Faiz would have to run too, this time from the assassins of Israel.

Notes

1. Salima Hashmi, personal recollection.
2. Muhammad Iqbal, *Payaam-e Mashriq: Manzoom Urdu Tarjuma*. Trans. Faiz Ahmed Faiz (Lahore: Sang-e-Meel Publications, 2011), p. 13.
3. Salima Hashmi, personal recollection.
4. Agha Nasir, 'Man-mohni shakhsiat', in *Teri Yaadon ke Naqoosh* (Lahore: Sang-e-Meel Publications, 2011), p. 19.
5. Salima Hashmi, personal recollection.
6. Faiz Ahmed Faiz, *Lao Tau Qatl Nama Mera* (Lahore: Kausar Publishers, 1985), pp. 120–1.
7. Alys Faiz, *Over My Shoulder* (Lahore: Frontier Post Publications, 1993), pp. 97, 98.
8. Syed Sibt-e Hasan, *Sukhan dar Sukhan* (Karachi: Maktaba Daniyal, 2009), p. 95.

9. Alys Faiz, *Over My Shoulder* (Lahore: Frontier Post Publications, 1993), p. 99.
10. Ibid., p. 100.
11. Ibid., p. 102.
12. Ibid., p. 105.
13. Salima Hashmi, personal recollection.
14. Alys Faiz, *Over My Shoulder* (Lahore: Frontier Post Publications, 1993), p. 107.
15. Ibid., p. 106.
16. Palestinian poet and author, recipient of numerous literary awards and regarded as Palestine's national poet.
17. The nom de plume of Ali Ahmad Said Esber, Syrian poet, author and translator, described as the greatest living poet of the Arab world.
18. Salima Hashmi, personal recollection.
19. From Faiz's Lenin Peace Prize speech in Moscow, 1962.
20. Salima Hashmi, personal recollection.
21. (d. 1985) noted South African novelist, ardent campaigner against apartheid, winner of the Lotus prize for literature in 1969.
22. Salima Hashmi, personal recollection.

19

Wanderer-II

We have triumphed over the plan to expel us from history.

—Mahmoud Darwish

On 6 June 1982, the Israeli army under the command of Defence Minister Ariel Sharon invaded Southern Lebanon. The official pretext for the invasion was the attempted assassination of Israel's ambassador to the United Kingdom, which the Israeli prime minister blamed on the Palestinian Liberation Organization (PLO). The Israelis planned to expel the PLO from Beirut, limit Syrian influence over Lebanon and install a pro-Israeli Christian government in Lebanon. Ariel Sharon, who would later be nicknamed 'the butcher of Beirut' for this operation, had planned the invasion a year in advance. The aim was to destroy Lebanon's refugee camps and bring about the mass expulsion of 2,00,000 Palestinian refugees.

Exodus

Before the final invasion, Faiz had already persuaded Alys to leave, which she had, reluctantly: 'We knew we had to leave as soon as possible. I packed a few things with a heavy heart; there were so many books on the shelves, clothes in the cupboard, essays, writings and notes in the desk, groceries in the kitchen, a carpet we had bought so lovingly with our hard-won savings; now, there would be only memories.'[1]

Alys had no trouble getting out of Beirut because of her British passport; the Israeli soldiers manning checkpoints could not stop her. But Faiz was a different matter. He had earlier flown to Japan for a UNESCO conference and had stopped over briefly in Karachi where he had been promptly detained by the military. Even though he was eventually released, it was obvious that he was still persona non grata in Pakistan. Back in Beirut, things had gone from bad to worse. It was only much later that the family found out what Faiz had gone through in his last days in Beirut. The apartment complex in which Faiz and Alys lived had been bombed in the run-up to the invasion and almost totally destroyed. For a time, the family feared for his life but his driver had managed to get him to Mu'in Bseiso's house. Faiz was still reluctant to leave but the Palestinian leadership warned him that his name was on the list of people wanted by the Israelis. They could not risk his life any longer. He had to go. Faiz recalls:

> People had been told to leave the city but I didn't think it wise to take refuge with the enemy, so I didn't go. After that, all the roads were closed. On the night of 24th or 25th June, a friend who worked in the United Nations sent a message that he was leaving with his family the next day and I could leave with them if I wished. I was living with my PLO friends and they insisted that I leave since they could not protect me any longer. I agreed to leave. We were stopped several times by the Israelis and the Phalangists[2] but my friend had a UN passport and he told them his family was with him. There were two cars; he was in one and his children and family were in the other. I was sitting with the children. They must have thought I was the grandfather or something. We were stopped six times but no one asked for my passport.[3]

Once out of Beirut, they headed north to Tripoli, then to Homs in Syria, Damascus and finally London. Later, Faiz said of his last days in Beirut that they were 'terrifying, horrific; there was continuous bombing'. His stay in Beirut had affected Faiz deeply and his last collections of poetry contained several poems in which he expressed his feelings for the struggle of the Palestinians. In poems like 'Love takes its prisoners in chains', 'Palestinian martyrs killed in foreign lands' and 'Don't cry child', Faiz gave voice to his anger and sorrow against what was being done to them. It is also important to remember that for Faiz, these poems were not simply reflections from afar. They were the voice of his heart since he had lived amongst the Palestinians, shared their joys and sorrows as well as their fear and anger. And the Palestinians reciprocated his feelings. In a special letter on the occasion of Faiz's seventieth birthday in 1981, Yasser Arafat had written:

> Revered poet and brother Faiz Ahmed Faiz! Our Arab Palestinian people have found in you a progressive, international poet, an

> untiring worker for world peace and a fighter for the rights of oppressed people struggling for their freedom, progress and welfare. Our Arab Palestinian people are proud of your friendship, your deep awareness and your efforts on behalf of Palestine and the legitimate struggle of the Palestinian people. Your sincere and authentic verses which talk of the Palestinian people, especially our children and our revolutionaries will live for all time and be an example of brotherly truth and sincere love.[4]

Faiz returned the compliment by dedicating his collection *Mere Dil Mere Musafir* to Arafat.

Condemned

Once the PLO had been chased out of Beirut, it became a shadow of its former self. The leadership relocated to Tunis, the capital of Tunisia, across the Mediterranean Sea, and its fighters dispersed. According to some accounts, the PLO was never the same again.

Faiz headed to London and then on to Moscow, homeless once again. Going back to Pakistan was out of the question. The brutal military dictatorship in Pakistan had tightened its grip over the country. Political repression was at its peak with public lashings and executions commonplace. A week after executing Pakistan's first popularly elected prime minister, Zulfiqar Ali Bhutto, in a trial widely condemned as a farce, General Zia-ul-Haq had convened a conference of writers in the capital city of Islamabad, in which he had harangued the assembled delegates in his presidential address. The general had threatened all those who did not march in step with him that there was no place in Pakistan for them. Faiz knew that he was included in the list and had written to a friend: 'I read about the matter of the writers [conference] in the newspaper. Just as well I am not there, otherwise I would have been condemned if I had not gone and blamed if I had. It is because of these shenanigans that I feel fed up and reluctant to return home.'[5]

Faiz continued from time to time to work as chief editor of *Lotus* while he was in Moscow, but he was increasingly weary of the task. The reasons for this have been pointed out by Faiz's dear friend and interpreter in Moscow, Ludmila Vasilieva. The Afro-

Asian Writers' Association (AAWA)was itself undergoing significant turmoil. The organization had been set up with the help of the Soviet government and was being funded solely by Soviet money. As such, the Soviet leadership expected its mission to be aligned with the goals of Soviet policy. This may have been easier to achieve in the decades immediately following the Second World War, but now, thirty years later, it was proving more difficult. The organization had encouraged writers and artists from all over the third world, especially countries that had recently won their freedom, to explore their own culture and history and work on emancipating their people from centuries of bondage. At some point, this began to come in conflict with the demands of the Soviet leadership that had its own ideas about how things should be done. The organization was getting 'out of control'. All this, of course, was a precursor to the upheavals of the late 1980s, which would see dramatic restructuring of the Soviet Union itself. At this point, though, there were just ripples of discontent under the surface. None of this was spoken about openly in Moscow, but Faiz was an intelligent man and he was, no doubt, aware of the discontent. He wanted to keep the peace and, as was his habit, find a compromise solution but he was also one of the founders of AAWA and the impending rift must have hurt him. In addition, the changes in the Soviet Union itself, its rigid bureaucracy, corruption and mismanagement must have been obvious to him for a while. Now, towards the end of his life, they were harder to ignore.

A large part of his time as chief editor of *Lotus* was spent in correspondence and writings reports and official documents, work that he probably found tedious and time-consuming. There was no editorial staff to speak of and he had to do a lot of the work himself. Many of the submissions from underdeveloped countries required significant editorial corrections, which must have been tiresome.

Shaam-e Shehr-e Yaaran *and* Mere Dil Mere Musafir

Faiz's sixth collection of poetry, *Shaam-e Shehr-e Yaaran* (Evening of the Beloved's City), was published in 1978. It was dedicated to his old friends, Colonel Majeed Malik and his wife, Amina behen (sister Amina). It contained poems composed over approximately seven years but, according to some, was not as creatively rich as his previous collections. The period in which these poems were written was a tumultuous one in Pakistan. The India–Pakistan war of 1971 and the creation of Bangladesh, the stormy years of the Bhutto government, the third Arab-Israeli war and many other changes on the international horizon provided fertile material for writers and artists but little of this was reflected in Faiz's poetry. One reason for this may have been Faiz's 'official' duties. He served for close to five years in the Bhutto government in an official or unofficial capacity and, as has been mentioned previously, most of those years were poetically barren. Faiz himself complained to his friends that he felt muzzled and suffocated because of his official position, unable to express his feelings in verse. Many of the poems of these years are 'inward looking', in which Faiz writes about his dissatisfaction and unease with the way things were.

Some poems in this collection are a departure from Faiz's usual style. 'Leningrad ka goristaan' ('Leningrad's cemetery') was Faiz's tribute to the millions of Soviet citizens who paid with their lives to defend the city known as the birthplace of the Russian Revolution from the Nazis during the Second World War:

> On frigid slabs
> On pale slabs
> Like fresh warm blood
> Are speckles of flower bouquets
> The gravestones are nameless but
> Every flower has a name
> Of the one who sleeps unperturbed
> The one who cries in remembrance
> Free of their duty
> Clasping their cloak of blood
> All the sons are sleeping
> Having beaded her necklace of sorrows
> Mother, alone, is awake.[6]

Mere Dil Mere Musafir (My Heart, My Traveller) was published in 1980. It contains as many poems as the previous collection, even though it was written over a period of just two years. This was Faiz's period of 'exile' and the entire collection, dedicated to Yasser Arafat, reflects this theme. The period from 1978 to 1980 was a dark one for Pakistan. The Zia military dictatorship, in attempting to strengthen its hold on the country, was encouraging the growth of religious fundamentalism, which would, in the decades to come, tear the country apart. In 1979, after a farcical trial, Zulfiqar Ali Bhutto, was hanged. Even though Bhutto had lost his way politically in the heady days after his first election, the execution of a popularly elected, serving prime minister was extremely traumatic for the people of Pakistan; it was meant to send a message to all those who dared to dissent or raise their voices. The mood in the country was gloomy and many of Faiz's poems reflected this. The pain of exile and homelessness forms another theme running through the collection. His stay in Beirut and his association with the Palestinians provided another impetus to his poetry and many of the poems in *Mere Dil Mere Musafir* spoke of the Palestinian people, their brave struggle and their sacrifices.

Ghubaar-e Ayaam (The dust of times) is included as a separate collection in Faiz's kulliyat, his complete collection of poetry, *Nuskha hai wafa*. It is more appropriately seen as an appendix to *Mere Dil Mere Musafir*. The themes in this, Faiz's last collection, are similar to the previous one: the pain of exile, the sorrows of the Palestinians, protest against oppression and tyranny in the Afro-Asian countries and all over the world.

Moscow, London and all over the world

For five years, from 1978 to 1983, Faiz spent most of his time outside Pakistan. Some of this was in service of the Afro-Asian Writers' Association which had chapters in over seventy countries. As already mentioned, Faiz was one of its founding members and on several of its committees. The list of cities that Faiz and Alys travelled to in connection with the activities of the organization, reads like an atlas: Moscow, Leningrad, London, Peking, Cairo, Ankara, Istanbul, New York, Washington, Chicago, Tokyo, Rome, Khartoum, Tehran, Cyprus, Delhi, Calcutta, Adis Ababa, Colombo, Tunis, Prague and Benghazi. Even though it must have been exhausting at times, Faiz was an avid traveller and never turned down an invitation to visit a new place.

Of all these cities, the ones he spent the most time in were London and Moscow. London was the city which most reminded him of home since it housed a vast population of expatriates from India and Pakistan. He had a sentimental affection for it since his father, Sultan Muhammad Khan, had spent several years of his life there and it was also the home of his in-laws. London was where Syed Sajjad Zaheer and his compatriots had first laid the foundation of the All-India Progressive Writers' Association. In addition, the largest community of Urdu lovers outside the subcontinent was located in London and its surrounding cities like Manchester, Birmingham and Oxford. In 1962, after he had received the Lenin Peace Prize when he and Alys had decided to not return to Pakistan immediately because of Ayub Khan's military dictatorship, London was the city they had chosen as home. This time around, London was a veritable galaxy of Urdu luminaries who had escaped the repression of the Zia government. Most progressive writers and poets from Pakistan had settled in London and many from India often visited. The Urdu Markaz was a cultural organization founded in London during those days and it became the centre of literary and poetic activities in the city and helped bind Indian and Pakistani writers and poets together in a common purpose.

Faiz did not like the pace of life in the West and he certainly didn't like London's weather. During his earlier stay in London he had said: 'What kind of country is this? It's always so cold here. Well, that might be tolerable since it's so hot in our country but here, in this gold-plated land, in the midst of this crowd of wage-slaves, no one is at peace. Everybody is running, running, running. Take a bus, take a train and keep running. There is no rest. And we can tolerate the rain but these clouds all the time; you never see the sky, the stars, the moon, the sun.'[7]

And in conversation with British scholar of Urdu, Ralph Russell, Faiz said: 'I miss my country, everything about it. Who can I meet here? Who can I talk to? Who should I write poetry for? Who will listen to it?'[8]

In spite of this, and despite the fact that he and Alys were living in Beirut, Faiz would always return to London every month or two to see friends and participate in the cultural activities taking place in the city.

Moscow, of course, had been one of his favourite nesting places for years. Faiz was considered 'royalty' in the Soviet Union and since he had received the Lenin Peace Prize, was feted and honoured in every city in the country. In Moscow, whenever there was an event that involved Faiz, the hall would be overflowing with people. He would recite his Urdu poems and then a Russian poet would present the translations to the audience. Although always an official state guest, Faiz was equally popular amongst the common people. Translations of his poetry were published regularly in large numbers and would immediately sell out. These Russian translations were regularly translated into regional Soviet languages, which would also sell out immediately. Faiz's birthdays were regularly celebrated in the Soviet Union, even when he was not able to attend. On the celebration of his seventieth birthday in 1981, Faiz was in Moscow. Hundreds of writers and poets had gathered to pay tribute to him and in his speech to the assembled audience, he said: 'I am not as happy to be celebrating my seventieth birthday as I am in celebrating it here, in Moscow. This city, and its inhabitants are very dear to us. I have made many friends here, loved many people, written many verses, enjoyed many feasts and learned many things from many people and the ideology that I have adopted had also been formed with the help of many friends here. The people of Moscow have taught me two things: to love peace and to fight for it.'[9]

It was in the Soviet Union that Faiz had met some of the giants of world literature, poetry and philosophy, including Jean-Paul Sartre, Alberto Moravia, Pablo Neruda and Nazim Hikmet.

Hawaii

Of all the countries in the world to which he and Alys travelled, the one conspicuously absent from the list was the United States of America. Faiz made only two trips to the USA in his life. The first was in 1948 to participate in the International Labour Organization conference in the Californian city of San Francisco. As already mentioned, since Faiz participated as a delegate rather than as the representative of a trade union. This meant that he did not have any voting rights at the conference, but this did not stop him from vigorously voicing his opinions.

In 1979, an international literary conference was organized in the Hawaiian city of Honolulu by the East-West Center, an educational and research organization established by the US Congress in 1960 to strengthen relations and understanding among the peoples and nations of Asia, the Pacific and the United States. Delegates from Australia, New Zealand, Fiji, Malaysia, North Korea, Japan, Bangladesh and India were invited. Faiz was invited to represent Pakistan since the invitation came directly from the University of Hawaii; if the invitation had been sent to the Government of Pakistan, no doubt an 'official' writer would have been chosen instead. It was in Honolulu that Faiz first met American poet Naomi Lazard, who later did the first English translation of his poetry to be published in the USA. In some ways, her translations, titled *The True Subject*, may be considered more authoritative than some other English translations since many of them were done under Faiz's personal supervision while he was in Honolulu. The book was published for the first time by Princeton University Press in 1988. Lazard's first-hand account of her close collaboration with Faiz, who she termed 'one of the few great poets of this century' on a par with Neruda, Cesar Vallejo, Nazim Hikmet and Ernesto Cardenal was also published as an essay after Faiz's death in 1985.[10]

Three score and ten

Faiz turned seventy in February 1981. Someone who reaches this age is, in many cultures, considered to have completed the natural lifespan of a human being. Living any longer is a bonus.

By the age of seventy, Faiz had been a world-renowned poet for some time. In Pakistan and anywhere in the world where Urdu-poetry lovers lived, he was an easily recognizable presence. He would often be stopped on the street by random strangers wanting to shake his hand or have a picture taken with him. The outpouring of popular love and affection that he was enjoyed was in stark contrast to the official constraints on him, especially in Pakistan. His hold on the popular imagination made his Left-wing ideas all the more dangerous for successive governments of the country.

As his seventieth birthday approached, his friends and well-wishers geared up to celebrate it in style. It had been a tradition for his birthday to be celebrated in many cities all over the world, including London, Moscow, Canada and of course, Lahore. Yasser Arafat had announced an official celebration in Beirut. Faiz, of course, wanted to spend this day with his family in Lahore. He had ardent fans and close friends in most of the major cities of Pakistan.

But the Zia military dictatorship in Pakistan was having none of it. The last thing they wanted were gatherings of people all over Pakistan celebrating Faiz and his poetry of resistance. As soon as it was announced that Faiz's friends and well-wishers in Pakistan had constituted a committee to plan his seventieth birthday celebrations (across the border, in India, too, a committee had been formed for the purpose), Pakistan's military junta declared all such activities subversive. Arrests and harassment quickly followed. In spite of this, the celebration went ahead in Lahore (without Faiz, who was in Moscow at the time). The master of ceremonies was noted Pakistani film actor Muhammad Ali, an avid fan of Faiz's, and a galaxy of literary luminaries participated. Similar events were held all over the country, and inside most of the country's jails as well! Faiz had become a symbol of resistance against the detested military dictatorship. Faiz heard the news of the celebrations abroad with a heavy heart. He would have preferred to have been amongst those celebrating. He was also worried about news of the arrest of his older son-in-law, Shoaib Hashmi, who was picked up and detained for several months along with many of Faiz's closest friends. The story goes that one of the policemen who arrested Shoaib Hashmi asked him which party he belonged to. He promptly replied, 'The birthday party'!

Canada

One place that Faiz visited frequently while he was in self-imposed exile was the Canadian city of Toronto which, even in those days, boasted quite a few people of a literary bent from the Indian sub-continent. Faiz first visited the city in 1978. In those days, there were few actual poets there so the literary gatherings included people who recited the poetry of well-known poets in lieu of original work. It was a way of remembering 'the old country', enjoying the sound of Urdu being spoken and recited and, in general, keeping the love of Urdu literature alive in a foreign land. Faiz's presence was like a shot in the arm for the Indian and Pakistani inhabitants of Toronto. He came back again in 1980 and this time, some of his old friends and comrades from the All-India Progressive Writers' Association were also invited. Faiz got a chance to meet and recite his poetry alongside Kaifi Azmi, Ali Sardar Jafri, Akhtar-ul Iman and many others. In his presidential address, Faiz made the audience aware of the fate of the Palestinian people in Beirut. Even the law of the jungle is governed by some principles, Faiz said, but in this conflict (the Israeli bombardment of Beirut), all human laws had been forgotten. Faiz called the conduct of Israel 'modern fascism'. He urged the assembled audience to do its part to bring these crimes to light. He reminded it that Canada had a free press, there was freedom of speech and freedom of assembly, which it must use to highlight the pitiable condition of the Palestinians as well as their brave and principled struggle.

In 1981, Faiz and Alys went together to the eastern Canadian city of Halifax at the annual conference of the Canadian Asian Studies Society. Faiz lectured at several universities during this visit and Faiz and Alys celebrated their fortieth wedding anniversary in Toronto. Alys also presided over a special event in Toronto about the Palestinian problem.

In 1982, Faiz went to Toronto to participate in the Aalmi [International] Urdu Conference. When asked to preside over the mushaira at the end of the conference, he gracefully suggested to the organizers that perhaps one of the younger poets should be given that honour, since 'I'm old, let the young people come forward'. As usual, he impressed everyone in Toronto with his warm-heartedness and generosity. Faiz had this effect on everyone who met him; it was as if a halo of warmth and love surrounded him and everyone wanted to bask in it wherever he went.

Faiz, though, was feeling the tug of home and family more and more. And perhaps like most people who experience old age, he was also sensing the end approaching. He wanted to go home.

Notes

1. Alys Faiz, *Over My Shoulder* (Lahore: Frontier Post Publications, 1993), p. 107.
2. Christian militias.
3. Asif Farrukhi, in *Makalmaat-e Faiz* (Lahore: Sang-e Meel Publications, 2011), p. 14.
4. Yasser Arafat, 'Faiz mere dost', in *Adb-e Latif*, Faiz number (Lahore: Maktaba Jadeed, 1988), p. 7.
5. Sarfaraz Iqbal, *Daman-e Yousaf* (Lahore: Mavra Publishers, 1989), p. 75.
6. Translation by this author.
7. Ayub Mirza, *Faiz Nama* (Lahore: Classic Publishers, 2005), p. 276.
8. Ibadat Barelvi, 'Chand yaadein, chandta'asuraat', in *Afkar*, Faiz number (Karachi: Maktaba Afkar, 1965), p. 188.
9. Ibid.
10. N. Lazard, 'Translating Faiz', *Annual of Urdu Studies*, vol. 5. Available at http://dsal.uchicago.edu/books/annualofurdustudies/toc.html?volume=5

20

Free at Last

> We shall not cease from exploration, and the end of all our exploring will be to arrive where we started and know the place for the first time.
>
> —T.S. Eliot

Faiz had already seriously started thinking of returning home to Lahore before his seventieth birthday in 1981. He was not getting any younger and his health was declining steadily. A lifetime of chain-smoking, travelling, lack of exercise and a generally unhealthy lifestyle had taken its toll. He was even willing to be constantly watched by the military regime in Pakistan if that was the price he had to pay for being close to family and spending more time with his daughters and grandchildren. He knew he would not be allowed to do much in Pakistan. The Zia dictatorship was at its zenith and there was widespread repression and surveillance of any activities which were not approved of by the government. Faiz felt, though, that he had done his part and deserved some rest in his last days. In a letter to a journalist friend in 1981, he had written:

> Friends like you miss me, I'm sure. But there are many others who are relieved that I am absent [from Pakistan]...you say that there is still room for us in literature and culture [in Pakistan], and bless you for saying that, but those I have mentioned [earlier] don't even spare us while we are [abroad] and fabricate God knows, all kinds of ridiculous stories. At any rate, I have no complaints; because of them, I am still remembered over there. You have written about religion and Islam; perhaps on your guarantee, they might admit me into their circle of faith but as Iqbal had said:'The narrow minded zealot termed me a "kaafir" (infidel)
>
> And the kaafir considered me a Musalman'.
>
> And these people are not even zealots, they are merely merchants of religion otherwise I have had the honor of learning in the company of many renowned religious scholars of our

> day: Shams-ul-Ulema Maulvi Mir Hasan, Maulvi Ibrahim Hussain [many others], and no one has dared say a word [against them]. This fashion of expelling believers from Islam is a new one…and the amazing thing is that one day Dr. Abdus Salam[1] is declared a 'kaafir' and heretic and the next day [after] he receives a prestigious Western award, the same people declare their slavish obeisance. And another thing, to our name is still attached the "Rawalpindi Conspiracy case convict" appendage. One of our friends and co-accused is now the Minister of Culture,[2] I wonder if that title is appended to his name as well. Anyway, forget it, we have lived our life; now it's just a matter of an invitation from the 'other side'.[3]

In the same letter, Faiz referred to the carnage that Alys and he were witnessing in Beirut. Israeli bombings were daily wreaking death and destruction on defenceless Palestinian civilians. Faiz described how, on one particularly horrific day, explosions reverberated all day, all around them; intermingled with the bombing was the wail of ambulance sirens, announcements on loudspeakers imploring people to donate blood for the wounded and the crying of those who had lost loved ones. In one bombing, an entire family of Palestinians, some of whom worked in Faiz's building, was killed. 'There is hardly a home which has not become a House of Mourning,' he wrote. In spite of this, he wanted to stay on. 'It doesn't seem right to run away', and so, he kept travelling with Beirut as his base.

In early February 1982, Faiz went to Lahore. Alys was already there. Faiz intended to stay for a few months and then return to Beirut and resume his travelling. He was very happy in Lahore and, unlike in the past, wanted to meet as many people as possible. There was no dearth of visitors, of course. Friends, admirers, young, old, men, women, journalists, they all wanted to spend time with Faiz. But he would lose his breath and tire easily. His doctors had forbidden him from smoking and he was trying to give it up. Alys and his daughters would try to keep him from smoking or tiring himself out, but it wasn't easy.

'I am wandering of my own free will'

Since people were so intensely interested in Faiz's life, it was natural on this trip that he was asked questions about his self-imposed 'exile', a word about which Faiz himself had always been coy. While he referred repeatedly to 'exile' in his poetry from this period, he refused outright to term his absence from the country as such in his interviews: 'I did not decide to leave the country because of any steps by the government. It was just that circumstances were such that I had to stay abroad for an extended period and when circumstances allow, I will return home.'[4]

And in an interview a few months earlier, about his 'exile poetry' and that of Nazim Hikmet, Mahmoud Darwish, and others, Faiz had said clearly that while the pain of separation from the homeland was similar, the difference between him and those other poets was that 'they were forcibly exiled while I am wandering of my own free will, I have not been forced out of my home, I can go back whenever I desire.'[5] Referring specifically to Palestine's Mahmoud Darwish, he said it was not just Darwish but the entire Palestinian people who had been forcibly turned out of their homeland. He also talked about Nazim Hikmet, who had been sentenced to fourteen years in prison and later had to flee Turkey in fear of his life. 'They had no way to return home,' said Faiz and thus their pain was much greater than his.

It might have helped dispel the speculation if Faiz had bothered to respond to his critics but it had been his lifelong habit to ignore his detractors and, in fact, greet them as friends if he ever came across them. It irritated those close to him who felt that he ought to at least answer some of these criticisms since his silence at times appeared to give credence to the rumours and innuendos. His younger son-in-law, Humair Hashmi, once complained to Faiz about one particular poet and writer who claimed great loyalty to Faiz, yet never lost a chance to take a dig at him behind his back. Faiz had said with a chuckle, 'You know God has said to try to develop His divine qualities in oneself; now take a look at all the people God has to endure. So what if we have to endure that one person?'[6]

'Come back home'

On 22 February 1982, one of Faiz's close friends, the poet Shabbir Hasan Khan popularly known as Josh Malihabadi, passed away in Islamabad. Faiz was in the city that day and was planning to attend the funeral. Before the funeral, though, he was due to meet Pakistan's military dictator, General Zia-ul-Haq. The meeting had been arranged by Faiz's friend Arbab Niaz, then minister of culture in the Zia government. After the meeting, Faiz said that the general had received him warmly and had admitted to an oversight when Faiz chided him that no one from his staff or the government had seen fit to attend the great Urdu poet, 'Josh's' funeral, even though General Zia professed to be a great supporter of Urdu. Later in the conversation, General Zia brought up the issue of Faiz living abroad and asked why he did not come back to Pakistan; that it was the wish of the government and Zia himself that Faiz live permanently in Pakistan. Faiz told him that he too wished to live in Pakistan but was concerned about the restrictions that might be placed on him. As an example, he told the general how, on his way from London to Tokyo, he had been stopped and harassed at Karachi airport and had only been given permission to continue after the minister of the interior had personally intervened. The general apologized and said he had no knowledge of the incident. Faiz told him that he would like to live in Pakistan but there should be no restriction on his travel abroad and General Zia assured him that it would be so. After some more chit-chat, the meeting ended.

This meeting was the source of some consternation amongst Faiz's friends. Faiz had served for a time in the previous government of Zulfiqar Ali Bhutto, and they objected to his meeting with the general who had deposed and later hanged Bhutto, suspended civil liberties and was leading an undemocratic, military dictatorship. Faiz, of course, was used to being disparaged by friend and foe alike. It had started when he was still chief editor of *Pakistan Times* before partition and had reached a crescendo when he had been arrested for the Rawalpindi Conspiracy Case. In a letter to his younger daughter, Moneeza, who was going through something similar in her work at the state-run Pakistan Television during the Zia dictatorship, he had written:

> There is no solution to the headaches of the office. As far as possible, use our 'switch-off' remedy. The late Malik Feroz Khan[7] had an even better remedy but perhaps only high officials can use that. When I was in Delhi,[8] Malik sahib was the Defense

> member of the Viceroy's Council. One day, the elder Bokhari[9] and I went to his office to meet him. We observed not a single paper on Malik sahib's desk while he was sitting idly smoking a cheroot. Bokhari sahib said; Malik sahib, there is a war going on and you are the Defense member, do you not have any work? Malik sahib said 'Shah-jee, don't ask about work. The more I do, the more there is, so I never bother with it!'[10]

In the years since the Rawalpindi Conspiracy Case, Faiz had become expert at 'switching off' the noise from outside.

One can speculate that now, past the age of seventy and in failing health, Faiz must have been nostalgic for family and home. In addition, the daily carnage all around him in Beirut must have been both physically and emotionally draining. He had already confessed to a friend in London that although he remained true to the humanist and socialist values for which he had struggled all his life, and that the struggle for social justice was far from over, he was now older and did not have the strength to endure imprisonment or worse. He wanted to go home, but he also wanted to make sure he knew what the military rulers of Pakistan had in store for him when he returned.

General Zia himself had said publicly more than once that Faiz should return home, that his government bore him no ill will and that he would not be restricted from travelling. Once he met the general, and heard it from his own mouth, Faiz knew he could go back with some measure of certainty that he would remain free of harassment.

Faiz was still in Lahore and preparing to leave for Beirut when he started having breathing problems and was rushed to Lahore's Mayo Hospital. He had to spend ten days in the intensive care unit. While in hospital, he wrote his haunting 'Iss waqt tau yun lagta hai' (It seems, at this time). Later, he called it 'the experience of a sleepless night':

> It seems at this time, that there is nothing
> The Moon, the Sun, neither darkness nor morning
> A veil of beauty on the windows of the eyes
> And a repose of pain in the havens of the heart[11]

After being discharged from hospital, he again headed for Beirut but he was clearly unhappy there and wrote to a friend a week after he arrived about how it felt strange to be back after a 'month and a half of festivities in Lahore'. He kept travelling and was in Moscow when Soviet leader Brezhnev died in November 1982. On the advice of his Soviet doctors, Faiz was admitted to a Moscow hospital where he was treated for a chest infection and his doctors finally prevailed upon him to stop smoking entirely. He was even forbidden from going to any gathering where people were smoking so as to prevent his exposure to cigarette smoke. After more than fifty years of chain-smoking, Faiz finally decided that he was ready to breathe easier and stopped smoking, with the result that his breathing and asthma attacks improved considerably. He also lost quite a bit of weight and felt better physically. Mentally though, to those around him, he appeared even more absent-minded than usual. He would occasionally lose his train of thought while talking. It was as if he was fading away.

Medically speaking, it can be surmised that Faiz, as a result of his lifelong chain-smoking, drinking and complete lack of physical exercise had developed what is today called 'minimal cognitive impairment', a precursor to the more severe condition known as dementia. Ageing and its related changes cause hardening and narrowing of the blood vessels in the brain (and the rest of the body). This leads to blood-circulation problems which can manifest as absent-mindedness, confusion, memory problems or other symptoms. Although one of his last poems 'Bahut mila na mila zindagi se gham kya hai' (Whatever we have received from life, why fret) is dated November 1984, the month that he died, indicating that his poetic abilities, at least, remained intact almost to the end, it is likely that had Faiz not succumbed to his breathing and heart problems when he did, he would have continued to decline mentally with increasing memory problems, confusion and other symptoms of poor brain function.

He arrived back in Lahore in February 1983 after another globetrotting tour in which he visited Toronto, Moscow, London, Tunis, Cyprus, Paris, and several other places. As usual, he was delighted to be back. His family had imposed strict limits on his meeting people in view of his health, but Faiz himself was very eager to meet old friends and acquaintances. He would lose his breath easily though, and still had fits of coughing, which tired him out. His friends and admirers in Pakistan and all over the world wanted to see him though, and invitations from poured in constantly. Other than Moscow and London, he turned down most invitations from outside Pakistan, pleading ill health. Discussions were on about moving the *Lotus* headquarters to Tunis, but Faiz had already decided that he would live in Lahore and manage his editorial duties from there.

The sum of a life: Saaray Sukhan Hamaray *and* Nuskha Hai Wafa

Faiz was still in London in 1982 when the idea of a 'collected' works of his poetry was floated by some of his friends. The idea was to come up with a 'special edition' that could be sold for a decent sum to raise money for a Faiz Foundation in London. After his *Sar-e Wadi-e Sina*, three other collections: *Sham-e Shehr-e Yaran*, *Mere Dil Mere Musafir* and *Ghubaar-e-Ayaam* had been published in quick succession. Of these, the last was the one in which Faiz's poetic expression was at its all-encompassing best.

*Ghubaar-e-A*yaam, which can, in some ways, be considered a supplement to *Mere Dil Mere Musafir*, reflects all those experiences that had found a voice in the latter: the pain of exile and its attendant sense of rootlessness, the brave struggle of the Palestinian people, sacrifice and renunciation, a maturation of the meaning of home and homeland, the rising global fury against tyranny and oppression, the ongoing Afro-Asian struggle against neocolonial exploitation, the shared pain of oppressed people all over the world and a belief in eventual victory, an impassioned plea against all kinds of fascism, the collective human struggle against an indifferent universe, one person's intense loneliness in the midst of a crowd and the indescribable pain of being apart from those one loves and holds dear; these are some of the themes that pervade the poetry of Faiz's last days.

Saaray Sukhan Hamaray (All Our Words) was published by one of Faiz's friends who had fled Pakistan following the Zia martial law and settled in London. Only 700 copies of the special edition were published, each numbered individually and inscribed with Faiz's signature. A sketch of Faiz's, characteristically with cigarette in hand, by renowned Indian painter M.F. Hussain, was included in the book. The edition was expensive and was meant for those of Faiz's friends and fans in North America and Europe who could afford it. It was hugely popular and sold out soon after its publication. Faiz loved the new book. He wrote to a friend: '[It] is something to behold regardless of the poetry. Never, after the reign of the Mughals, has an Urdu book been published with such fanfare.'[12]

Almost simultaneously, the Pakistani edition of Faiz's collected works was published under the title *Nuskha hai Wafa* (Destinies in Love). The name was taken from a verse by Faiz favourite, Mirza Asadullah Khan Ghalib. While *Saaray Sukhan Hamaray* remained limited mainly to Europe and North America, *Nuskha hai Wafa* was widely welcomed in Pakistan, India, Bangladesh and all over the Indian subcontinent. Special celebrations were held all over Pakistan to mark the publication of the book. In one memorable meeting in Islamabad, the crowd was such that there was no room to even squeeze into the main hall. When Faiz arrived at the venue, he was carried into the hall on the shoulders of his adoring readers and well-wishers. In his speech, a clearly emotional Faiz thanked the crowd and said: 'How could I have known that all of you loved me so much; if only I had realized it earlier, I would have tried to write more and better.'[13]

Similar scenes were repeated all over the country whenever Faiz was in Pakistan.

Saaray Sukhan Hamaray and *Nuskha hai Wafa* are almost identical in their content except for one significant omission: ten verses from Faiz's beautiful poem, 'Sar e Waadi e Seena', were expunged from *Nuskha Hai Wafa*, perhaps because of some Arabic terms and references to the Divine. The right-wing press in Lahore had had a field day excoriating Faiz for his 'irreligious' outlook and for insulting Islam when the poem was first published in the collection *Sar-e Wadi-e Sina*, even though the verses appear to contain nothing objectionable. Since it was the beginning of a new era of religious revivalism in Pakistan though (and this time, it was being fully supported and encouraged by a military dictatorship), Faiz's Lahore publisher had thought it would be prudent to edit the poem. Faiz had refused point blank and had, instead, given the collection to his Karachi publisher, who published the poem in its entirety in *Sar-e Wadi-e Sina*. When the collected works, *Nuskha hai Wafa'* was published from Lahore, to Faiz's astonishment, the ten controversial verses were missing. To this day, the poem continues to be published in its censored version in the collected works.

'What will it be like the day death comes'

By 1983, Faiz had settled more or less permanently in Lahore. Salima and Moneeza lived close by with their families and Faiz and Alys could spend time with the grandchildren to their heart's content. Faiz was doing as well as could be expected, given his long-standing heart and breathing problems. As already mentioned, he had stopped smoking on strict instructions from his doctors and was even forbidden from being around anyone who was smoking. He had undergone a medical check-up in Moscow in 1982 where, according to him, 'They dusted me off, tightened a few nuts and bolts, changed the oil and water, that's about it,' meaning he had been given a clean bill of health notwithstanding the medical problems which were now part and parcel of his life.

On his last birthday, 13 February 1984, Faiz was in Lahore and his friends and well-wishers wanted to celebrate the day with their usual fervour. Faiz, though, was unusually glum. The recent death of his friend, the Palestinian poet Mu'in Bseiso, from a heart condition, had greatly saddened him and he did not want a big celebration. But his friends would have none of it and gathered at the home of Salima and Shoaib Hashmi. Faiz sat in a separate room so as to avoid cigarette smoke, while people came in and offered birthday greetings. Everyone wanted their photograph taken with him and, as usual, Faiz obliged. The noted singer Iqbal Bano came as a guest and sang Faiz's poetry for hours while Faiz sat lost in thought. Salima and Moneeza were concerned about his health and so he was taken home to get some sleep while the festivities went on late into the night.

In April, he headed off to Moscow as he did every year for a medical check-up and also in connection with *Lotus*. Faiz was interested in bringing out an Urdu edition of the journal from Pakistan, as a prelude to reorganizing the Afro-Asian Writers' Association, also from Pakistan. The international office of *Lotus* was in the process of being set up in Tunis when Mu'in Bseiso passed away in London and the matter was delayed. After spending time in Moscow and Tashkent, Faiz went on to London where, in July, he presided over an international Faiz seminar in which noted Urdu scholars from all over read papers about his poetry and his craft.

His friends remembered that he was very happy that summer. In an essay, one of his friends later wrote how Faiz met them at Pakistani poet Zehra Nigah's house and said, 'Come, I'll take you to paint the town red' and took them to a pub, then to a restaurant and chatted and laughed with them for hours. He dwelt on old memories, recalled his meeting in the USSR with Nazim Hikmet and Pablo Neruda and recited some of his new verses.

From London, Faiz headed to Germany to look over the printing of the latest edition of *Lotus*, then to Beirut, back to Moscow and finally back to Lahore. This time, he appeared in such good health that his family and friends were delighted to see him.

The spirits of ancestors

By late summer of 1984, Faiz and Alys were back in Lahore in their small, comfortable home close to their family. The house overlooked a front and back lawn filled with trees and flowers of all kinds. Faiz would get up each morning and after getting dressed, sit in his verandah and receive his friends and visitors. He would tire easily and would retire for a rest in the afternoon. He had never been one to stay in one place too long though, and, in September, headed to Islamabad for yet another conference in his honour.

As already mentioned, he was also worried about his old friends. He wanted to put together a trust to arrange some money for a house for his friend Ustad Daman.[14] Another old friend, acclaimed music director Khwaja Khurshid Anwar, was sick and in hospital. When Faiz went to see him, he told Faiz, 'Listen yaar, let me go on first. I'll wait to welcome you over there.' When Khwaja Khurshid died on 30 October 1984, Faiz was inconsolable.

In those last days, Faiz was impatient to go to his village. He had helped fix up the village mosque and his ancestral home and had used his influence with the village administration to open up a school and a dispensary, as well as a health centre for women. On the way from Lahore to Kala Qader, as the car in which Faiz was riding bumped along dusty country roads, Faiz remarked, 'I have always said that the distance between our cities and our villages is 5000 years.'[15] It was a pointed comment on the lack of development in Pakistan's (and India's) rural areas, where the benefits of modernity were yet to penetrate.

Faiz had only visited the village a few times in the last several decades, although Alys and the grandchildren had been there a few times. His cousins had been informed of Faiz's visit and the whole village (it seemed) as well as dozens of people from neighbouring villages had turned up to welcome him. He did not know many of the people by name but, of course, they all knew him. Everyone wanted him to use whatever influence he had with the district government to help them in their problems and Faiz promised to do so. Faiz visited the ancestral mosque and, at the villagers' insistence, led the evening prayers. He then headed over to the neighbouring village of Jessar, his mother's home, to pay a visit.

On the way back, Faiz was very happy. He had asked the villagers to build him a room overlooking the mustard fields where he could stay when he came to the village and was toying with the idea of spending more time there. He had even broached the idea with Alys. They could open a school there and spend time reading and writing. Alys had reminded him tartly about his breathing problems and the dust in the village and the fact that there would be no one in the village to come visit him in the evening and chat with him. Nevertheless, Faiz remained enthusiastic about the idea, mentioning it repeatedly to Salima as well.

'May nothing haunt your heart but sleep'

Moneeza and Humair Hashmi's seventeenth wedding anniversary was on 19 November 1984 and they had invited some friends over for dinner. Faiz fell sick the same night, during the party, and was rushed to Lahore's Mayo Hospital where he succumbed to a combination of his heart and breathing problems the next day.

The news of Faiz's death on the afternoon of 20 November

1984 flashed around the world despite the fact that this was well before the era of mobile phones, the Internet or instant media. By the time Faiz was brought home to be buried, all of Lahore was in mourning and scores of people had already gathered at his Model Town home. By evening, people from surrounding cities like Rawalpindi, Gujranwala, Faisalabad and Sargodha had started gathering as well, including workers' organizations complete with their red flags. The streets of the quiet neighbourhood were choked with people.

Alys, who was besides herself with grief, had been given a sedative and was in bed. Faiz's two sons-in-law, Shoaib and Humair Hashmi, were shooing away photographers who were trying to take pictures of Faiz's body, 'He is alive, please don't show him lifeless.' Representatives from the state-run Pakistan Television and Radio Pakistan had also shown up and been turned away. The family had decided not to allow the state-run media, which had blacklisted Faiz while he was alive, to show him after his death.

Faiz was hoisted onto the shoulders of his family and friends to begin his last journey to the graveyard. The funeral procession was more than a mile long. Once, Alys and Faiz had argued about where they wanted to be buried. Alys had claimed that she was an internationalist and would be buried wherever she was when she died, while Faiz had expressed his fervent desire to be buried in his homeland. Finally, the procession reached the graveyard. Faiz was lowered into the freshly dug grave for his final rest.

The journey was over.

Notes

1. Mohammad Abdus Salam (1926–1996), Pakistani theoretical physicist; the first Pakistani (and second Muslim) to win the Nobel Prize in physics in 1979; friend and admirer of Faiz's. Gave the first Faiz Memorial Lecture after Faiz's death in 1988 in Lahore.
2. Lieutenant Colonel Niaz Muhammad Arbab, one of the fifteen co-accused in the Rawalpindi Conspiracy Case.
3. Faiz Ahmed Faiz, Letter to Mohammad Shafi (Meem Sheen), dated 22 July 1981, in *Lao tau Qatl Nama Mera* (Lahore: Kausar Publishers, 1985), p. 28.
4. Ashfaq Hussain (comp.), *Faiz ke Maghrabi Hawalay* (Lahore: Jang Publishers, 1995), p. 212.

5. Ibid.
6. Humair Hashmi, personal recollection.
7. Malik Sir Feroz Khan Noon (1893–1970), noted politician and, briefly, prime minister of Pakistan. The first Indian to serve in the Viceroy's Council before independence, he held the defence portfolio from 1941 to 1943.
8. Faiz served in the British Indian Army during the Second World War and was posted in Delhi during that time.
9. Ahmad Shah Bokhari 'Patras', Faiz's beloved teacher and mentor, one of the greatest humorists of the Urdu language.
10. Unpublished letter to Moneeza Hashmi, April 1980.
11. Translation by this author.
12. Hussain, *Faiz ke Maghrabi Hawalay*, p. 808.
13. Ibid.
14. Real name Chiragh Deen (1911–1984), Punjabi poet and mystic, a persistent critic of military dictators and the most celebrated Punjabi poet at the time of partition; close friend of Faiz's.
15. Ahmad Salim, *Faiz: Yaadein, Baatein* (Lahore: Sang-e-Meel Publications, 2011), p. 78.

21
Man and Myth-I

> I do not accept the claim of saintliness...I am prone to as many weaknesses as you are. But I have seen the world. I have lived in the world with my eyes open.
>
> —Mahatma Gandhi

Faiz was never averse to talking about all aspects of his life, including personal ones. People who had read his poetry were curious to know more about him, particularly because of the notoriety following his imprisonment. It would be rare to find anyone among his contemporaries as willing as Faiz to speak about himself. This was not something he enjoyed. He was an intensely shy man, someone who was quite happy sitting quietly in a roomful of people. He also had an aversion to talking about himself, calling it a 'favorite occupation of bores'. He recognized though that, because of the notoriety he had gained for his poetry and his political activism, people wanted to know more about him, both as a person and a poet.

As a result of his willingness to 'go on the record', there is a wealth of material available about his likes and dislikes, his habits and beliefs and, in general, about many aspects of his life.

He was of average height, with a darkish complexion. Standing next to Alys, who was taller than the average Pakistani woman, Faiz looked short. The most striking feature of his face was his large expressive eyes, which, in photographs, always seem to be smiling. It is universally reported that he was calm, with a supremely serene temperament. Except for close family members who might have seen him express some irritation at a minor matter, no one can recall ever having seen him angry (or dejected or frustrated). In fact, the moniker of 'Happy Buddha', bestowed upon him in later years, seems quite apt.

Friends and well-wishers would often chide him for not responding to the frequent vitriolic attacks on his work and personal life. Faiz would always call such a response a waste of one's creative energies which could be better utilized in practising one's chosen craft. And for those who had made it their stock in trade to abuse him, including in print, his response would always be, 'If it helps them make a living, let them do it.' He was humble to a fault. This was not the false humility of someone who thought a great deal of himself; Faiz knew he was a good poet, technically sound and with a deep knowledge of poetry, but he was genuinely uncomfortable when he was compared to those he considered the masters: Iqbal, Ghalib, Mir. His response would be, 'Leave it be, I am nothing. Ghalib, Iqbal, Mir, these people were poets, what am I? I have written a few poems, a few ghazals, what great achievement is that?'[1]

Of course it can be argued that this humility is a natural consequence of having achieved something worthwhile in life. After all, it was Faiz himself who wrote about human life being an unending endeavour to elevate oneself beyond one's limits.

As a leading intellectual of his age, Faiz would often be called upon to pronounce judgement on the pressing issues of the day, including making predictions about when or how such and such thing would happen. It was his lifelong habit to refuse to be drawn into arguments on 'non-issues'. He would either brush a question off with his usual 'choro bhai' (leave it) or would make a gentle joke to change the subject. Once a dedicated 'comrade' asked him rather insistently when the long-promised revolution would come, in answer to which Faiz smiled his serene smile and responded placidly, 'Well, it will come sooner or later; you're still young'!

He also made it a point never to demean or deny a contrary point of view.

Life of the party

On the personal front, while his penchant for late-night parties was legendary (and some of these would last well into the morning hours), he was always an early riser who would be up and out of bed by 6 a.m. His daughters remember how he would always be freshly shaved and smelling of his favourite cologne (Paco Rabane or Old Spice) whenever he stepped out of his bedroom. He was something of a 'dandy'; his clothes would always be clean and freshly laundered, his shoes shining, everything about his external appearance primly in place.

His penchant for drink is well known, with scotch whiskey being his favourite, although he was not averse to trying more exotic concoctions such as a cocktail of rum, vodka and lime cordial. He loved to eat saag and pulao and one of his favourite dishes was shabdegh, the rich Kashmiri dish of meat, turnips and spices cooked overnight. It was a favourite of his old friend and mentor, Sufi Ghulam Mustafa Tabassum's as well. Their mutual friend, the renowned singer Farida Khanum, would often cook it at Sufi Tabassum's house at his insistence. Faiz also was in the habit, since his youth, of eating a fixed number of almonds or almond paste first thing in the morning with water; an age-old recipe in the subcontinent said to strengthen memory and to provide all manner of health benefits. He loved to eat sweets, one of his favourites being 'gajrella', a thick, sweet concoction made of carrots and milk. He was also fond of gosh-e feel, literally ears of the elephant, an Afghan dessert of crumbly, papery pastry sprinkled with powdered sugar; he had developed a taste for it because his mother used to make it often. She, in turn, had learned it from the Afghan women who lived in their house and had accompanied Faiz's father back from his travels.

He was never averse to an invitation for a dinner or a party and would often be invited to the houses of the 'movers and shakers' of Pakistan; high-ranking bureaucrats, industrialists, feudal lords, and the like. Some of them he knew from his days at *Pakistan Times*, others were fans of his poetry, still others he had known in Government College or had met later in life. All of them were entranced by his affectionate, erudite personality, his always cheerful demeanour, and, of course, his total command over literature, language and poetry. Inevitably, at such gatherings, he would be asked to recite some of his poetry. Alys would teasingly refer to it as Faiz 'singing for his supper', to which he would serenely respond that he was of peasant stock, so if the lord of the realm (or its modern-day equivalent) summoned him, of course he had to go and 'sing for his supper'. It was his lifelong habit to never allow his political beliefs to interfere with his personal friendships.

He had a wide circle of friends and admirers and it did not take long, whenever he was in town, wherever he was, for word to get out and people to start gathering. Faiz welcomed them all, old and young, male and female, rich and poor, accomplished and obscure, and, of course, persons of letters, poets, novelists, short-story writers, film and TV people and everyone connected with the 'finer arts'. He rarely spoke much even in the midst of a crowd, usually sitting quietly, smiling and drinking. His fondness for a drink stayed with him till his last years, even when his health did not allow it any longer. Someone once remarked that Faiz's going to 'Scotch Mission' high school may have been an omen, since he was particularly fond of that drink!

Salima remembers though that in spite of being able to put away prodigious quantities of alcohol, she can never remember seeing him drunk, certainly not unpleasantly so. In fact, the more he drank, the quieter he would become. He was never a talker anyway, preferring to sit and listen to others, something he did par excellence, seeming to pay attention to even the most inane talkers, making them feel wanted and appreciated. As the evening would wear on, Faiz, a drink in his hand, would become mellower. One way to tell that he was enjoying his drink was that he would laugh more, but that was about it. Towards the end of his life, when his doctors forbade him from drinking anymore, he stopped abruptly and was none the worse for it.

Alys used to nag him about his chain-smoking. Salima remembers how her mother used to try and limit Faiz's cigarette smoking, 'She never forced him to stop but she would always try and limit the amount he smoked. He would keep lighting one after the other, sometimes a 100 cigarettes a day!'[2] Later in life, when his health would not permit him to smoke, he once joked to a friend, 'The doctors say if I keep smoking and drinking I will die; I think I will die if I don't smoke and drink so this is life's dilemma right now!'[3]

Women: The splendour of the world

Faiz was extremely fond of the company of women. He would greet them with a hug and a kiss on the forehead, make space for them next to him and generally give them attention. Women, of course, as with all poets, responded ardently to his affection. In any case, Faiz had been raised mainly by women: aunts, cousins, half- and stepsisters, and remembered affectionately how they had 'forced him to become civilized'. This was also a window into his serene personality. 'While growing up, they [the women] taught me to never utter an abusive word; I still can't.'

The circle of his women admirers stretched from his native Pakistan to the UK, the USSR and all over the world. His collection *Sar-e Wadi-e Sina* is dedicated to Maryam (Mira) Salganik, the distinguished Russian writer, scholar and friend. Ludmila Vasilieva, the Russian and Urdu scholar [and author of the very comprehensive *Faiz: Hayaat aur Takhleeqat* (Faiz: Life and Creations)] fondly remembered her first meeting with Faiz when she was a young student at Moscow University in 1967, and his affection for her throughout his life, in her eulogy delivered in Moscow a few months after his death. In Pakistan, too, there were countless women who loved and admired Faiz.

This must have tested Alys's patience at times but there is no record of any discord between the two of them on this issue. Writer and poet Amrita Pritam once asked him about this in an interview: Did Alys know of all his loves? Faiz answered that she did but 'she is not only my wife, she is also my friend. That is why we have stayed together for so long. Love is painful, friendship is peaceful.'

After sharing that, Faiz put his cigarette in the ashtray and became serious. He paused for a while and then said, 'I decided a while ago not to fall in love with any woman ever again. I will make friends, though, provided she is worthy of friendship.'[4]

Many of Faiz's most popular poems were set to music and sung by some of the biggest names in the Indian subcontinent. Two marsiyas (elegies) written by Faiz in memory of his close friend Dr Shaukat Haroon in 1968 were, 'Chand niklay kisi jaanib teri zebaai ka' ('Let the moon of your countenance rise somewhere') and 'Kab tak dil kee khair manain' ('How long must we guard our heart'). Both were sung beautifully by Pakistan's Farida Khanum, an ardent Faiz admirer.

Humair Hashmi remembers how Faiz and his beloved teacher, Sufi Ghulam Mustafa Tabassum (also an accomplished poet and the only one Faiz considered worthy of critiquing his own poetry), came over to his and Moneeza's house one winter afternoon.

While lunch was being laid, they had a drink, which turned into two and then three, and Faiz mentioned Farida Khanum and expressed a wish to see her. She was called on the phone and a car was sent to fetch her and she came over, all dressed up, smiling and joyous to be with him. Of course, the lunch stretched into evening and the gathering became bigger and bigger as news spread about the three of them (Faiz, Tabassum and Farida) being in one place.

Another Faiz admirer was the Queen of Melody (Malika-e Tarannum), Noor Jehan herself. Humair Hashmi remembers another time, while passing by her house, in Lahore's Liberty Market, Faiz decided on impulse to go in and see her. She had sung his famous 'Mujh se pehli si muhabbat meri mehboob na maang' ('Do not ask of me, my darling, that love of old'). Faiz had been so happy with her rendition of it that he had 'gifted' the poem to her, telling her it was now 'her' poem. When Faiz and his companions went into her house, she was singing accompanied by a harmonium to an audience of music and film personages. As soon as Noor Jehan saw Faiz, she stopped singing, shrieked with joy, hugged and kissed him and introduced him to her guests. Drinks were ordered and, upon Faiz's insistence, she resumed her singing, and it went on till early dawn the next day.

One of the women with whom Faiz was extremely close was the poet Zehra Nigah. Her house in London was where Faiz would stay every time he was there. Now in frail health, her eyes still sparkle and her memory is strong when it comes to the time she spent with Faiz:

> They [women] loved him. I only saw two poets who had that kind of effect on women: Faiz and Faraz;[5] there used to be an avalanche [of women] when they were around. It was always amazing to me, no matter which city, where he [Faiz] was, it was the same. In Hindustan, they would line up as if for a 'darshan'. I feel the reason for that was his generosity of heart, his graciousness and his humility. He was such a great man but so humble, never one to put on airs. Someone would say 'recite something' and he would say 'alright, I'll try to recall something' and then he would do it. Poets are known for being pompous but not Faiz sahib.[6]

And upon being pressed to name the women Faiz was particularly close to, she almost whispers the name 'Maryam Bilgrami;[7] he was very close to her, there was a stack of letters [gestures with her hands], and such beautiful letters...' And then, like Faiz, she refuses to say anymore.

> Whatever it was, with whichever woman, he handled it perfectly, very gracefully. He never discussed it with anyone. We would tease him about it and say, 'Faiz sahib, so and so has come especially to be close to you,' and he would just laughingly chide us and tell us to stop. I asked him one time about his vision of the perfect woman, what would she be like, what qualities should she have? And you know, he didn't say she should be beautiful. He said she should be intelligent and alluring ['dil-kash']. Now this has many meanings but the first thing he said was she should be intelligent. That was his standard of beauty. If he saw it in anyone, he would be happy.

And then, in a sign of her own devotion to him, she says:

> His eyes were so luminous and expressive. When he was happy, you could see it in his eyes and the same when he was sad. When he was upset, he would go very quiet and just smoke one cigarette after another, he would pick up a piece of paper, then put it down, then pick it up again. When Majid [her husband] would go to Dubai or somewhere on business, I would say to him, 'Faiz sahib, let's go to the cinema,' to cheer him up, but he would say no. He was always ready to go to the theatre though.[8]

One friend who had a 'licence' to tease Faiz was journalist and translator, Khalid Hasan. He was a part of Bhutto's government and was posted in London when General Zia-ul-Haq's military coup happened and chose to stay on in London. About him, Zehra Nigah remembers:

> He [Khalid Hasan] used to come to our house [in London] every evening. In those days, Naomi[9] was doing her translations of his poetry. She would sit at our dining table and one day, Khalid Hasan came and [Faiz] was explaining something to Naomi and he was holding her hand and Khalid Hasan said to him in Punjabi, 'Sir ji, does this "gori" understand anything or are you just wasting your time?' And Faiz said, 'No, no; she understands

> everything, she just has a little difficulty writing it properly,' and Khalid Hasan said, 'Well, how can she write unless you let go of her hand!' [chuckles]; and he [Faiz] just reddened and said 'What are you talking about!?' and that poor American girl, she was mystified about what was going on. You know, that was the pinnacle of love, holding hands, because he was so shy. He had such a cultured, refined attitude about expressing his affection. It's so rare in our poets [laughs].[10]

And again, talking about his affection for her, she recalls:

> He would always eat an omelette one morning, then the next day, he would eat cereal and then maybe a toast and tea another day. Anyway, he would always have an omelette on one of the days. Some nights, we would be up until 4 a.m. talking and then he would say, 'Tomorrow is our cereal day,' and I would remind him that it was omelette day but he would say no, so I wouldn't have to wake up early? It was little things like that which made him so endearing. He would never leave a newspaper open. There were all these thick newspapers but he would always read them, then fold them back up perfectly and put them on the table. My younger son, Nomi, always admired this green dressing gown that Faiz sahib wore and one time, when he left London, he folded it up and left it in Nomi's room. Nomi still has it and he still remembers Faiz sahib fondly for it. It used to be such a festival when he was in London. Our house used to be packed with visitors. People would show up at all hours to see him, and he would welcome all of them, no matter what time it was. He used to try and make his bed and clean up the room, he would really try and I would get cross and would tell him off because he would just mess it up. I would tell him just leave it, Carmen will come and do it. She was a Spanish girl who used to come to clean our house. She was very pretty and he was always pleased to see her. She would bounce in and say 'Good morning sir,' and he would have this big smile on his face, 'Good morning Carmen,' and he would say, 'How nice it is to see this girl; she lights up the place' [chuckles]. He did have a soft spot for a pretty face.[11]

Notes

1. Abdul Rauf Malik, *Faiz ki Sha'eri ka Naya Daur* (Lahore: People's Publishing House, 1988), p. 142.
2. Salima Hashmi, interview with Rubina Sarwar, *Jeddo Jehd*, Faiz number, vol. 20, issue 6, 14 February 2008, p. 15.
3. Khaleeq Anjum (comp.), *Faiz Ahmed Faiz: Tanqeedi Jaaeza* (New Delhi: Anjuman Taraqqi Urdu [Hind], 1985), p. 36.
4. Sheema Majeed (comp.), *Batein Faiz se* (Lahore: Rohtas Books, 1990), p. 20.
5. Syed Ahmad Shah 'Faraz' (1931–2008), Pakistani Urdu poet whose poetry has often been compared to Faiz's for its simplicity and elegance.
6. Zehra Nigah, unpublished interview with the author.
7. Originally from Hyderabad, Deccan; visited Faiz more than once in Lahore.
8. Zehra Nigah, unpublished interview with the author.
9. American poet and translator Naomi Lazard. The only American poet to translate Faiz's poetry under Faiz's personal supervision. Later published as *The True Subject* by Oxford University Press.
10. Zehra Nigah, unpublished interview with the author.
11. Ibid.

22

Man and Myth-II

I warm'd both hands before the fire of Life;
It sinks; and I am ready to depart.

—Walter Savage Landor

Love of books and music

Faiz had been an avid reader since a young age. He had started reading both Urdu prose and poetry since before his teens, including classics like *Fasana-e Azad* by Ratan Nath Sarshar and fiction by Abdul Halim Sharar. By his own account, his study of poetry started with Ghalib's contemporaries, Amir Meenai and Nawab Mirza Khan 'Dagh Dehlavi', whom he found easier to read than the notoriously difficult Ghalib. Later, on the advice of his father, he added English books to his reading, starting with Dickens, Arthur Conan Doyle and H. Rider Haggard, while still in school. In college, since he studied literature and poetry, he said that he had read all European fiction 'from Hardy to Tolstoy'. Tolstoy was one of his favourite writers and he had read *War and Peace* 'about 12 times'!

This love of reading remained with him all his life. When he was imprisoned the second time in Lahore Fort, he took two large trunk of books with him saying, 'There are books [in there]. There is no opportunity to study seriously outside [prison]. Now that I have a chance, I want to catch up on many years' worth of reading'![1]

Faiz also loved music. He attributed his love of music to

> my dearest friend Khwaja Khursheed Anwar [Pakistan's greatest music director—died 1984]. He used to be a terrorist in the times of Bhagat Singh. After being released from prison, he suddenly got obsessed with music and immersed himself in it. He introduced me to music. I remember the first musical experiment. I used to listen to Ashiq Ali Khan and Abdul Waheed Khan, and other teachers before as well, but there was not much substantial impact on my mind. Once I heard my friend Rafiq Ghaznavi singing a *thumri* 'Puppi-haa raa pi ki boli na bol', a *thumri* of

> [Raag] *Peeloo*. That suddenly made me appreciate music. Often I and Khursheed Anwar used to visit the mountains in summer vacations. He would sing and I would listen. So I have been interested in this field since the beginning.[2]

Salima remembers: '[He] was very fond of listening to classical music and had a very refined taste; everything from Western classical to African music. Among singers, he was friends with Roshan Ara Begum, Nazakat Ali Khan, Salamat Ali Khan, Amanat Ali Khan and Fateh Ali Khan. He was also close to Bade Ghulam Ali Khan.'[3]

Of things undone and forgotten

Like the prototypical poet, he was dreamy and absent-minded. His close friend Ludmila Vasilieva recites an incident to illustrate it:

> Faiz had once come over to my house as he so often did when he was in town [Moscow] and as usual, he was writing something. He gave it to me before he left and asked me not to show it to anyone until he'd spruced it up the next time he visited. It was his famous ghazal 'Aakhir-e Shab'.
>
> Two years passed before he came again. I gave the ghazal to him reminding him of his intent to brush it up for publishing. He looked it over and exclaimed, 'This is a good ghazal! Who wrote this?' I told him he had [laughs].
>
> There was a verse in that ghazal,
>
> 'Lams-e jaanaanliyey, masti-e paimaanaliyey
> Hamd-e Bari koutheydast-e duaaakhir e shab'
>
> He asked me whether he should use 'Lams' [consciousness] or 'Aks' [reflection] and I exclaimed 'Aks! Aks!' He'd crossed over 'Lams' and wrote 'Aks' in its place before he left. Later when he showed me the ghazal that was included in his compiled works, 'Merey Dil, Merey Musafir', I thumbed through it to find 'Akhir-e Shab' and saw that he had used 'Lams' after all. He was just being nice to me before, but I still have that piece of paper on which he'd crossed out 'Lams' and written 'Aks'.[4]

Faiz expressed regrets for many things that he had planned to do but never got around to. These ranged from boyhood dreams of becoming a cricketer (which every youth in the subcontinent dreams of) to writing a comprehensive history of Urdu poetry. For this project, he had even prepared a written outline and at one time, had thought of submitting it as a PhD project but it never saw the light of day.

Like the quintessential poet, he was also famously forgetful. Alys was very careful about money while Faiz was the opposite. He would send off his cook to get something from the bazaar and then forget how much money he had given him and never ask for change. He would take tongas to people's houses and get busy talking to the hosts and completely forget about the tonga, which would stay around and charge him extra fare. One of his friends recounts how the family would have to remind Faiz to turn on the ignition in the car before attempting to start it. One time, the fuel gauge on the car was out of order. Just to be on the safe side, it was decided that every time the car was taken out of the house, two gallons of petrol would be put in it. One day, Faiz took it to the petrol pump only to be told that the petrol tank was full. He was delighted and had totally forgotten that every day he had been putting two gallons in it and only using about half a gallon. 'He was so happy, as if he had found treasure!'[5]

Laugh as if there's no tomorrow

Despite Faiz's commitment to the most serious political causes of his time and despite going through some devastating personal losses, he never lost his sense of humour. Even while he was in jail, away from his young family, he could make them laugh, cheering them up as well. In a letter to Alys from jail in 1951, he wrote: 'Listen to a joke about one of our Ministers. It is said that in a function, there was a Muslim girl wearing a frock sitting next to a religious minded minister. The minister remarked crossly to a person sitting next to him "Look how shameless our girls have become. They don't even bother to hide their private parts". The man remarked "What are you saying? The poor girl is wearing a frock that goes down to her knees". To which the minister replied "so what? A Muslim girl's private parts go all the way down to her ankles!".'[6]

Another time, Faiz and his old friend, Abdullah Malik were sitting chatting about something when a high government official came in and joined them. Faiz had been his teacher. He asked Faiz what his greatest accomplishment in life had been. Faiz replied without missing a beat, 'Undoubtedly, helping you pass your BA exam!'[7]

As already mentioned, when Faiz's collection *Dast-e Saba* was published and he dedicated it to 'Kulsoom' (Alys's married name), there was a good measure of curiosity amongst his friends and acquaintances about the identity of the mysterious 'Kulsoom'. This was while Faiz and his companions were incarcerated during the Rawalpindi Conspiracy Case. Faiz let his friends stew for a few days before merrily revealing that 'Kulsoom' was his wife, upon hearing which his friends were quite dejected. Faiz thought their moroseness was quite hilarious: 'Look what things have come to,' he said, 'If a poet dedicates his collection to his wife, everyone feels let down; all these oafs are in search of a girlfriend!'[8]

Poetic inspiration

There were a few people who saw Faiz in the process of conceiving a verse or a poem and described it in their own words. His dear friend, Major Ishaq Muhammad, who spent a considerable amount of time with Faiz while they were imprisoned together in the Rawalpindi Conspiracy Case, said: 'When he would be immersed in [composing] poetry, Faiz sahib would go silent. Sometimes he would be restless, sitting down, getting up. We would realize that he needed listeners so we would go to him and start demanding that he recite something. If something was ready, he would recite a verse or two, otherwise he would tell us to be off.'[9]

Another friend described it in a different way:

> He [Faiz] would look at the trees, then at the flowers; he would be walking around, smiling to himself. Once he said 'I feel like reciting some poetry'. He reached for his cigarettes but the pack was empty. He started looking lost. I went inside and got him some cigarettes. He took a few puffs, looked up at the sky, smiled and started humming to himself. I realized that this was how poetry was born. I excused myself and went in to make some tea. I came out after half an hour and saw that he was still strolling and humming to himself. I left the tea there and went back inside. When I came out again after a long while, he looked very happy.[10]

Faiz himself described the process of poetic creation in an interview:

> There is no one form it [creativity] takes. Take the example of the poems I wrote in prison. Obviously the topic that weighed on my mind the most at that time was the jail cell, and it started with:
>
> *Nisar mae teri galiyon pe ay watan k jahan*
> [Blessings on the streets of my land where...][11]
>
> This came first...a vague restlessness appears in the mind. A hemistich or tune or idea comes to mind and then one starts weaving around it. The whole form never materializes at once...after a while the pattern begins to crystallize. In a way it is a conscious process. Then one writes it in a number of ways. Ghazal is a more confined format. This doesn't apply to that, I am talking about Nazams. There is no such thing in ghazal, it has more to do with rhyme. In a nazam, however, it happens that you write many half-verses, you make one skeleton, then make another, and so on, in a continuity. After this the extent of the subject is determined in its own manner and sometimes it happens that the topic which you have set changes not once, but twice or thrice during writing. This is because you planned to write in a particular way and then realized later that it doesn't match with the rest...There is a topic in mind but the final form it takes keeps changing with words, because words are autonomous to an extent. At times they are not under our control, and they determine what form of expression the subject will take.[12]

Regarding the commonly held misconception that an artistic creation appears spontaneously, fully formed, out of the artist's mind, Faiz was quite clear that nothing happens without concentrated hard work. An idea still has to be reworked, polished and improved for its final artistic form.

While Faiz's poetry worked magic on his admirers, the same cannot be said of the way he recited his verses. Many people commented on this. Unlike other poets of his era, including Iqbal, Faiz always recited new verses in a rather austere, unembellished, style, almost as if he were reciting prose. This was in stark contrast to the bombastic style of some of the poets of the time and was a reflection of his shyness and his self-effacing personality. One time, a brash admirer criticized his recitation style to Faiz's face, contrasting the beauty of the poem with the stark manner that Faiz had recited it. He even went so far as suggesting that Faiz take diction lessons to improve his delivery. Faiz took a serene puff of his ubiquitous cigarette and said playfully, 'Well young man, should I be the one to do everything? Perhaps you should help as well!'

The embrace of those we love

Faiz grew up in a large, loving family and was particularly close to his father when he was young. Perhaps Sultan Muhammad Khan, his father, was drawn to Faiz because of their shared love of intellectual pursuits. His father's death, when Faiz was in Government College, hit Faiz hard because it was not just the death of a loving and indulgent father; it was also the death of his life of ease and nonchalance. As would happen later, Faiz withdrew into himself and retreated to his room for days on end. The same thing would happen many years later when his beloved mother died.

The sudden, unexpected death of his older brother Tufail, who died while on his way to visiting Faiz in jail, was another shattering blow for Faiz. Once, when asked what the most painful experience of his life was, Faiz identified this incident. Even years later, when talking about it, his eyes would moisten and his voice would go hoarse with emotion. And when the time came to translate his prison letters for publication, he refused to dictate the translation of letter no. 45 (in which he described his brother's death to Alys), preferring to do the translation himself in solitude. When another friend was recording Faiz's poems in his own voice, Faiz regretfully declined to record the elegy, 'Mujh ko shikwa hai mere bhai' ('I beseech you brother'), which he had written in memory of Tufail. This was twenty years after Tufail's death, but the wound was still raw.

Faiz doted on both his daughters and, later, his grandchildren. His letters to Moneeza and Salima at various times and from all over the world are filled with a father's affection interlaced with friendly, sometime humorous advice. He named all his grandchildren himself, taking great care to select names that he felt were appropriate, and would write postcards or brief letters to them from wherever he was in the world. When in Lahore, he would make it a point to take the family out for lunches or dinners. All the grandchildren looked forward eagerly to this since this used to be a special treat. Whenever 'Nana' was in Lahore, we could all expect little gifts (chocolates and the like) as well as one or two meals in our favourite Chinese restaurants.

The call of the unseen

Faiz's religiosity (or its lack thereof) was a subject of much debate throughout his life. It could not be otherwise, since religion remains a pervasive part of everyday life in Pakistan and India and throughout the subcontinent and, for that matter, all across the economically underdeveloped third world. This, of course, as Marx pointed out long ago, is a consequence of the helplessness of those who have no recourse in the face of an unjust social and political system. Faiz, as a socialist, was often accused of being irreligious, even though his deep knowledge of religion and faith is evident from his poetry and his writings. This started with his early childhood tutelage in Arabic and Islam, as is traditional in all Muslim households. In an interview, he recounted how he memorized the first four chapters of the Quran but then had to stop when he developed eye problems. He also expressed regret that he had not been able to continue and memorize the Quran fully.

Faiz always described himself as attracted to the Sufi version of Islam as preached by Muslim mystics and saints. Even today, the vast majority of Muslims in India and Pakistan adhere to this moderate version of their faith. Amongst the great Sufi mystics, Faiz singled out Rumi[13] as his spiritual guide, once humorously deflecting a question in jail about what religion he belonged to by saying that his religion was the same as that of Rumi. The story goes that Islamic scholars belonging to dozens of different sects once descended on Rumi. They demanded to know which sect out of a total of seventy-two in Islam he believed in. Rumi calmly replied that he agreed with all seventy-two! The group, which was bent on picking a fight with the old man, persisted, insisting that this meant he was an infidel and a fire-worshipper, to which Rumi promptly replied that he agreed with this as well![14]

Faiz's first collection of poetry begins with a 'hamd', an ode to the Almighty; and in answer to an interviewer's question about religious traditions in the subcontinent, Faiz replied: 'This [religion] is an integral part of our [social] system. However, this tradition has been expressed in two ways: the way of the Sufis and the customary, outward way [based on religious rituals]. In the customary way, the emphasis has been on outward observance of religion [prayers, fasting, etc.] while the way of the Sufis is completely different. I have said many times that my [spiritual] mentor is Rumi.' On another occasion, Faiz reiterated how religious mud-slinging has been a time-honoured way of besmirching a person's reputation in the subcontinent and how this is in total opposition to the spirit of religious teaching.[15]

Faiz was once asked about his relations with well-known, traditional religious scholars of his time, to which he replied, 'I have met Maulana Maududi[16] a number of times, both in and out of jail but we have never exchanged ideas because in addition to his religious leanings, he has a specific political agenda and I have never felt that there is any common ground between us on that. He has never discussed religious matters with me and I try not to argue about those either.'[17]

In answer to an interviewer's question about having visited the mazaars (shrines) of Sufi saints, Faiz replied: 'This is part of our culture. I grew up in a village and used to spend my holidays in my village. In those days, at night, people would gather by the light of lanterns and "Saif-ul-Mulook"[18] and "Yousaf-Zuleikha"[19] would be recited with great relish. We would go to the shrines in all the surrounding areas and this was part of our rural culture.'[20]

And in response to a question about the supposed 'superiority' of an 'Islamic' system over socialism (a question that still lingers in Muslim countries), Faiz had this to say:

> The real question is: what exactly are you calling an 'Islamic system'? There are many Muslim countries in the world today, each with a different social and political system: Egypt, Syria, Saudi Arab, Pakistan, Indonesia. So what is this 'Islamic system' that no one can see? Moscow [in the former USSR] and China are in front of you, everyone can see for themselves. In those countries, people can get an education, they have jobs, they have food to eat and the daily comforts of life. Can you tell me which

> Muslim country in the world today offers even a fraction of that to its inhabitants? So how is their system better than the system in China or the USSR? This has nothing to do with the 'Islamic system' being inherently wrong. It's just that the system that has been devised in these Islamic countries is terribly flawed. If it is fixed, there is no reason that people in Islamic countries cannot get the same benefits as people in the USSR or China and if that were to happen, everyone would be content. So instead of criticizing China and the USSR [for being 'un-Islamic'], what we should be criticizing are the governments in our own countries who have failed to create a workable system.[21]

While Faiz's poetry contains numerous references to the Divine, there is (like Iqbal) always an exhortation to humans to rise above their challenges and even (again like Iqbal) to challenge an unjust God. Once, while describing the evils of an unequal, class-based social system like capitalism, Faiz pointed out: 'Instead of lecturing people on morality, it is far better to provide them with three square meals a day so they can stay alive and perhaps realize these things on their own. If an empty house is a devil's abode, how can the hungry stomach and weary mind of a poor man accommodate God's light?' And coming back to so-called 'Islamic countries', Faiz remarked, 'There still exist economic slaves in all these "Muslim" countries. The real Jihad is to eradicate this evil [of economic slavery] and this is what Revolution aspires to as well.'

While Faiz made it a point to avoid religious arguments, aware, no doubt, that people who engaged in such arguments were not open to reason anyway, he was quite sure of his own stand on these matters and did not shy away either from expressing his personal religious views (while carefully avoiding hurting the religious sentiments of others) nor of pointing out how religion was being used to uphold brutal and exploitative social systems all over the so-called 'Islamic' world.

Notes

1. Syed Sibt-e Hasan, *Sukhan dar Sukhan* (Karachi: Maktaba Daniyal, 2009), p. 45.
2. Faiz Ahmed Faiz, 'Guftagoo—Faiz Ahmed Faiz', *Dunyazad*, no. 35 (Karachi: Scheherzade Publications, 2012), p. 63.

3. Salima Hashmi, Interview with Rubina Sarwar, *Jeddo Jehd*, Faiz number, vol. 20, issue 6, 14 February 2008, p. 15.
4. Ludmila Vasilieva, unpublished interview with the author, Lahore, 2014.
5. Hameed Akhtar, *Faiz ke Baad...Ab Kuch Bhi Nahin Hai. Teri Yaadon k Naqoosh* (Lahore: Sang-e-Meel Publications, 2011), pp. 280–1.
6. Faiz Ahmed Faiz, *Saleebain Mere Darichay Main* (Karachi: Maktaba-e Daniyal, 2011), pp. 24, 25.
7. Syed Taqi Abedi, 'Faiz ka aqeeda', in *Faiz Fehmi* (Lahore: Multimedia Affairs, 2011), p. 1280.
8. Ibid., p. 1282.
9. Ishaq Mohammad, 'Roodaad-e Qafas', in *Nuskha hai Wafa* (Lahore: Maktaba-e Karvan, 1985), pp. 207–8.
10. Khadija Begum,'Yaadon se muattar', in Mirza Zafarul Hasan (comp.), *Khoon-e Dil ki Kasheed* (Karachi: Maktaba Asloob, 1983), pp. 60–1.
11. Translation by this author.
12. Faiz, 'Guftagoo--Faiz Ahmed Faiz', p. 67.
13. Jalaluddin Muhammad 'Rumi' (1207–1273), thirteenth-century Persian poet, scholar, theologian, jurist and Muslim mystic whose influence extends throughout Central and South Asia across national, ethnic and linguistic boundaries.
14. Fateh Mohammad Malik, *Faiz: Shairi aur Siasat*. (Lahore: Sang-e-Meel Publications, 2008), pp. 17–18.
15. Khaleel Ahmed, *Makalmat-e Faiz,* (Lahore : Sang-e-Meel Publications, 2011), p. 25.
16. Abul Ala Maududi (1903–1979). Influential religious scholar, journalist and Islamist, founder of the 'Jamaat-e Islami', one of the largest Islamic political parties in South Asia with organizational methods inspired by the early communist parties.
17. Ahmed, *Makalmat-e Faiz*, p. 227.
18. Devotional poetry.
19. The Prophet Yousaf (Joseph), sixteenth century BCE; he is revered in all three 'monotheistic' religions, Judaism, Christianity and Islam. The story of Yousaf and Zuleikha, the woman who lusted after him, has been a staple of the religious folklore of all three religions.
20. Ahmed, *Makalmat-e Faiz*, p. 29.
21. Abedi, 'Faiz ka aqeeda', p. 817.

Destinies in Love: Faiz Today

Well, then, let's follow
the peal of bells to the
yonder shore.

—Hakurin

It is one of the many ironies of history that those who lead the most controversial lives are imperceptibly absorbed into the mainstream following their deaths; their lives and ideas moulded and softened to fit prevailing beliefs. The most potent symbol of resistance to the prevailing world order, the Argentinian revolutionary, physician and author Ernesto 'Che' Guevara (1928–1967), one of the architects of the Cuban Revolution and a perpetual thorn in the side of those opposed to the Cuban experiment, was tortured and murdered in the jungles of Bolivia. He had become restless after the success of the Cuban Revolution and wished to bring the same change to the rest of Latin America. Unfortunately, his creative and revolutionary energies ran ahead of the existing social conditions and he was captured and executed at the young age of thirty-nine. Even though he was reviled by many during his life (and adored by an equal, if not greater, number), today, he has been sanitized and 'commoditized', his likeness on T-shirts, posters, and any number of goods being used for a variety of causes of which he may or may not have approved.

Closer home, one of the most controversial writers of recent times, Saadat Hasan Manto, has seen a sudden resurgence of interest in his life and work with the Government of Pakistan even bestowing a top state award on him and putting his face on a postage stamp. This is the same Manto who was prosecuted six separate times on charges of obscenity during his lifetime (and honourably exonerated each time) and who eventually drank himself to death because of his legal and financial difficulties. As if to underline the point, Manto's dear friend and fellow writer, Ismat Chughtai (no stranger to controversy herself) recalled how she had teased Manto about his legacy: 'One day, just to tease him, I said, "Manto, when you die, people will worship you and call you a standard-bearer of all greatness. People will permanently attach the word 'great' to your name. They'll call you an expert psychologist and a national reformer."Manto got very mad at all of this and began to shout while trying to scowl at me as best he could with his very large eyes. "By God," he said, "if that happens, I'll come out of my grave and haunt them."[1]

Something similar seems to be happening with Faiz. His poetry, perceived as a symbol of resistance to oppression and injustice during his lifetime, now appears in school textbooks, political rallies, television programmes and even advertisements for various products. It has been shorn of its political and social context and is in the process of being 'commoditized' to suit commercial and political interests. Some of the blame for all this rests, perhaps, on Faiz himself. Soon after independence, it became evident that the new rulers of Pakistan were not inclined towards the socialistic aspirations of the mass of people. The independence struggle had willy-nilly unified people of all political beliefs into a 'common front' against the hated British. Once the British were gone, though, class differences between the rich and the poor inevitably began to come to the fore. Faiz and his companions had dreamed of a new country, Pakistan, in which oppression, hunger, injustice and tyranny would be a distant memory but, like all dreamers, they had no concrete plan to bring such a world into existence. Faiz admitted as much in an interview many years later. His seminal poem, 'Subh-e azadi' (Dawn of freedom), written in August 1947 already speaks of this disillusionment and exhorts his countrymen to 'go on, our goal is not reached yet'.

For close to four years after independence, Faiz continued his political activism along with his poetry. He wrote scathing editorials in his two newspapers about the ineptitude of the new Pakistani government; about the dangers to workers' rights, womens' rights and democracy; about the short-sightedness of Pakistani foreign policy and about the increasing dangers of dictatorship at home. Once the clampdown came and he was imprisoned (along with anyone else remotely considered a danger in official circles), he had time to think about his situation. The imprisonment itself must have been stressful enough with Alys having to care for their two young daughters by herself, although even in prison, Faiz's innate optimism, his staunch faith in the goodness of human nature and his resolute idealism persisted, as evident in his letters to Alys from prison. Once he was released, Pakistan had changed beyond recognition. The Left was in tatters. The Communist party, which had been decimated at partition by the migration of its most committed and experienced cadres to India, had effectively ceased to exist and the few who remained in Pakistan were in hiding or lying low.

Faiz had never been a slogan monger anyway. His temperament was not suited to it. Now that there was no movement to speak of, he decided to concentrate on the arena he knew best and was comfortable in: culture and literature. One Left critic wrote rather harshly that Faiz's political stand following his imprisonment in the Rawalpindi Conspiracy Case was 'one of an avoidance of full commitment to any clear cut standand one which therefore enabled him to steer clear of anyone's strong disapproval'.[2] The same author describes Faiz's politics as 'a blend of Marxism and a kind of secular Pakistani nationalism', close enough to the communists to win their respect, but not so much as to alienate the liberal Pakistani establishment.

Faiz continued to write poetry that highlighted the burning social and political issues of the day, both within Pakistan and internationally and, after he was awarded the Lenin Peace Prize in 1962, he was fortunate to find a hugely sympathetic and receptive audience in the Soviet Union where his poetry was widely translated and read.

While he was alive, he had his share of detractors, especially in Pakistan. After his death, with the passage of time, the 'topical' issues in his poetry have faded away, leaving only the universal message. This, as Faiz himself pointed out, resonates only if a poet captures the inner essence of his reader's feelings, what is in his or her heart. Since injustice, tyranny and oppression have continued, and in some way intensified since the fall of the Soviet Union, Faiz's poetry remains relevant and widely read. The theoretical political debates of the decades since Faiz was born have faded away but people can still feel the indignation, the protest and the hope in his poetry and this is what they respond to.

The fact that his poetry has been expropriated by the Pakistani establishment (and in some cases by the religious right) for their own purposes is less a failure of Faiz than of the Left movement in Pakistan, a project that was strangled in its infancy by a combination of state repression and its own theoretical and practical inadequacies.

How is one to explain the enduring popularity of Faiz?

One explanation is to be found in Faiz's use of language. Even though some of his poems retain the classical Persianized language of the ghazal, most of his poetry is fairly easy to understand, even for the average reader. There is some 'sloganeering' in a few of his poems but even these retain their poetical quality and are pleasing to the senses. Like all good poets, his best poems pull at one's heartstrings and resonate with one's inner experiences. Unlike his predecessor Iqbal, there are no overt calls to the heavens or references to angels and the Divine (a fact that endears Iqbal more to the religiously inclined than Faiz). Although there are numerous references to the Quran and to the Divine in Faiz's poetry, they stay rooted in the struggles of *this* world, as befits a 'socialist humanist'. For those repelled by the barbarity of religious fundamentalism, this is a key attraction of Faiz's poetry.

Another explanation of Faiz's enduring popularity might simply be the recentness of the themes of his poetry. We are still less than a generation away from his death and a little over a hundred years away from his birth. The burning issues of the twentieth century, especially as they pertain to Pakistan and India, are still with us. Partition and its attendant mutual suspicion and hostility remain a 'festering sore, dripping corruption' on the body of the Indian subcontinent. For Pakistan, especially, the dismemberment of the original dream in 1971 remains another unhealed wound. And, of course, for millions of people in both Pakistan and India, 'Azadi' remains a cruel joke while they are 'yoked to the wheel of fate' as Faiz wrote in his only English-language poem,'The unicorn and the dancing girl':

And the wheel was fate
And the yoke was 'karma'
And fear and want and pain
And withering of age
And death with its mercy
And the tyrant with no mercy in his heart.

Further on in the poem, Faiz writes of the present:

> Time present is still time past
> in faces
> in places
> in custom and ritual and the grave of the nameless saint
> In hunger and want and pain and the withering of age
> And its birth in Pakistan as elsewhere in
> the newly liberated countries of Asia and Africa
> is as yet only a small flag of freedom raised against
> The bannered and embattled host of
> Fear and want and hunger and
> pain
> and the death of human hearts.

For the purists, including poets and writers, a key attraction of Faiz's poetry is his supreme command over technique and language. Faiz was well versed in all three 'root' languages of Urdu poetry—Arabic, Persian and Urdu—and this is evident from his diction. In addition, he was fortunate during his youth to have had teachers who had mastery over poetry and languages such as Sufi Tabassum, an acknowledged master of Persian and Urdu. Not even the most accomplished poets can find fault with Faiz's mastery of his poetical craft.

For the casual reader, the themes resonate but so too do the language, the melody and the romantic lyricism, the core of classical Urdu poetry. One does not have to be a Marxist or a litterateur to enjoy Faiz's most beloved poems. They are enjoyable even in casual reading. This was the reason that popular singers of Faiz's era, including Noor Jehan, Farida Khanum, Mehdi Hassan and many others sang a number of Faiz's poems for radio, television and films. This helped popularize his poetry even more and with the increasing advent of mass media (a process that started in Faiz's youth and blossomed after partition), his poetry found a new and more receptive global audience. Now, in its 'second incarnation' with the coming of the Internet and social media, Faiz is being reborn yet again for another generation, although his poetry is now shorn (in most cases) of its political and social context. Those who take the trouble to dig a little deeper, though, can easily find the underlying subtext, which links the poem to its original 'cause'.

In the end, two interrelated themes can best explain why Faiz and his poetry continue to be adored by millions, not just in South Asia but around the globe.

With his technical and linguistic proficiency and his complete mastery over the canon of Urdu and Persian poetry, including the likes of Hafez of Shiraz and even the seventh-century Arab master, Ta'abbata Sharra, Faiz had the ability to comprehensively express all manner of themes and ideas in his poetry, including 'new' ideas like socialism, humanism and the various permutations of politics. With practise, he also became a master of 'political lyricism'. This was one of his innovations and his particular contribution to this genre was to create poetry that adhered to the rules of classical Urdu poetry while still showcasing the struggles, hopes and aspirations of the teeming masses of colonized (and newly liberated) nations of Asia and Africa.

The second was, of course, his conscious commitment to being a spokesman for ordinary people: workers and peasants, women and children, all those who have no voice in the oppressive societies of underdeveloped, third-world nations. He made the decision to speak for them, in his own way, early on in his life and, by and large, upheld this commitment. This alone would have been enough to endear him to a large majority of the people in all countries where Urdu poetry is read and appreciated. In Pakistan, India and the subcontinent, where poets are revered just a little less than prophets, it has won him millions of ardent followers.

As he aged and the times changed, his poetry also became more reflective (and less overtly 'political'), but then this is common to all of us. A person is no more and no less, as Marx said, than the sum of his or her 'historical conditions'. Our worldview, including our view about ourselves, changes as we move through life. What may have seemed urgent and insistent at one stage may appear trivial at best and laughable at worst at another time. This is what it means to be human.

But while we understand and often forgive this trait in ourselves and those around us, it is more difficult to do so in those whom we adore and idealize. In the end, though, they are just as human as we are and to ask more of them than we do of ourselves seems rather churlish.

Faiz is gone but his voice is still with us in his poetry, and so are those things in the world that so rankled and infuriated him: exploitation, injustice, tyranny, oppression.

If we can remember that the best tribute we can pay him is to dedicate ourselves, in whatever small way we can, to ending these cruelties, Faiz would be happy that he had succeeded in his mission.

Notes

1. Ismat Chugtai, A talk with one of Urdu's most outspoken women writers, *Mahfil*, vol. 8, nos 2–3 (Summer-Fall 1972), pp. 169–88. Available athttp://www.columbia.edu/itc/mealac/pritchett/00urdu/ismat/txt_ismat_interview_mahfil1972.html?
2. Ralph Russell, 'Faiz Ahmed Faiz—Poetry, Politics and Pakistan', in *The Pursuit of Urdu Literature: A Select History* (London: Zed Books, 1992). Available at http://www.columbia.edu/itc/mealac/pritchett/00urdu/3mod/

Acknowledgements

This book would never have happened without the help and encouragement of a number of people: my family members who were always there with a helpful comment as well as with their invaluable personal memories of Faiz and Alys; my aunt Salima Hashmi, an extraordinary treasure trove of Faiz stories; my mother Moneeza and father Humair Hashmi. I am indebted, besides, to two people in particular who made my life so much easier with their diligent research and scholarship: Syed Mazhar Jameel whose tome *Zikr-e Faiz* was the backbone of this book and my friend and researcher Dr Rai Imran Zafar, a meticulous scholar and Faiz aficionado without whose help and gentle pushing I might still have been fretting about starting the book. I am grateful to all those friends and colleagues who read parts of the book and offered helpful comments: Dr Khalid Sohail, a 'friend of the heart', Dr Rakhshanda Jalil, Musharraf Ali Farooqi whose dual skills as an author/translator and a publisher never cease to amaze me, all those friends and acquaintances who shared their memories of Faiz and Alys; Dr Asim Allahbakhsh, friend and 'spiritual guide' who insisted that I slog on even when I didn't want to; my agent Kanishka Gupta and the editorial staff at Rupa especially Shalini Shekhar; Mr Muhammad Umar Memon, who encouraged me to resume serious writing after a long hiatus and continues to remain a source of inspiration for all of us.

And Mavra, who knows why.

Index

Made in the USA
Las Vegas, NV
05 September 2025

27481700R00187